MEDIA ORGANISATION AND
PRODUCTION

The *Media in Focus* series provides students and lecturers with an authoritative, that is, balanced and informed account of the media communication field and its many sub-fields of contemporary research. The editor of each volume, an expert in the media sub-field in focus, contributes an introductory 'mapping essay' charting the perspectives, debates and findings of major studies before introducing the reader to a carefully commissioned and structured range of chapters authored by international researchers. In this way, readers gain a relatively compact and structured overview of the media sub-field in question as well as exposure to a judicious range of writings selected to illuminate theoretical and methodological frameworks, key research findings, and defining debates. The *Media in Focus* series, then, is informed by strong pedagogical and scholarly emphases throughout and provides media communication lecturers and students with an accessible and authoritative resource for teaching and learning.

Simon Cottle, Series Editor

Edited by
Simon Cottle

MEDIA ORGANISATION AND
PRODUCTION

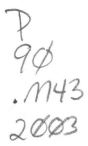

SAGE Publications

London • Thousand Oaks • New Delhi

SAGE Publications Ltd
6 Bonhill Street
London EC2A 4PU

SAGE Publications Inc
2455 Teller Road
Thousand Oaks, California 91320

SAGE Publications India Pvt Ltd
B-42, Panchsheel Enclave
Post Box 4109
New Delhi – 100 017

British Library Cataloguing in Publication data

A catalogue record for this book is available from the British Library

ISBN 0 7619 7493 8
ISBN 0 7619 7494 6 (pbk)

Library of Congress Control Number:

Typeset by Mayhew Typesetting, Rhayader, Powys
Printed and bound in Great Britain by the Athenaeum Press, Gateshead

Contents

List of figures vi
List of tables vii
Notes on Contributors viii
Acknowledgements x

PART I **Introduction** 1

    1 Media organisation and production: mapping the
    field *Simon Cottle* 3

PART II **Global Corporations, Local Alternatives** 25

    2 Corporate media, global capitalism *Robert W. McChesney* 27
    3 Organisation and production in alternative
    media *Chris Atton* 41

PART III **Corporate Change and Organisational Cultures** 57

    4 Strategising technological innovation: the case of news
    corporation *Timothy Marjoribanks* 59
    5 Organisational culture inside the BBC and
    CNN *Lucy Küng-Shankleman* 77

PART IV **Producers, Practices and the Production of Cultural Forms** 97

    6 The *Brains Trust*: a historical study of the management
    of liveness on radio *Paddy Scannell* 99
    7 Journalists with a difference: producing music
    journalism *Eamonn Forde* 113
    8 Cultures of production: the making of children's
    news *Julian Matthews* 131

PART V **Changing International Genres and Production Ecologies** 147

    9 International TV and film co-production: a Canadian
    case study *Doris Baltruschat* 149
    10 Producing nature(s): the changing production ecology
    of natural history TV *Simon Cottle* 170

References 188
Index 198

List of figures

5.1   The BBC's cultural paradigm   78
5.2   The BBC's assumption and attitude map   83
5.3   The 'fit' between the BBC's environment, strategy and culture   85
5.4   CNN's cultural paradigm   86
5.5   CNN's assumption and attitude maps   91
5.6   The 'fit' between CNN's environment, strategy and culture   93
8.1   Job advertisement in the *Guardian*   134
9.1   Mean scores for local and co-produced programmes   160
9.2   Place/location mean scores for television and film   160
9.3   Co-produced feature film, *The Red Violin*: narrative breakdown   163
9.4   Locally produced feature film, *The Hanging Garden*: narrative breakdown   164
9.5   Co-produced television drama series, *The Secret Adventures of Jules Verne*: narrative breakdown   165
9.6   Locally produced television docudrama, *Milgaard*: narrative breakdown   166

List of tables

7.1 'Hard' news and music journalism compared   114
7.2 Sales figures of music magazine titles (Jan–June 2002)   115
9.1 Canadian co-production activity 1992–2000 in film and television   153
9.2 Canadian production activity 1992–2000 in film and television   154
9.3 Categories of film and television programmes   158
9.4 Five-scale measure establishing *global* or *local* forms   159
9.5 Summary of scores for both prodution modes   162

Notes on Contributors

Chris Atton teaches in the School of Communication Arts at Napier University, Edinburgh, Scotland. He is the author of *Alternative Literature* (Gower, 1996), *Alternative Media* (Sage, 2002) and has published widely on alternative and radical media. He is currently researching radical media coverage of September 11, its aftermath and Operation Enduring Freedom. His next book, *An Alternative Internet*, will be published in 2004 (Edinburgh University Press).

Doris Baltruschat has extensive experience in the production and distribution of international film and television programmes. She is also an independent researcher with a particular interest in globalisation and culture, international film and TV co-productions and media literacy. As a member of media and democracy associations in Canada, she is actively involved in media education and digital media production. She has an MA in Mass Communications from the University of Leicester.

Simon Cottle is Professor and Director, Media and Communications Programme at the University of Melbourne, Australia. His books include: *TV News, Urban Conflict and the Inner City* (Leicester University Press, 1993), *Television and Ethnic Minorities: Producers' Perspectives* (Avebury, 1997), as co-author *Mass Communication Research Methods* (Macmillan, 1998) and as editor *Ethnic Minorities and the Media: Changing Cultural Boundaries* (Open University Press, 2000), and *News, Public Relations and Power* (Sage, 2003). He is the Series Editor of the Sage Media in Focus series. He is also currently writing *Media Performance and Public Transformation: The Case of Stephen Lawrence* (Praeger, 2003) and conducting a major study entitled 'TV Journalism and Deliberative Democracy: An International Study of Changing Forms, Communicative Architecture and "Democratic Deepening"'.

Eamonn Forde conducted his PhD research at University of Westminster, UK. His publications include 'From Polyglottism to Branding: on the Decline of Personality Journalism in the British Music Press' in *Journalism: Theory, Practice & Criticism* (Sage, 2001). He is editor of *Five Eight*, a monthly music business and strategy title. His research interests include all areas of the global music industry.

Lucy Küng-Shankleman is Senior Lecturer and Project Manager at the Media and Communications Management Institute at the University of St. Gallen, Switzerland. She is the author of *Inside the BBC and CNN: Managing Media Organizations* (Routledge, 2000). Her current research specialises on the strategic and organisational options facing media firms as they confront a changing technological landscape and consumer tastes.

Timothy Marjoribanks is T.R. Ashworth Lecturer in Sociology at The University of Melbourne, Australia. His publications include *News Corporation, Technology and the Workplace: Global Strategies, Local Change* (Cambridge, 2000), and articles in journals on the media and health professions. In the media field, he is currently undertaking research on media and sport, and a collaborative comparative study of defamation/libel law and news production processes.

Julian Matthews is a lecturer in Media Communication at Bath Spa University College, England. He has recently completed and is in the process of publishing his doctoral research that examines the production of the children's news programme *Newsround*. His interests include the sociology of news production, political communication and new technologies.

Robert W. McChesney is a professor in the Institute of Communications Research at the University of Illinois at Urbana-Champaign. He is the author of nine books, including (with John Nichols) *Our Media, Not Theirs: The Democratic Struggle Against Corporate Media* (Seven Stories Press, 2002), and (with John Bellamy Foster) *The Big Picture: Understanding Media Through Political Economy* (Monthly Review Press, 2003). McChesney's work has been translated into more than a dozen languages. He also serves as co-editor of *Monthly Review*, the New York based socialist magazine started by Paul Sweezy and Leo Huberman in 1949.

Paddy Scannell is a Professor of Broadcasting at the University of Westminster where he has worked for the last 35 years. He is a founding editor of *Media Culture and Society* (now in its 25th year), and co-author, with David Cardiff, of *A Social History of British Broadcasting, 1922–1939* (Blackwell, 1991). Other works include *Broadcast Talk* (Sage, 1991) and *Radio, Television and Modern Life* (Blackwell, 1996). His current research interests include broadcasting history, theories of communication and language, communication and culture in Southern Africa, broadcast music and phenomenology.

Acknowledgements

The chapters in this book, in line with the pedagogical and cutting-edge aims of the Media in Focus series, present and summarise current arguments and recent findings within the research field of media organisation and production. These have sometimes been published at greater length elsewhere, and where this is so is acknowledged by the various authors in their respective chapters. All chapters in this volume, however, have been carefully prepared especially for this volume. I would like to thank Mugdha Rai, once again, for her detailed eye and diligent help in preparing the manuscript for publication.

PART I

INTRODUCTION

CHAPTER 1
Media Organisation and Production: Mapping the Field

Simon Cottle

To understand media today we need to study media organisation and production in global and local contexts. This is so whether we are concerned with transnational corporations such as AOL-Time Warner, Disney, Sony, Bertelsmann, Viacom and News Corporation, media giants whose commercial operations traverse the globe and extend into the satellite heavens; whether we are focusing on national public service organisations besieged by forces of technological change, industrial convergence and political deregulation; or whether we are examining alternative forms of media production in which the commercially disenfranchised and politically hungry make innovative uses of communication technologies, both old and new, in their struggle to make a difference on the contested terrain of civil society. This book examines how and why media organisations and production are structured in particular ways, how media producers and professionals manage creativity and constraint within these organisational settings and, importantly, with what consequences for the forms and representations produced.

Media organisation and production can be approached from diverse perspectives. In their own terms, media industries are businesses, sites of investment and sources of employment. Today a growing army of media professionals, producers and others work in this expanding sector of the economy, many of them in freelance, temporary, subcontracted and underpaid (and sometimes unpaid) positions. Life chances and opportunities for growing numbers of media and communications workers around the world are thereby affected, as well as for those in associated industries. Transnational media corporations, such as those above, also increasingly occupy the 'commanding heights' of national economies and have national flagship status bestowed on them by exchange markets in recognition of their continuing rise (and occasional falls) of speculative profits and their 'path-breaking' operations in opening up world marketplaces. They are also often at the forefront of processes of organisational change including new flexible work regimes, reflexive corporate cultures, and the introduction of digital technologies, multimedia production and multiskilled practices. Important as these features undoubtedly are, they do not capture the central importance of media organisation and production as an object of enquiry within the field of media and communications study. Above all else it is their status and operation as 'cultural industries' that inform the central thrust of academic study and investigation. Media industries and organisations are different from most other businesses and organisations in that they characteristically produce and purvey commodities and content that are essentially symbolic in nature – and these symbols enter into the life of society.

In late-modern societies the symbolic forms of media output are implicated in the constitution of society: in its routines and rhythms of daily life, in the representation of social relations and in the conduct of politics, as well as in the affirmation (or challenge to) wider cultural values, traditions and identities. In subtle, 'naturalised' and taken-for-granted ways, as well as in sensationalist and 'in-your-face' claims for attention, media representations enter into public and private life. They contribute images and ideas, discourses and debate for the conduct of social relations and the wider engagements of social, cultural and political power. Governmental and other forms of administrative power routinely seek public legitimation on the media stage, and the voices of the marginal and dispossessed also struggle for the media spotlight to draw attention to their plight, though with noticeably less success. In such ways cultural industries can prove to be influential allies in processes of democratic deepening or base supporters of information management, 'spin' and propaganda, and thereby injurious to democracy. Through its symbolic forms and representations, cultural industries also help to constitute and redefine the historically shifting boundaries of 'public' and 'private spheres' and address us as citizens or consumers. Herein lies their principal interest for media communication scholars and students, but herein also lie the seeds of theoretical dispute about how best to proceed in examining and explaining their operations and output.

Political economy and cultural studies, two overarching theoretical traditions discussed below, have tended to dominate discussion of how we can best approach and explain the output of media organisations. But though both are necessary for improved understanding of the wider commercial and cultural forces that undoubtedly circumscribe and penetrate the material and discursive practices of media organisations and producers, they by no means exhaust the field of relevant theoretical frameworks. Other approaches and levels of insights are needed for a more encompassing and grounded understanding of the complex 'mediations' involved in cultural production. In between the theoretical foci on marketplace determinations and play of cultural discourses, there still exists a relatively unexplored and under-theorised 'middle ground' of organisational structures and workplace practices. This comprises different organisational fields and institutional settings, and the dynamic practices and daily grind of media professionals and producers engaged in productive processes. Attending to how these producers practically manage and 'mediate' a complex of forces (economic, political, regulatory, technological, professional, cultural, normative) that variously facilitate, condition and constrain their forms of media output reveals further levels of insight and understanding. Studies here are often based on in-depth qualitative modes of exploration – ethnography, semi-structured interviews – as well as documentary searches and archival methods that invite a deeper and possibly more humanistic understanding of the culture, practices and performances of media producers and how these give expression to the complexities and contingencies involved. This ethnographic approach often proves invaluable as a corrective to speculative and abstract theory and the generalising claims to which this can give rise. Too often the complex and multi-dimensional nature of media production is short-circuited by those holding a priori theoretical commitments, or rigid political views and expectations. Generalising and simplistic explanations of media output and portrayal often come in two variants.

The first *instrumental* explanation suggests that the operations and performance of the media can adequately be explained in terms of proprietorial intervention and the instrumental pursuit of ruling interests and/or political allegiances, a position often aligned to forms of conspiracy theory. The second *structural determination* position inverts this focus on agency, and maintains that media personnel, whatever their position within organisational hierarchies, are compelled by impinging determinants – economic, technological, ideological – to reproduce media forms and content unconsciously and routinely in predetermined ways. Important issues of agency versus structure, creativity versus constraint, conspiracy versus convention are thereby raised but often in mutually exclusive and absolute terms, that fail to consider the possibility of the complex interplay between these different factors and the dynamics that come into play within particular fields of production. Such bold claims, then, remain insufficient as fully fledged theories of media organisation and practice – which is not to suggest that structural determinations, class interests or even, on occasion, conspiracies do not figure in the explanatory equation. These commonly heard positions also have the unfortunate result of either inflating the responsibility or 'culpability' of media producers in the construction and circulation of particular discourses in society, or marginalising their involvement entirely and seeing them as little more than puppets of an overbearing and overdetermining system. Both instrumentalist and structural determinist positions can thereby give rise to the so-called 'problem of inference'.

It is disconcerting how many studies of media output are conducted with a complete disregard for the moment of production and the forces enacted or condensed inside the production domain. When the analyst infers, as is often the case from a textual interpretation alone, the possible explanations, motivations or reasons that have informed their production, angels are often to be found dancing on a pinhead of textual analysis. If we want to understand why media representations assume the forms that they do as well as the silences found within media discourse, we cannot rely upon readings of media texts alone, no matter how analytically refined and methodologically sophisticated these may be. Studies of media organisation and production powerfully address the 'problem of inference' head-on by attending empirically to the often complex articulation of differing influences and constraints, both material and discursive, intended and unintended, structurally determined and culturally mediated, embedded within the moment of production – and which can be recovered by research.

Media Organisation and Production, then, sets out to review the field of media and communication studies and the different theoretical and empirical approaches attending to production practices and media organisations now operating at global to local levels. It demonstrates how the insights generated from studies of production contexts, domains and professional practices are invaluable for building a more encompassing and adequate understanding of the complex nature of today's media industries and organisations operating in different fields and markets. This thereby helps to qualify and correct the sometimes speculative and generalising claims of abstract media theories as well as the assumptions of common sense. The book draws on the latest work of international academics, both new and established, based in the UK, USA, Australia, Switzerland and Canada. Together they address a wide range of global–local media organisations, production domains, media and genres. These include transnational and national, commercial and public service corporations (News International, CNN, BBC, Canadian Broadcasting Company); mainstream and independent television and film production companies and international co-productions; the production of children's television news, historical radio, and press music journalism, and the changing production ecology of natural history television; as well as the politics and organisational forms of alternative media production including radical newspapers, video and the Internet. These are examined through a variety of theoretical and conceptual frameworks and via a range of methodologies.

Some of the contributions to this book focus specifically on news organisations, news production environments and journalist practices. This reflects the continuing prominence of news study within media production research in general, and the continuing centrality of journalist forms to processes of democratic representation and citizenship. In contrast to earlier news production studies, these more recent studies help to encourage a differentiated understanding of today's news ecology, its organisations, cultural forms and associated practices. Intensified market competition, corporate conglomeration and convergence, new technologies, digitalisation and globalisation also feature across many of the chapters and are necessary points of discussion for understanding the operations and structures of today's media organisations. How these and other forces are 'mediated' by different organisations and become enacted and/or negotiated by corporate managements, organisational structures, workplace cultures and professional practices are subject to close scrutiny. Through this encounter with a wide range of up-to-date empirical materials, detailed case studies, and informed theoretical frameworks and levels of analysis, *Media Organisation and Production* aims to underline the essential significance of media production and organisation for understanding today's media as well as the complex interrelationships and levels of analysis involved.

Before introducing each of the chapters that follow, it is first useful to map some of the main theoretical contours, debates and studies that have characterised the field in the recent past and which continue to contribute frameworks of use for the study of media organisation and production today. To begin, we briefly review the overarching frameworks of political economy and cultural studies, two mutually antagonistic approaches, yet each contributing a powerful theoretical optic through which to view the operations and output of the media, before turning to more closely engaged studies of media organisation and production.

Overarching Traditions: Political Economy and Cultural Studies

Political economy and cultural studies have generated heated debates about where the explanatory emphasis should be placed when studying media communication: whether on 'the economic determinants at work' or 'the cultural discourses at play'. Implicit to these exchanges are deep-seated differences about social ontology (the nature of social reality), epistemology (what constitutes valid 'knowledge' of this social reality), methodology (of how we can proceed to investigate this social reality), as well as conflicting political values and normative outlooks (how we can change this social reality for the better). These two traditions also encompass a myriad of disputes as well as more refined differences of approach within each camp. They also draw, in part at least, on shared intellectual antecedents.

Encapsulated in an oft-quoted statement from *The German Ideology*, written by Karl Marx and Friedrich Engels in 1846, is a view of the social organisation of power that has direct relevance for subsequent approaches to the study of media organisation and production. It bears repeating.

> The ideas of the ruling class are in every epoch the ruling ideas, i.e. the class which is the ruling *material* force of society, is at the same time its ruling *intellectual* force. The class which has the means of material production at its disposal has control at the same time over the means of mental production, so that thereby, generally speaking, the ideas of those who lack the means of mental production are subject to it. (Marx and Engels [1846] 1976)

Here a fundamental connection is made between the way in which social relations of production are historically organised and how this invariably provides the ruling class(es) with an important advantage in terms of controlling the forms of 'mental production'. Whoever owns and controls material production, it is stated, will also generally have control over 'mental production', that is the production of ideas, values and beliefs circulating in society – ideas that can help to justify and legitimise their position of social dominance. This statement was never fully worked through in the corpus of Marx's later writings, though later commentators have interpreted it in different ways. What is generally centre-stage in all of them, however, is the part played by the mass media in today's societies and, following the Marxist historical materialist view of history, how this is thought to support ruling-class interests. Three different Marxist emphases have subsequently come to the fore.

Sometimes the media have been conceived as an instrument deployed in class struggle. This *instrumentalist* view informs, for example, Ralph Miliband's (1969) *The State in Capitalist Society* (subtitled '*The Analysis of the Western System of Power*'). Miliband identified the mass media as a key institution in processes of capitalist legitimation and postulated a close coincidence between the social composition of media owners, interlocking elite networks, shared cultural and educational backgrounds, and forms of socialising (and socialisation) as a principal explanation for why and how the media routinely served as 'an expression of a system of domination' and 'as a means of reinforcing it' (1969: 198). Similar views also inform the 'propaganda model' of US authors Edward Herman and Noam Chomsky (1988). Occasional developments in the media suggest that these instrumentalist views of the media are not without explanatory purchase on the operations of today's media. Consider the following press articles.

BBC chief denies being Labour crony	Berlusconi tightens grip on Italian TV
Tories were furious to learn of the appointment of Gavin Davies, a multi-millionaire former Labour Party member and financial supporter, as chairman of the BBC. Critics accused Mr Blair of packing the corporation with cronies and mounting a 'final takeover' of the organisation following the appointment of another former Labour donor, Greg Dyke, as its director-general.	Italy's state broadcasting service tumbled into Silvio Berlusconi's control last weekend when the term of the board of directors expired, giving the prime minister an opportunity to seal his dominance of television.
But Mr Davis, whose wife runs the office of the Chancellor, Gordon Brown, insisted that he would tackle the job without bias. Labour pointed out that many former BBC chairmen had had Tory links and added that Mr Davis, who made his fortune as chief economist with Goldman Sachs, had been appointed by an independent panel.	A board sympathetic to the ruling centre-right coalition is expected to be appointed soon, paving the way for a political tilt in news, current affairs and drama programmes. Mr Berlusconi owns Italy's largest private television network, Mediaset, and with the state-owned Rai he will directly or indirectly control about 90 per cent of the television market.
(*Guardian Weekly*, October 2001)	(*Guardian Weekly*, February 2002)

Developments such as these strongly suggest that examples of 'instrumental' uses of the media are not difficult to find, notwithstanding protestations to the contrary from those immediately involved. The question, however, is whether such examples constitute a general theory of the operations, organisation and output of the media on a routine and daily basis.

Others have interpreted the role of the media not so much as an instrument of ruling-class interests strategically deployed, but more as an expression of a generalised culture of consumerism underpinned by 'commodity fetishism'. This view is less indebted to Marx the author of class warfare, pursued in works such as *The Eighteenth Brumaire of Louis Bonaparte* (1852), and more Marx the author of *Capital* (see volume one, chapter one, section iv) (1867) and, before that, the theory of alienation outlined in *The Economic and Philosophic Manuscripts* (1844). Here ideas are developed about how a generalised system of capitalist production reproduces itself, alienating both workers and the ruling class from their true humanity, and where the intrinsic use-value of things becomes replaced by pursuit of the exchange value of commodities in the marketplace.

Capitalist production is realised in the moment of consumption and the capitalist system extends itself on the basis of the generation of 'false' needs. Unintentionally, but no less powerfully for that, capitalism ingratiates itself into the very core of individual human existence and desires. For these theorists, Marx's faith in the contradictions produced by the constantly revolutionising forces of production as the motor force of historical change takes a dark and terminal detour towards the ultimate systemic manipulation of human 'needs'. The 'culture industry', according to Theodor Adorno and Max Horkheimer, standardises culture, debases artistic creativity and undermines humanity through the production and circulation of commodified culture: 'The whole world is made to pass through the filter of the culture industry', and enlightenment becomes mass deception (Adorno and Horkheimer [1944] 1972) These ideas have been formulated by others across the years (Lukacs [1922] 1968; Marcuse 1968), and echoes can still often be heard within contemporary postmodernist writings.

A third emphasis, also developing on the original writings of Marx, attends more closely to the actual operations and dynamics of the 'cultural industries' analysed for the most part in terms of competitive market relationships and how this delimits and shapes the production of media output, and 'ideology'. Graham Murdock and Peter Golding, for example, have consistently argued that a political economy approach is absolutely necessary for an understanding of media communications.

> For us the mass media are first and foremost industrial and commercial organizations which produce and distribute commodities within a late capitalist order. Consequently we would argue, the production of ideology cannot be separated from or adequately understood, without grasping the general economic dynamics of media production and the determinations they exert. (Murdock and Golding 1974)

Here the impersonal laws (economic determinants) of the marketplace rather than the ideological motivations (instrumental agency) of media bosses and tycoons are said to explain much of the organisational structures, routine operations and output of the media. Competitive forces of the marketplace determine the success and long-term viability of media industries. This involves an inherent tendency towards media concentration through buying up (or outpricing and ruining) competitors, processes of vertical integration (extending control over the entire production and distribution processes), and horizontal integration (combining related or complementary businesses) as a way of reducing costs, increasing market share and corporate control. A number of other consequences flow from this same logic of economics.

As processes of concentration and conglomeration result in ever bigger media corporations, so new market entrants find it increasingly difficult to match the economies of scale and market penetration already achieved by established large companies, thus lessening opportunities for new alternative forms of media output and minority representation. Media corporations in pursuit of profits and continuing investor loyalty and/or advertising revenue will generally produce commodities for the largest possible market and for those with a disposable income who are thereby attractive to advertisers. In consequence, those without disposable income or who hold minority or oppositional views are less likely to be catered for through extant media organisations seeking out the 'middle ground' where the largest audience resides. Lifestyle, sports and consumerism, in contrast to politics and the contests and conflicts within civil society, are thereby destined to find increased media prominence. Similarly, 'successful' (that is profitable) commercial products – whether film, books, music, magazines or computer games – will tend to be replicated *ad nauseam*, producing formulaic cultural products that leave little room or opportunity for cultural creativity, expressions of cultural diversity or the development of autonomous and sustainable spheres of artistic activity. By such impersonal means of the marketplace, and not the ideological machinations of the powerful, culture becomes defined in terms of consumerism not citizenship, standardised products not expressions of cultural creativity, and audiences are positioned by income and technological access not citizenship rights or cultural needs.

Moreover, these same general economic determinants extend beyond national frontiers with the pursuit of new markets and profits thereby shaping international communication dynamics, media forms and products. Observing the Western, and principally US-led, dominance of international corporations and communication flows, theorists of 'cultural imperialism' have long criticised the importation of consumerist products and values into underdeveloped countries around the globe and how this is thought to have undermined authentic cultures and ways of life and furthered capitalistic processes of underdevelopment (Schiller 1991, 2000; Tomlinson 1991). These ideas have recently been debated and qualified in terms of a more complex theorisation of processes of globalisation (Sreberny-Mohammadi et al. 1997; Sreberny 2000; Mohammadi 1999; Tomlinson 1999; Thussu 2000). In recent years market processes have been accelerated and deepened at both national and international levels through new technologies of delivery and digitalisation. Digitalisation, or the process of translating different forms of communication into a common code, technically facilitates multimedia production and delivery and prompts mergers between different media industries and sectors, thereby further extending opportunities for media concentration and market dominance (Murdock 1990; Hamelink 1996; Schiller 2000).

In such ways as these, political economy approaches theorise the operations and organisation of the cultural industries. There is no doubting the considerable explanatory power of this theoretical approach when confronting the latest corporate merger or takeover, the operations of the world's ever growing media conglomerates, or the struggles and market failures of small-scale and alternative forms of media production commercially disenfranchised by the inequalities of the marketplace; simply, the 'fit' between theoretical claims and real-world developments is all too evident (Thussu 1998, 2000; McChesney 1999; Golding and Murdock 2000). Even so, this broad approach is not without its critics.

Cultural studies – our second overarching framework – raises a number of objections to political economy approaches. Principal amongst these are: questions of economic determinism; the conceptualisation of ideology; the lack of a theory of the subject; as well as the seeming privileging of production over the moment of consumption and the political focus on class at the expense of other social divisions within society – 'race', ethnicity, gender, sexuality, age/youth. These criticisms, needless to say, have all been hotly debated. The critique has been mounted on the basis of cultural studies' own theoretical underpinnings based in the humanities rather than in the social sciences, and therefore disposed to interrogate how messages and meanings are generated within texts and signifying practices, rather than economic or sociological investigations of social structures and the strategic deployments of organised power (Grossberg et al. 1992; Turner 1996; During 1999; Durham and Kellner 2001). Rooted in a philo-sophical stance to language and discourse and the signifying capacity of media representations to 'construct' social realities, not simply 'reflect' them, as well as radical political commitments to intervene in processes of hegemonic struggle and change 'from below', cultural studies has progressively sought to interrogate the politics of opposition and the struggles played out within the moment of the text. This has also more recently been extended to address processes and contexts of audience consumption and the ways in which identities are constituted, or contested, within and through media involvement in everyday life. Questions of pleasure, the private sphere and popular culture have here generally found increased salience over those of politics (institutionally defined), the public sphere (rationally conceived) and professional discourses (as carriers of official 'knowledge'). This set of theoretical co-ordinates and political alignments ques-tions the social ontology of the political economy approach in which 'production', 'class' and 'economic determinants' appear to position ordinary people (in theoretical patronising ways) as the passive recipients of 'ideology' conceived in terms of 'false consciousness'.

> Production, narrowly understood as the practices of manufacturing, and abstractly understood as the mode of production, is too easily assumed to be the real bottom line. Perhaps cultural studies has overemphasised the pleasure, freedom and empowerment of consumption (and reception), but . . . I fear that what is operating behind such claims is the desire to return to a simpler model of domination in which people are seen as passively manipulated 'cultural dopes'. (Grossberg 1995: 74–5)

These theoretical differences of approach, based within different ideas of social ontology, epistemology, methodology and politics, cannot be theoretically wished away nor simply accommodated in a new theoretical synthesis: their differences are too deep-seated for that (Golding and Murdock 1979; Garnham 1986, 1995a, 1995b; McGuigan 1992; Carey 1995; Grossberg 1995; Murdock 1995; Ferguson and Golding 1997; Born 2000). None the less, each arguably brings something of use to the table and each also helps (by omission as well as commission) to identify significant lacunae or blind-spots in respect of cultural production. These blind-spots concern the relatively underexplored and theor-etically underdeveloped 'middle ground' of media organisation and production.

Cultural studies' sensitivity to the forms and features of media representa-tions, the play of discourses and 'imagined audience' inscribed within media texts, as well as the fluid nature of cultural power exercised in and through these, all help to question earlier rigid views of 'ideological domination' as the presumed end-point prefigured in media ownership and control and market forces. On the other hand, these same strengths can sometimes lead to a celebratory endorsement of popular cultural forms, and a less than critical interrogation of important silences within their discourses as well as their possible dependence on material forces that by definition are not best accounted for with reference to 'discourse' or 'culture'. (In this respect, simply inverting the research emphasis signalled in the phrase 'production of culture' to 'cultures of production', as some cultural studies commentators are now apt to do, does not suffice as a means of engaging with the multiple complexities of media production enacted within organisational and production domains.)

The political economy approach, on strong empirical grounds, counsels against attending to the symbolic nature of media representations alone as the sole means of recovering the explanations and reasons for the 'play of power' enacted in the moment of textual representation. Indeed, some variants of political economy ignore the symbolic nature of media texts, content to theorise media output as nothing more than a 'bribe' or 'a free lunch' to entice audiences who are thereby delivered and sold to advertisers as the real 'product' on offer (Smythe 1980) – a position that has not gone uncontested by other political economy approaches (Murdock 1978). Even so, political economy's commitment to a social realist ontology based on the historically changing nature of the social relations of production and how these inform 'the cultural' compels it to delve behind the manifest appearances of media representations – important though these are in the dynamics of power – and explore the ways in which media forms and representations have been produced and shaped within limits set by wider social and economic forces. This approach can tend toward generalising economic explanations that ride roughshod over countervailing tendencies and the complexities of symbolic forms.

General processes of media concentration and standardisation of output, for example, can be qualified by the rise of new niche markets, the production of successful minority media products, as well as the actions of venture capitalists buying and fragmenting media industries. The 'symbolic value' of uneconomic or costly media services and 'flagship' productions (public service broadcasting, commercial TV news provision, or spectacular one-off TV dramas or natural history programmes for example) all qualify the generalised explanatory power of economic determinants alone, as can politicised regulatory environments and the outcomes of political struggles countering marketplace forces. The marketplace is never static and the pursuit of profits can both stimulate and stifle cultural innovation. Moreover, marketplaces can often accommodate simultaneously different forms of media organisation that co-exist as well as compete within symbiotic relationships internal to particular fields of cultural production, pointing to further layers of complexity and 'production ecologies' that have yet to receive detailed analysis.

Perhaps in acknowledgement of some of these criticisms, Murdock and Golding have recently rebranded their influential approach as 'critical political economy' and sought to extend its reach to structuring processes informing audience involvement and cultural consumption as well as production. Today they are more likely to refer to questions of 'discourse' rather than concerns of 'ideology' classically conceived as 'false consciousness'.

What distinguishes the critical political economy perspective . . . is precisely its focus on the interplay between the symbolic and the economic dimensions of public communication. It sets out to show how different ways of financing and organizing cultural production have traceable consequences for the range of discourses and representations in the public domain and for audience access to them. (Golding and Murdock 2000: 70)

Many researching the field of media organisation and production will probably concur with the general thrust of this approach whilst none the less wanting to examine and explore further the complexities and multilayered processes and practices involved in media production and organisation, and give these their explanatory due – a position that some political economists, for their part, generously concede: 'Critical political economy is a necessary precursor to an adequate sociology of cultural production; it is not a substitute for it' (Murdock 1995: 92; see also Mosco 1996).

Between the economic determinations of the marketplace and the cultural discourses within media representations, then, lies a terrain that has yet to be fully explored and adequately theorised (Born 2000; Curran 2000). Studies of media organisation and production generally sail between the Scylla of marketplace determinations and the Charybdis of the unmediated play of cultural power. Where the former can all too often begin and end with a materialist presumption of the determinacy of the marketplace, the latter too often substitutes an idealist interpretation of the play of discourses divorced from a grounded analysis of exactly how these were selected and shaped in the processes and practices of media production – or outside them. Questions of organisation and production have yet to be fully opened up to empirical analysis and interpretation and in ways that are analytically sensitive to the 'mediating' agency of cultural producers.

One area of production research, exceptionally, has contributed detailed empirical findings and discussion to the wider field of media communication studies: the field of news production.[1] This literature is of interest in its own terms but it also serves to highlight the complexities and different levels of 'mediation' involved in processes of cultural production more generally. Currently news organisations and journalism practices are undergoing fundamental change, prompting a re-evaluation of earlier findings and also new theorisation of this important area of cultural production. For these reasons it is useful to focus on news production studies. The following now reviews this research effort and points to new and productive departures for future research – many of which are represented in the chapters that follow.

Studies in the Sociology of News Production

If the ideas of Marx still register in the traditions of political economy and cultural studies, so the ideas of Émile Durkheim with respect to processes of professional socialisation and the establishment of group norms, and Max Weber with respect to the nature of modern bureaucracies and views of social action, have informed the sociological study of news production.

Early 'formative' studies of news focused on particular news processes, whether the gatekeeping selections of news editors (White 1950); the reasons for journalist conformity to a news policy (Breed 1955; Warner 1971); the effects of collective journalist expectancies upon reporting behaviour (Lang and Lang 1953; Halloran et al. 1970); the strategic use of 'objectivity' by journalists as a means of warding off criticism (Tuchman 1972); the journalistic reliance upon typifications in routinising the unexpected nature of news (Tuchman 1973); or the role of organisational policies in conflict avoidance between reporters and their superiors (Sigelman 1973). These early studies, all worth reading to this day, pointed to the explanatory potential of attending to aspects of the news production process and becoming familiar with the journalist's working environment. Other studies did likewise, though these relied mainly on professional interview testimonies and retrospective accounts of media production and organisational factors. Thus early studies of Westminster correspondents (Tunstall 1970), crime reporters (Chibnall 1977), the institution of the British Broadcasting Corporation (BBC) (Burns 1977), and political programme-makers (Tracey 1978), all made numerous references to the determining influences of organisational contexts and production practices – as recounted by the professionals themselves. These early studies, then, indicated some of the insights that could be achieved from attending to professional practices and the news production domain.

Throughout the 1970s and 1980s a number of 'substantive' ethnographies developed this interest in the organisational, bureaucratic and professional nature of news production and news manufacture processes (Epstein 1973; Altheide 1976; Murphy 1976; Schlesinger 1978; Tuchman 1978; Gans 1979; Golding and Elliott 1979; Bantz et al. 1980; Fishman 1980; Gitlin 1980; Ericson et al. 1987; Soloski 1989). Based on extensive and intensive periods of newsroom observations and interviews, sometimes conducted across many years and different news outlets, researchers became fully conversant with news-making processes. How news was subject to temporal routines, how newsroom layouts were organised spatially, and how news processing was organised in relation to a newsroom division of labour, corporate hierarchy and professional cultural milieu all became basic building blocks to understanding. The ideological consequences of the organisational character of news production was often stressed:

> The organisational imperatives of network news, and the logics that proceed from these demands, irresistibly shape the picture of society in consistent directions. (Epstein 1973: 265)

> The routines of production have definite consequences in structuring news . . . The doings of the world are tamed to meet the needs of a production system in many respects bureaucratically organised. (Schlesinger 1978: 47)

> It is the organisation of news, not events in the world, that creates news. (Ericson et al. 1987: 345)

Researchers also observed the professional pursuit of deep-seated news values and the operation of a journalistic culture and milieu sustaining of colleague relationships, journalist professionalism and news policies. But it was the bureaucratic necessity of 'routine' that became the explanatory key for many of these theorists. In contrast to earlier studies of news gatekeepers, with their tendency towards individualist and subjectivist explanations of news selection (White 1950), these studies collectively emphasised how news was an organisational accomplishment guaranteeing that sufficient amounts of news were produced on time and to a predetermined form (Rock 1981).

A number of unintended consequences were said to flow from this. First, the characteristic 'event orientation' of news gives expression to the temporal routines of production (Halloran et al. 1970) and this, in turn, displaces from public view wider issues of social structure and longer-term processes of change (Schlesinger 1978). Second, a newsroom division of labour is required to monitor 'the news net' of other news media and sources (Tuchman 1978); specialist journalists and correspondents are therefore organised into 'news beats', and news bureaux are established in certain locations (Rock 1981; Fishman 1980). Third, this places journalists in a position of dependency on 'official' sources, which are thereby granted 'routine' entry into the news media and become the 'primary definers' of important events (Hall et al. 1978). Fourth, 'routine' also features in the journalists' deployment of a 'vocabulary of precedents' that help them to recognise, produce and justify their selection and treatment of 'news stories' (Ericson et al. 1987: 348) and so helps to create the professional journalist's 'news sense'. In all these ways, then, the bureaucratic and organisational expediency of 'routine' was said to help account for the relatively 'unconscious' role played by news journalists in news manufacture, the relatively standardised form of news produced across news outlets, and also the generally ideological nature of news and its orientation towards social and political elites and the endorsement of the capitalist social system.

A related finding concerned the identification of a shared professional ideology of objectivity. This too, it was concluded, contributed to the reproduction of elite views. John Soloski argued, for example, that, 'objectivity is the most important professional norm, and from it flows more specific aspects of news professionalism such as news judgment, the selection of sources and the structure of news beats' (Soloski 1989: 213; see also Hall et al. 1978). Importantly, this also ensures that 'authoritative' (typically 'authority') sources are routinely sought out and granted privileged access to the news media as a way of buttressing the journalists' professional claims to objectivity and keeping potential critics at bay. This 'strategic ritual' (Tuchman 1972), in social constructionist accounts, can also be theorised as a pragmatic response to the philosophical elusiveness of 'objectivity', as well as to the difficulties of reporting on contending social interests and their conflicting interpretative claims. Professional claims to 'objectivity' also obviate the need for explicit organisational policies as a form of control. The norm of 'objectivity' is internalised and journalists police themselves and 'discretion becomes predictable' (Larson quoted in Soloski 1989: 210; cf. Breed 1955).

In summary, then, these studies argued that the organisational requirements of news combine with the professional ideology of objectivity to routinely privilege the voices of the powerful, and this further reinforces the tendency towards the standardised and ideological nature of news. These studies in the sociology of news production represent a substantive literature, rich in empirical detail and theorisation of the mechanics of news production. Together they produced an invaluable sociological record and analysis of news production and the forces constraining news output and demonstrated how in-depth study of news producers, their cultural milieu and professional domains could help to explain the dynamics and determinants of news output. As such, they served to qualify the generalising and largely speculative theories current at the time. Both 'underdeveloped' instrumentalist ideas of news control and conspiracy, for example, as well as structurally 'overdetermined' theories of news as ideological reproduction, came up against their more grounded theorisation of news manufacture. Since many of these ethnographies were conducted, however, much news ink has dried up for good under the bridge of technological change, and economic, regulatory and cultural forces have all played their part in the radical, (often professionally traumatic), reconfiguration of news corporations, news production and journalist practices. New(s) departures are thereby opened up for today's researchers.

New(s) Departures

Today, digital technologies, satellite and cable delivery systems and the opportunities for convergence that these provide, have stimulated the pursuit by corporate news players of new(s) synergies and profits through the simultaneous production for multimedia news outlets (Murdock 1990; Herman and McChesney 1997; Boyd-Barrett 1998; Thussu 1998). These changes, in turn, have paved the way for 'multiskilled' (or is it 'deskilled'?) journalists who are now often obliged by short-term contracts, casualisation and flattened career structures to turn their hand to 'flexible' work practices, and 'package' news according to conventionalised formats (Altheide and Snow 1991; Franklin 1994; Cottle 1995, 2001b; Bromley 1997; Franklin and Murphy 1998). Today's 'news culture' (Allan 1999) is arguably no longer confined to the professional milieu inhabited by news workers and their immersion within an impinging web of 'news facticity' plied by competitor colleagues; rather, it also informs the strategic promotional interventions of organised and alternative interests (Ericson et al. 1989; Manning 2001; Cottle 2003), as well as audiences and readers more generally (Bardoel 1996). News also now comes in many different forms, both 'serious' and 'popular', and is variously lamented and celebrated for doing so (Franklin 1997; Langer 1997). It is delivered by on-line technologies (Jankowsjki and Selm 2000; Hall, J., 2001) as well as traditional print and global broadcasting media with increased 24-hour, 'real-time' capabilities (MacGregor 1997; McNair 1998; Volkmer 1999). A complex and more differentiated field of news production therefore characterises today's news ecology.

A few studies only have begun to pursue the differentiated nature of news forms and professional practices into their production domains and, in so doing, have also begun to explore how news production 'contexts' and news 'texts' can be productively approached as mutually interpenetrating, and not as analytically separable moments (Bell 1991; Cottle 1993a; Hellend 1995; Clausen 2001; Matthews 2002). Implicit to such studies is a questioning of the received wisdom of earlier ethnographies. The different forms of news now on offer, for example,

qualify earlier generalising claims that the organisational nature of news production exerts a determinacy moving toward ideological closure (see also
Eliasoph 1988). The earlier theoretical and explanatory emphasis placed upon
routine tended towards a form of *organisational functionalism* in which ideas
of journalist agency and practices became lost from view in the workings of
bureaucratic needs and professional norms. This may have helped to qualify
easy ideas of conspiracy and ideological partisanship as the principal explanation of news output, but at the cost of denying human actors their central role in
the purposeful construction and reproduction of differentiated news products –
products characteristically differentiated and defined in conformity to the particular parameters and agendas of news selection, distinctive textual conventions
of storytelling, and particularised audience appeals and modes of address.

A conceptual shift from 'routine' to 'practice' is therefore required. The conceptualisation of 'practice', borrowing in part from Michel Foucault, is preferable
in that it can accommodate both a sense of the 'discursive' and the 'administrative' in the enactments and regulation of social processes – including those of
cultural production. Moreover, negative ideas of power, control and regulation
as imposed from outside or from above, are also broadened to include a more
discursive appreciation of the role of human agency and meanings within pre-
vailing administrative procedures and/or 'regimes of truth'. Practices and
discourses can thereby be seen as productive and facilitative, as well as repres-
sive or imposed. On the basis of recent observations of news production (Cottle
1993a, 1999; Pedelty 1995; Clausen 2001; Forde 2001; Matthews 2002), this more
'productive' stance to journalist behaviour certainly finds empirical support.
Journalists arguably do what they do for the most part knowingly and purposefully, which is not to say they are on an 'ideological mission' or, in idealist terms,
that they somehow escape the structures in which they work. But it is to argue
that they are more 'consciously' and 'knowingly' involved and purposefully
'productive' of news texts and output than they are often theoretically given
credit for. They are not, in other words, simply 'unwittingly, unconsciously'
serving 'as a support for the reproduction of a dominant ideological discursive
field' (Hall 1982: 82).

Based within a phenomenology of everyday life, the work of Paddy Scannell
(1992, 1994) also makes a compelling case for seeking to understand the 'communicative intentionality' of programme producers, and demonstrates historically how this has informed the production of programme forms.

> News intends to provide information. Adverts intend to persuade. But even where there is a
> manifest content with obvious strategic-purposive intentions (most obviously, as we shall
> see, in the propaganda that saturated every area of programming in the Second World
> War), there is a necessary prior sociable commitment in the communicative form of every
> programme . . . The character of broadcasting as necessarily sociable lies in the form of its
> communicative context. (Scannell 1994: 23)

In terms of production, news 'text' and production 'context' need not be seen as
separate analytical moments but rather as mutually constitutive and interpenetrating. They can therefore be productively explored both phenomenologically

(Tuchman 1978; Morrison and Tumber 1988; Morrison 1994) and sociologically by examining the cultural practices of news workers and the reproduction of distinctive forms of news. This shift of approach helps to move beyond the seemingly static and homogenising sense of news interrogated through the theoretical prism of bureaucratic routines, and can also help to bridge the theoretical divide between the principal approaches to the study of news – political economy, organisational studies and cultural studies (Berkowitz 1997; Schudson 2000) – since market forces, professional practices and cultural forms all interpenetrate in the moment of production.

Today's differentiated news ecology also qualifies earlier claims that professional journalists subscribe to a prevalent, perhaps universal, ideology of 'objectivity'. This generalises what in fact may be a far more variegated and often journalistically circumspect set of epistemological positions. The ethnographies referenced above, for the most part, focused their empirical sights on high-profile, mainstream national news outlets. These prestigious journalist outlets certainly demand careful scrutiny, given their prominent position within the ecology of news, but they cannot be taken as representative of all news forms; and nor do they necessarily reveal a shared journalistic commitment to 'the' notion of objectivity. Even within prestigious news outlets publicly espousing a commitment to news 'objectivity', such as the BBC, we can encounter journalists and investigative reporters who are reflexively aware of the philosophical difficulties involved as well as the pragmatic conventions and artifices that they and their colleagues deploy when constructing a semblance of news balance, impartiality and 'fair play'. Too often, it seems, journalists are patronised by academics who assume that they alone have an omniscient insight into such difficult representational issues, and who fail to recognise the range of practitioners' views on offer. Ideas of 'objectivity' and its closest correlates – 'balance', 'impartiality', 'fairness', 'truthfulness' and 'factual accuracy' – do not exhaust the epistemological claims of journalism (cf. Glasser and Craft 1998). Today, confronted by the different textual means that serve to underpin claims to news 'knowledge', researchers are better advised seriously to consider, and ethnographically to explore, the full range of news epistemologies on offer across the news field. Tabloid and populist forms of journalism, for example, tend to underwrite their claims 'to know' and the seeming 'truthfulness' of their news stories by an inscribed 'subjectivist epistemology'; championing a position of moral partisanship, if not outrage, for example, and appealing directly to sentiment and feelings, rather than expert rationalities and statistical corroboration (Bird 1990; Dahlgren and Sparks 1992; Cottle 1993a). This work has barely begun. It demands careful, comparative ethnographic research, and it promises a deeper appreciation of how text, talk and visuals are professionally inscribed into, and serve to underwrite, the differing epistemological 'truth' claims of news.

Exploring the construction of distinct forms of news can also reveal how patterns and forms of news access and participation sometimes depend on the deliberate 'emplotments' of news producers in conformity to the pursuit of established textual appeals as much as the strategic interventions originated by outside interests – again qualifying generalising predictions about routine and privileged elite access (Jacobs 1996; Langer 1997; Cottle 2003). There is a textual

complexity here awaiting ethnographic exploration. Similarly, how news producers visualise their 'imagined audience' and inscribe this into their news
selections and inflections and characteristic forms of news presentation and with
what impact on their treatment of news stories and forms of portrayal, can also
be productively pursued into the news domain – whether that of a populist
commercial TV news programme (Cottle 1993a), commercial and public service
Japanese news stations (Clausen 2001), magazine music journalism (Forde 2001),
or a BBC children's news programme (Matthews 2002).

We need to explore further how news is professionally produced and differentiated according to the established sub-genres of the wider news field, how
these may serve corporate strategies and the pursuit of niche markets, and how
different news forms address the 'imagined' cultural horizons of their audiences.
This more encompassing, holistic approach to the news field has barely begun to
be explored and theorised. Here Pierre Bourdieu's ideas in respect to the
differentiation of the literary field and its cultural production may help:

> The science of the literary field is a form of *analysis situs* which establishes that each position
> – e.g. the one which corresponds to a genre such as the novel, or within this, to a sub-
> category such as the 'society novel' (*roman mondain*) or the 'popular novel' – is subjectively
> defined by the system of distinctive properties by which it can be situated relative to other
> positions; that every position, even the dominant one, depends for its very existence, and for
> the determinations it imposes on its occupants, on the other positions constituting the field.
> (Bourdieu 1993: 30)

In some respects, this approach to the literary field can be considered homo-
logous to the news field and is suggestive of today's complex 'news ecology'.
The term 'news ecology' helps to signal (a) the under-theorised, and ethnographically under-explored, dimension of news differentiation, and (b) how this
is constituted in important respects by a system of internally defined relations of
difference – differences that are consciously monitored and reproduced by
practising journalists both as a means of managing personal career moves within
and across the field, but also as a professional means of reproducing specific
forms of news as required. How differentiated news forms are professionally
reproduced and inscribed into the selections and inflections of news has a
bearing not only on the ecology of news, of course, but also on the representations (and silences) of news output.

The differentiated nature of the news field to date has been under-theorised;
other powerful, countervailing forces of homogenisation have tended to attract
the critical spotlight. This is understandable. Political economy perspectives are
today as relevant as ever in the interrogation and explanation of the dynamics of
the marketplace, corporate change and commercial conglomeration (Murdock
1990; Thussu 1998; McChesney 1999) and their impact on news production
(McManus 1994; Ehrlich 1995; Altshull 1997). Even so, it is noteworthy how
ideas of 'post-Fordism', 'disorganised capitalism' and 'flexible specialisation'
(Hall and Jacques 1989; Lash and Urry 1987; Murray 1989) as well as observations of the rise of 'vertical disintegration' (Lash and Urry 1994) and 'venture
capitalism' within sectors of the media industry (Murphy 1998) all point to

economic trends that do not always, inexorably, further trends of global media conglomeration and news homogenisation. The complexities and contradictory tendencies of the marketplace, it seems, must also be kept under constant scrutiny and cannot always be predicted a priori.

Complexity and contradiction also obtain in respect to the introduction of new technologies, processes of digitalisation and technological convergence that are currently reconfiguring newsrooms and changing journalist practices (Bromley 1997; MacGregor 1997; McNair 1998). Close-up, empirical studies of the technological and associated changes under way in 'downsized', 'multi-media' and 'multiskilled' 'news centres' are relatively few (Beamish 1998; Pilling 1998; Cottle 1999), as are studies of how new technologies become a site of political struggle and 'corporate strategising' that is played out differently in national contexts and in relation to shifting balances of force within the work-place (Marjoribanks 2000a) and through distinct organisational cultures (Küng-Shankleman 2000). We need to know much more, for example, about processes of 'technological embedding' and the 'social (and professional) shaping' of news technologies in use by journalists, as well as the impact of these technological changes upon working practices, source involvement and news output.

We also need to examine, as a matter of considerable interest and potential insight, the production of alternative and minority forms of news serviced by the new on-line and old technologies of production and distribution (Giffard 1998; Atton 1999, 2002; Browne 1999; Downing 2001). These too are contributing to today's changing ecology of news within the communication flows of the 'net-work society' (Castells 1997). They present their own complex differentiations and often problematise the distinction between news producers and news consumers. They demand careful ethnographic work also. And we must also continue to explore news production domains in respect of divisions of labour and considerations of gender and minority ethnicity (Byerly and Warren 1996; Carter et al. 1998; Cottle 2000b; Ross 2001), as well as news production and practices across different national contexts and political systems (Manzella 2000; Pan 2000; Koltsova 2001). Of course there is much more to media production than news production, but the study of news production, as the most developed field of work in this area, affords some of the most penetrating insights into many of the complexities and levels of analysis required in the empirical exploration of cultural production. These range, as we have heard, across:

- *the micro-level* of cultural milieux and interactions of producers situated within norm-governed and hierarchical production settings and the relationships entered into with technologies, professional colleagues and outside sources;

- *the meso-level* of impinging organisational cultures, corporate strategy and editorial policies informing production practices and the reproduction of conventionalised (and changing) cultural forms; and

- *the macro-contexts* and surrounding regulatory, technological and competitive environments conditioning the operations and output of media organisations at global to local levels.

Plan of the Book

Media Organisation and Production is structured into four parts, each addressing general themes raised above. Following this introduction, Part II: **Global Corporations, Local Alternatives** includes two chapters emphasising different developments in the contemporary world of global–local media. Robert McChesney in Chapter 2 'Corporate media, global capitalism' provides an authoritative overview and critical analysis of the latest processes of corporate media concentration and the increasingly global operations of these media giants as well as the synergies of interest these have for powerful capitalist interests. The chapter demonstrates the continuing relevance of a political economy approach for mapping and explaining the latest corporate media dynamics and trends and also provides a searing critique of how these same processes are profoundly injurious for democracy. Chris Atton in Chapter 3, 'Organisation and production in alternative media', reminds us of the historical development and current vitality of alternative forms of media production and how these alternatives often struggle to counter the dominant media trends charted by McChesney. The discussion examines three very different approaches to alternative media organisation and production in contemporary society – case studies that help us to understand how different alternative media forms of organisation work in practice. Specifically the chapter attends to the production and organisational forms of a radical newspaper (*Counter Information*), an activist video magazine (*Undercurrents*) and a radical Internet project (*Indymedia*).

Part III, **Corporate Change and Organisational Cultures**, also comprises two complementary chapters, each adding further levels of insight for the analysis of contemporary corporate behaviour and their operations in times of change. Chapter 4, 'Strategising technological innovation: the case of news corporation' by Timothy Marjoribanks, analyses how Rupert Murdoch's global business News Corporation has sought to incorporate and exploit the latest developments in print-based technologies of production – technologies that have transformed the nature of newspaper work relations and production. Marjoribanks argues that how these technologies are implemented has a profound impact on the organisation of relations between management and the workforce in the newspaper production process, and that control of strategies for technological innovation has shifted to management with a consequent reduction in the role of unions in workplace negotiation processes. Despite these broad trends, the chapter also illustrates how work sites located within different national contexts (in the UK, US and Australia) have experienced the implementation and strategies for technological innovation differently, and thereby points to key differences at work and how these too inform corporate processes of change. Chapter 5, 'Organisational culture inside the BBC and CNN' by Lucy Küng-Shankleman, explores a further level of corporate complexity and organisational differentiation. The chapter provides unique insights into two of the world's best-known media organisations, during a period of challenge and change. The BBC and CNN have very different histories, remits and identities, but both must now compete to provide news in a media environment shaped by increasing competition, globalisation, digitalisation and convergence. Drawing on intensive research carried out among senior managers in both organisations, Küng-Shankleman explores the beliefs and attitudes that shape management priorities and broadcasting policy. Specifically, she examines how each organisation has distinct organisational cultures and how they differently position these organisations in their responses to surrounding forces of change.

Part IV, **Producers, Practices and the Production of Cultural Forms**, comprises three chapters each deliberately focused on producers and their practices and how these inform the production of distinctive cultural forms. Paddy Scannell in Chapter 6, 'The *Brains Trust*: a historical study of the management of liveness on radio', provides a fascinating recovery of the production of a historical radio programme and how the 'communicative intentionality' of the producers involved purposefully and creatively led to the creation of a new form of public expression – a form that has subsequently become 'naturalised' as part of the apparatus of broadcasting. By attending to the original moment of its creation and the phenomenological aspects of producing 'liveness', Scannell opens up a fresh and necessary vista on the human complexities of production. Chapter 7, 'Journalists with a difference: producing music journalism' by Eamonn Forde, charts the changing market forces of music journalism and how the practices and professionalism of music journalism are in many fundamental respects quite different from those of 'mainstream' journalism. Attending to these differences permits new insights into an empirically under-explored area of a distinctive arena of journalism, and also how journalism generally is oriented towards the production of distinctive forms – forms that demand different types of organisational arrangements, production practices and professional self-identities. This theme is also explored and empirically substantiated in Chapter 8, 'Cultures of production: the making of children's news', by Julian Matthews. Based on ethnographic research into the BBC children's news programme, *Newsround*, Matthews helps to signal the importance of analysing at a micro-level the relationship between news workers and the construction of distinctive forms of news text. This makes the case for a more differentiated understanding of news forms and how producers reproduce these informed by a sense of their imagined audiences. Here the producers' imagined audience of children is found to shape and inflect the representations of the environment in unnecessarily 'infantilised' ways – ways that are thought to be unhelpful for a more encompassing and adequate understanding of contemporary environmental risks.

Finally Part V, **Changing International Genres and Production Ecologies**, includes two chapters that also attend to the production of distinctive genres, but here exploring how and why these are changing in relation to wider forces of change and with what impact on the organisation of their production. Chapter 9, 'International TV and film co-production: a Canadian case study' by Doris Baltruschat, examines how Canadian TV programmes and film production are currently being shaped and (deleteriously) conditioned by the necessity for producers to participate in international co-productions as a means of securing funding and commissions. Here the author explores how both professional and textual practices are changing in response to the requirements of international co-productions, which, by definition, tend not to address audiences as nationally and locally differentiated or as culturally distinct. Considerations of changing genre are thereby implicated in the commercial 'advantages' of international co-production arrangements and the way in which producers professionally enact these.

The theme of changing genres is also pursued in Chapter 10, 'Producing nature(s): the changing production ecology of natural history TV' by Simon Cottle. Here the author documents how an established 'production ecology' of natural history TV production is currently responding to the changing commercial and scheduling priorities of TV broadcasters. Composed of different players, including established public service and commercial natural history programme units, satellite television and cable distributors, and small and medium-sized independent production houses, this 'production ecology' demonstrates a complex set of relationships characterised by competition and co-existence, rivalry and mutual dependency. How these various organisations and players negotiate their respective positions in the field of natural history programme production and manage and creatively respond to the changing demands of the TV marketplace is found to impact on the nature of their programme productions, and also how 'nature' is constructed for public consumption.

The chapters that follow will collectively provide a wide range of theoretical and analytical responses to the field of media organisation and production, demonstrating both the multiple and interrelated complexities involved and the explanatory gains that can be achieved from attending to this under-researched field. On this basis it is hoped that the reader will be encouraged to see how media organisation and production are always structured and conducted in relation to impinging contexts and determinants of change, and how these same forces are inscribed, managed and creatively negotiated by media professionals and producers in their practices, in different organisational settings, and in the production of distinctive and changing cultural forms. Media organisation and production cannot be usefully theorised as hermetically sealed behind institutional walls or as confined to organisational decision-making and professional routines, much less simply the unmediated expression of market forces or the surrounding field of contending discourses. As the chapters in this book attest, media 'organisation' and 'production' involve all of these forces in dynamic combination and played out at local and global levels.

CHAPTER SUMMARY

- To understand media today, we need to study media organisation and production in global and local contexts. It is only by this means that we can overcome the 'problem of inference' and better appreciate the complexities involved in processes of cultural production.

- Media organisation and production can be approached from a number of different theoretical perspectives. Overarching traditions of political economy and cultural studies have tended to dominate discussion of how we can best approach and explain the operations and output of media organisations.

- Though political economy and cultural studies approaches are necessary for improved understanding of the wider commercial and cultural forces that undoubtedly circumscribe and penetrate the material and discursive practices of media organisations and producers, they by no means exhaust the field of relevant theoretical frameworks. In between the theoretical foci on marketplace determinations and play of cultural discourses, there still exists a relatively unexplored and under-theorised 'middle ground' of organisational structures and workplace practices.

- Studies of news organisation and production, exceptionally, have contributed detailed empirical findings and theoretical discussion of the complex structures and levels of mediation often involved in cultural production. Over time these findings invariably reflect changing research traditions and approaches as well as significant changes on the ground of news production and practice. Today's news ecology is complex and differentiated.

- Complexities and levels of media production include, at the *micro-level*, the cultural milieux and interactions of producers situated within norm-governed and hierarchical production settings and the relationships entered into with technologies, professional colleagues and outside sources; at the *meso-level*, impinging organisational cultures, corporate strategies and editorial policies informing production practices and the reproduction of conventionalised (and changing) cultural forms; and, at the *macro-level*, surrounding regulatory, technological and competitive environments conditioning the operations and output of media organisations globally and locally.

- The study of media organisation and production analyses how both are structured and conducted in relation to impinging contexts and determinants of change, and how these same forces are inscribed, managed and creatively negotiated by media professionals and producers in their practices, in different organisational settings, and in the production of distinctive and changing cultural forms.

Note

1 For further discussion of the methodology of news ethnography, and a more detailed case for a 'second wave' of news production studies, see Cottle (1998, 2000a, 2001b). For further overview discussions of the sociology of news, see Schudson (2000) and Tuchman (2002). For useful edited collections of 'classic' news studies, see Berkowitz (1997), Boyd-Barrett and Newbold (1995) and Tumber (1999).

PART II
GLOBAL CORPORATIONS, LOCAL ALTERNATIVES

CHAPTER 2
Corporate Media, Global Capitalism

Robert W. McChesney

When one considers media, the role they play in society, and how they affect our economy, culture and polity, there are several approaches one may take. In the United States the dominant approach for much of the past few decades has been 'mainstream' and quantitative. By mainstream, I mean that the research accepted the existing media system (and social structure) as a given and unalterable (and, in effect, highly desirable); research then tended to emphasise measuring how the media system affected personal behaviour. More recently, in the United States and worldwide, there has been a surge in cultural studies approaches to media. This approach tends not to be 'mainstream', and it eschews quantitative methodologies. But the work has a tendency to examine texts and audience reception over production, and rarely places the entire media experience in a broader context. Like mainstream quantitative research, cultural studies is well suited for some sorts of questions, but poorly suited for others.

It is the 'big' questions about media and society that the field of the political economy of communication is particularly and uniquely suited to address. Political economy of communication entails two main features. First, it is concerned with the relationship of media systems to the broader social and power relations of society. Nowadays that means possibly the question: what is the relationship of media to capitalism and the global corporate economy? Political economy immediately and always asks the question that is all but forgotten in mainstream quantitative research: what role do the media play in reinforcing and/or undermining political and economic inequality? To what extent are media a democratic force? Cultural studies has a distinct interest in these questions as well.

The second feature of political economy is what makes it distinct from cultural studies. Political economy of communication specifically examines the structure of media industries – questions of ownership, market structure and commercial support – and how these affect media content, performance and impact. The crucial role of the profit motive in shaping media performance must be at the centre of any study of media that attempts to answer the fundamental questions that begin with 'why'. Those approaches to media that ignore this basic structural fact tend to drift off course and lose sight of the big picture. Political economy of communication cannot answer every question in media studies by a long shot, but it can provide a necessary context to promote better answers for almost all of them, and it is ideally suited to tackle others. Political economy, for example, is particularly concerned with how these structures of corporate control, markets and advertising set limits on what can be done by media workers, be they journalists or those toiling in the entertainment realm.

Above all, and far more than any other branch of communication research, political economy of communication is explicitly critical. Critical does not necessarily mean that it is 'radical' or 'left-wing': indeed, one may be a card-carrying conservative and yet employ political economy of communication. Political economy regards the state sceptically and is directly concerned with issues of censorship. What 'critical' means is that the very nature of the communication system as a whole – including the role of the government – is never taken as a 'given', as something natural and therefore off-limits to hard examination. The starting point for political economy of communication is the recognition that all media systems are the direct and indirect result of explicit public policies. Powerful interests invariably attempt to make the media system appear as if it is 'natural' and therefore necessary, but that is never the case. For that reason, the political economy of communication takes particular interest in examining the nature of political debates over media and communication policies. Much of this research is historical in nature.

So this is the intellectual pedigree for this chapter (and for this book). In what follows I will briefly lay out the contours of the global media system, how it developed, its relationship to global capitalism, and its implications for democracy. As you will see, political economy of communication is no mere academic exercise. Its orientation is to understand the world so as to change it; to promote or protect those values we deem most important.

The Media System Goes Global

In the past, media systems were primarily national; but recently, a global commercial media market has emerged. To grasp media today and in the future, one must start by understanding the global system, and then factor in differences at the national and local levels. 'What you are seeing', says Christopher Dixon, media analyst for the investment firm PaineWebber, 'is the creation of a global oligopoly. It happened to the oil and automotive industries earlier this century; now it is happening to the entertainment industry'.

This global oligopoly has two distinct but related facets. First, it means the dominant companies – roughly one-half US-based, but all with significant US, operations – are moving across the planet at breakneck speed. The point is to capitalise on the potential for growth abroad and not get outflanked by competitors, since the US market is well developed and only permits incremental expansion. As Viacom CEO Sumner Redstone has put it, 'Companies are focusing on those markets promising the best return, which means overseas.' Frank Biondi, former chairman of Vivendi's Universal Studios, asserts that '99 per cent of the success of these companies long-term is going to be successful execution offshore.'

The dominant media firms increasingly view themselves as global entities. Bertelsmann CEO Thomas Middelhoff bristled when, in 1998, some said it was improper for a German firm to control 15 per cent of both the US book publishing and music markets. 'We're not foreign. We're international', Middelhoff proclaimed. 'I'm an American with a German passport.' In 2000 Middelhoff proclaimed that Bertelsmann was no longer a German company: 'We are really the most global media company.' Likewise, AOL-Time Warner's Gerald Levin stated, 'We do not want to be viewed as an American company. We think globally' (Schechter 2000). Second, convergence and consolidation are the order of the day. Specific media industries are becoming more and more concentrated, and the dominant players in each media industry increasingly are subsidiaries of huge global media conglomerates. As one small example demonstrates, the US market for educational publishing is now controlled by four firms, whereas it had two dozen viable players as recently as 1980 ('Scardino's way', *The Economist*, 2000).

The level of mergers and acquisitions is breath-taking. In the first half of 2000, the number of merger deals in global media, Internet, and telecommunications totalled US$300 billion – triple the figure for the first six months of 1999, and exponentially higher than the figure from ten years earlier (Mermigas 2000a). The logic guiding media firms in all of this is clear: get very big very quickly, or get swallowed up by someone else. This is similar to trends taking place in many other industries. 'There will be less than a handful of end-game winners', the CEO of Chase Manhattan announced in September 2000. 'We want to be an end-game winner' ('Talk Show' 2000.) But in few industries has the level of concentration been as stunning as in media. In short order, the global media market has come to be dominated by nine transnational corporations: General Electric (owner of NBC), Liberty Media, Disney, AOL-Time Warner, Sony, News Corporation, Viacom, Vivendi, and Bertelsmann. None of these companies existed in their present form as recently as fifteen years ago; today nearly all of them will rank among the largest 200 non-financial firms in the world for 2000 ('The World's 100 Largest Public Companies' 2000). Of the nine, only five are truly US firms, though all of them have core operations there. Between them, these nine companies own: the major US film studios; the US television networks; 80–85 per cent of the global music market; the majority of satellite broadcasting worldwide; all or part of a majority of cable broadcasting systems; a significant percentage of book publishing and commercial magazine publishing; all or part of most of the commercial cable TV channels in the US and world-wide; a significant portion of European terrestrial television; and on and on and on.

By nearly all accounts, the level of concentration is only going to increase in the future. 'I'm a great believer that we are going to a world of vertically integrated companies where only the big survive', said Gordon Crawford, an executive of Capital Research & Management, a mutual fund that is among the largest shareholders in many of the nine firms listed above (Bianco 2000). For firms to survive, *Business Week* observes, speed is of the essence. 'Time is short' (ibid.). 'In a world moving to five, six, seven media companies, you don't want to be in a position where you have to count on others', Peter Chernin, the president of News Corporation states:

> You need to have enough marketplace dominance that people are forced to deal with you
> . . . There are great arguments about whether content is king or distribution is king. At the
> end of the day, scale is king. If you can spread your costs over a large base, you can outbid
> your competitors for programming and other assets you want to buy. (Hansell 2000)

By 2000, massive cross-border deals – like Pearson merging its TV operations with CLT and Bertelsmann, or Vivendi purchasing Universal – were increasing in prominence (Mermigas 2000b).

Chernin's firm, Rupert Murdoch's News Corporation, may be the most aggressive global trailblazer, although cases could be made for Sony, Bertelsmann or AOL-Time Warner. Murdoch spun off Sky Global Networks in 2000, consolidating his satellite TV services that run from Asia to Europe to Latin America (Goldsmith and Dawtrey 2000). His Star TV dominates in Asia with thirty channels in seven languages (Jacob 2000). News Corp.'s TV service for China, Phoenix TV, in which it has a 45 per cent stake, now reaches 45 million homes there and has enjoyed an 80 per cent increase in advertising revenues in the past year (Groves 2000). And this barely begins to describe News Corp.'s entire portfolio of assets: Twentieth Century Fox films, Fox TV network, HarperCollins publishers, TV stations, cable TV channels, magazines, over 130 newspapers, and professional sport teams.

Why has this taken place? The conventional explanation is technology or, in other words, radical improvements in communications technology that make global media empires feasible and lucrative in a manner unthinkable in the past. This is similar to the technological explanation for globalisation writ large. However, this is only a partial explanation, at best. The real force has been a shift to neoliberalism, which means the relaxation or elimination of barriers to commercial exploitation of media, and concentrated media ownership. There is nothing inherent in the technology that required neoliberalism; new digital communications could have been used, for example, simply to enhance public service media, had a society elected to do so. With neoliberal values, however, television, which had been a non-commercial preserve in many nations, suddenly became subject to transnational commercial development and was thrust into the centre of the emerging global media system.

Once the national deregulation of media took place in major nations like the United States and Britain, it was followed by transnational measures like the North American Free Trade Agreement (NAFTA) and the World Trade Organization (WTO), all intent on establishing regional and global marketplaces. This has laid the foundation for the creation of the global media system, dominated by the aforementioned conglomerates. Now in place, the system has its own logic. Firms must become larger and diversified to reduce risk and enhance profit-making opportunities, and they must straddle the globe so as never to be outflanked by competitors. The upside is high; this is a market that some anticipate will have trillions of dollars in annual revenues within a decade. If that is the case, those companies that sit atop the field will almost certainly rank among the two or three dozen largest in the world.

The development of the global media system has not been unopposed in elite policy-making forums. While media conglomerates press for policies to facilitate their domination of markets throughout the world, strong traditions of protection for domestic media and cultural industries persist. Nations ranging from Norway, Denmark and Spain to Mexico, South Africa and South Korea keep their small domestic film production industries alive with government subsidies. In the summer of 1998 culture ministers from twenty nations, including Brazil, Mexico, Sweden, Italy and Ivory Coast, met in Ottawa to discuss how they could 'build some ground rules' to protect their cultural fare from 'the Hollywood juggernaut'. Their main recommendation was to keep culture out of the control of the World Trade Organization. A similar 1998 gathering, sponsored by UNESCO in Stockholm, recommended that culture be granted special exemptions in global trade deals. Nevertheless, the trend is clearly in the direction of opening markets.

Proponents of neoliberalism in every country argue that cultural trade barriers and regulations harm consumers, and that subsidies inhibit the ability of nations to develop their own competitive media firms. There are often strong commercial-media lobbies within nations that believe they have more to gain by opening up their borders than by maintaining trade barriers. In 1998, for example, when the British government proposed a voluntary levy on film and theatre revenues (mostly Hollywood films) to benefit the British commercial film industry, British broadcasters, not wishing to antagonise the firms who supply their programming, lobbied against the measure until it died. If the WTO is explicitly a pro-commercial organisation, then the International Telecommunication Union (ITU) has only become one after a long march from its traditional commitment to public service values in telecommunications (Molony 1999).

The European Commission (EC), the executive arm of the European Union, too, finds itself in the middle of what controversy exists concerning media policy, and it has considerably more power than the ITU. On the one hand, the EC is committed to building powerful pan-European media giants that can go toe-to-toe with the US-based giants. On the other hand, it is committed to maintaining some semblance of competitive markets, so it occasionally rejects proposed media mergers as being anti-competitive (Stern 2000c). The wave of commercialisation of European media has put the EU in the position of condemning some of the traditional subsidies to public service broadcasters as 'non-competitive', which is a source of considerable controversy (Stern 2000a, 2000b). Public service broadcasting, once the media centrepiece of European social democracy, is now on the defensive and increasingly reduced to locating a semi-commercial niche in the global system (Goldsmith 2000; Larsen 2000). Yet, as a quasi-democratic institution, the EU is subject to some popular pressure that is unsympathetic to commercial interests. Indeed, when Sweden assumes the rotating chair of the EU in 2001, it may push for its domestic ban on TV advertising to children under 12 to be extended across Europe. If it does, it will be the most radical attempt yet to limit the prerogatives of the corporate media giants that dominate commercial children's television (Hatfield 2000).

Perhaps the best way to understand how closely the global commercial media system is linked to the neoliberal global capitalist economy is to consider the role of advertising. Advertising is a business expense made preponderantly by the largest firms in the economy. The commercial media system is the necessary transmission belt for businesses to market their wares across the world; indeed globalisation as we know it could not exist without it. A whopping three-quarters of global spending on advertising ends up in the pockets of a mere twenty media companies ('Star turn' 2000). Ad spending has grown by leaps and bounds in the past decade as TV has been opened to commercial exploitation and is growing at more than twice the rate of GDP growth (Tomkins 2000). Latin American ad spending, for example, is expected to increase by nearly 8 per cent in both 2000 and 2001 ('Ad spend growth' 2000). Five or six super-ad agencies have emerged in the past decade to dominate this $350 billion global industry. The consolidation in the global advertising industry is just as pronounced as that in global media, and the two are related. 'Mega-agencies are in a wonderful position to handle the business of mega-clients', one ad executive notes (Elliott 2000). It is 'absolutely necessary . . . for agencies to consolidate. Big is the mantra. So big it must be', another executive stated (Teinowitz and Linnett 2000).

A second tier of less than 100 firms that are national or regional powerhouses rounds out the global media market. Sometimes these second-tier firms control niche markets, like business or trade publishing. Between one-third and one-half of these second-tier firms come from North America; most of the rest are from Western Europe and Japan. Many national and regional conglomerates have been established on the back of publishing or television empires, as in the case of Denmark's Egmont. Each of these second-tier firms is a giant in its own right, often ranking among the thousand largest companies in the world and doing more than $1 billion per year in business. The roster of second-tier media firms from North America includes Dow Jones, Gannett, Knight-Ridder, Hearst and Advance Publications. Those in Europe include the Kirch Group, Mediaset, Prisa, Pearson, Reuters and Reed Elsevier. The Japanese companies, aside from Sony, remain almost exclusively domestic producers.

This second tier has also crystallised rather quickly; across the globe there has been a shakeout in national and regional media markets with small firms getting eaten by medium firms and medium firms being swallowed by big firms. Compared with ten or twenty years ago, a much smaller number of much larger firms now dominate the media at national and regional levels. In Britain, for example, one of the few remaining independent book publishers, Fourth Estate, was sold to Murdoch's HarperCollins in 2000 (Kirkpatrick 2000a). A wave of mergers has left German television – the second largest TV market in the world – the private realm of Bertelsmann and Kirch (Rohwedder 2000). Indeed, a wave of mergers has left all of European terrestrial television dominated by five firms, three of which rank in the global first tier (Reed 2000). The situation may be most stark in New Zealand, where the newspaper industry is largely the province of the Australian-American Rupert Murdoch and the Irishman Tony O'Reilly, who also dominates New Zealand's commercial radio broadcasting and has major stakes in magazine publishing. Murdoch also controls pay television. In short, the rulers of New Zealand's media system could squeeze into a closet.

Second-tier corporations, like those in the first tier, need to reach beyond national borders. 'The borders are gone. We have to grow', the chairman of Canada's CanWest Global Communications stated in 2000. 'We don't intend to be one of the corpses lying beside the information highway' (Brooke 2000).

'We have to be Columbia or Warner Brothers one day' (Cherney 2000). The CEO of Bonnier, Sweden's largest media conglomerate, says that to survive, 'we want to be the leading media company in Northern Europe' (Brown-Humes 2000). Australian media moguls, following the path blazed by Murdoch, have adopted the mantra 'Expand or die'. As one puts it, 'You really can't continue to grow as an Australian supplier in Australia.' Mediaset, the Berlusconi-owned Italian TV power, is angling to expand into the rest of Europe and Latin America. Perhaps the most striking example of second-tier globalisation is Hicks, Muse, Tate and Furst, the US radio/publishing/TV/billboard/movie theatre power that has been constructed almost overnight. Between 1998 and 2000 it spent well over $2 billion purchasing media assets in Mexico, Argentina, Brazil and Venezuela (Sutter 2000).

Second-tier media firms are hardly 'oppositional' to the global system. This is true as well in developing countries. Mexico's Televisa, Brazil's Globo, Argentina's Clarin and Venezuela's Cisneros Group, for example, are among the world's sixty or seventy largest media corporations. These firms tend to dominate their own national and regional media markets, which have been experiencing rapid consolidation as well. They have extensive ties and joint ventures with the largest media transnational corporations (TNCs) as well as with Wall Street investment banks. In Latin America, for example, the second-tier firms work closely with the US giants who are carving up the commercial media pie among themselves. Televisa or Globo can offer News Corp., for example, local domination of the politicians and the impression of local control over their joint ventures. And like second-tier media firms elsewhere, they are also establishing global operations, especially in nations that speak the same language. As a result, the second-tier media firms in the developing nations tend to have distinctly pro-business political agendas and to support expansion of the global media market, which puts them at odds with large segments of the population in their home countries.

Together, the sixty or seventy first- and second-tier giants control much of the world's media: book, magazine and newspaper publishing; music recording; TV production; TV stations and cable channels; satellite TV systems; film production; and motion picture theatres. But the system is still very much in formation. The end result of all this activity by second-tier media firms may well be the eventual creation of one or two more giants, and it almost certainly means the number of viable media players in the system will continue to plummet. Some new second-tier firms are emerging, especially in lucrative Asian markets, and there will probably be further upheavals among the ranks of the first-tier media giants. And corporations get no guarantee of success merely by going global. The point is that they have no choice in the matter. Some, perhaps many, will falter as they accrue too much debt or as they enter unprofitable ventures. However, we are in all probability closer to the end of the process of establishing a stable global media market than to the beginning. And as it takes shape, there is a distinct likelihood that the leading media firms in the world will find themselves in a very profitable position. That is what they are racing to secure.

The global media system is fundamentally non-competitive in any meaningful economic sense of the term. Many of the largest media firms have some of the same major shareholders, own portions of one another, or have interlocking boards of directors. When *Variety* compiled its list of the fifty largest global media firms for 1997, it observed that 'merger mania' and cross-ownership had 'resulted in a complex web of interrelationships' that would 'make you dizzy'. The global market strongly encourages corporations to establish equity joint ventures in which the media giants all own a part of an enterprise. This way, firms reduce competition and risk and increase the chance of profitability. As the CEO of Sogecable, Spain's largest media firm and one of the twelve largest private media companies in Europe, expressed it in *Variety*, the strategy is 'not to compete with international companies but to join them'.

In some respects, the global media market more closely resembles a cartel than it does the competitive marketplace found in economics textbooks. This point cannot be overemphasised. In competitive markets, in theory, numerous producers work hard and are largely oblivious to one another as they sell what they produce at the market price, over which they have no control. This fairy tale, still regularly regurgitated as being an apt description of our economy, is ludicrous when applied to the global media system. The leading CEOs are all on first-name terms and they regularly converse. Even those on unfriendly terms, like Murdoch and AOL-Time Warner's Ted Turner, understand that they need to work together for the 'greater good'. 'Sometimes you have to grit your teeth and treat your enemy as your friend', the former president of Universal, Frank Biondi, concedes (Grover and Siklos 1999). The head of Venezuela's huge Cisneros group, which is locked in combat over Latin American satellite TV with News Corporation, explains about Murdoch: 'We're friends. We're always talking' (Hoag 2000). Moreover, all the first- and second-tier media firms are connected through their reliance upon a few investment banks like Morgan Stanley and Goldman Sachs that quarterback most of the huge media mergers. Those two banks alone put together fifty-two media and telecom deals valued at US$450 billion in the first quarter of 2000, and 138 deals worth US$433 billion in all of 1999 (Mermigas 2000b). This conscious co-ordination does not simply affect economic behaviour; it makes the media giants particularly effective political lobbyists at national, regional and global levels.

Global Corporate Media, Culture and Politics

But what about media content? Global conglomerates can at times have a progressive impact on culture, especially when they enter nations that had been tightly controlled by corrupt, crony-controlled media systems (as in much of Latin America) or nations that had significant state censorship over media (as in parts of Asia). The global commercial media system is radical in that it respects no tradition or custom, on balance, if it stands in the way of profits. But ultimately it is politically conservative, because the media giants are significant beneficiaries of the current social structure around the world, and any upheaval in property or social relations – particularly to the extent that it reduces the power of business – is not in their interest.

The 'Hollywood juggernaut', or the spectre of US cultural imperialism, remains a central concern in many countries for obvious reasons. Exports of US films and TV shows increased by 22 per cent in 1999 (Guider 2000), and the list of the top 125 grossing films for 1999 is made up almost entirely of Hollywood fare (D'Alessandro 2000). When one goes nation by nation, even a 'cultural nationalist' country like France had nine of its top 10 grossing films in 1999 produced by the Hollywood giants (Grey 2000). 'Many leftist intellectuals in Paris are decrying American films, but the French people are eating them up', a Hollywood producer noted (Lyman 2000). Likewise, in Italy, the replacement of single-screen theatres by 'multiplexes' has contributed to a dramatic decline in local film box-office revenues (Rooney 2000). The moral of the story for many European film-makers is that you have to work in English and employ Hollywood movie-making conventions to succeed (Foreman 2000). In Latin America, channels controlled by media giants overwhelm local cable television and the de facto capital for the region is Miami ('US cable channels . . .' 2000).

But there are problems with leaving the discussion at this point. The notion that corporate media firms are merely purveyors of US culture is ever less plausible as the media system becomes increasingly concentrated, commercialised and globalised. The global media system is better understood as one that advances corporate and commercial interests and values and denigrates or ignores that which cannot be incorporated into its mission. There is no discernible difference in the firms' content, whether they are owned by shareholders in Japan or France or have corporate headquarters in New York or Sydney.

As the media conglomerates spread their tentacles, there is reason to believe they will encourage popular tastes to become more uniform in at least some forms of media. Based on conversations with Hollywood executives, *Variety* editor Peter Bart concluded that 'the world film-going audience is fast becoming more homogeneous'. Whereas action movies had once been the only sure-fire global fare – with comedies considerably more difficult to export – by the late 1990s, comedies like *My Best Friend's Wedding* and *The Full Monty* were doing between US$160 million and US$200 million in non-US box-office sales.

When audiences appear to prefer locally made fare, the global media corporations, rather than flee in despair, globalise their production. Sony has been at the forefront of this, producing films with local companies in China, France, India and Mexico, to name but a few (Brodesser 2000; Duke 2000b). India's acclaimed domestic film industry – 'Bollywood' – is also developing close ties to the global media giants ('Growing up' 2000). This process is even more visible in the music industry. Music has always been the least capital-intensive of the electronic media and therefore the most open to experimentation and new ideas. US recording artists generated 60 per cent of their sales outside the United States in 1993; by 1998 that figure was down to 40 per cent. Rather than fold their tents, however, the four media transnationals that dominate the world's recorded-music market are busy establishing local subsidiaries in places like Brazil, where 'people are totally committed to local music', in the words of a writer for a trade publication. Sony, again, has led the way in establishing distribution deals with independent music companies from around the world.

With hypercommercialism and growing corporate control comes an implicit political bias in media content. Consumerism, class inequality and individualism tend to be taken as natural and even benevolent, whereas political activity, civic values and anti-market activities are marginalised. The best journalism is pitched to the business class and suited to its needs and prejudices. With a few notable exceptions, the journalism reserved for the masses tends to be the sort of drivel provided by the media giants on their US television stations. In India, for example, influenced by the global media giants, 'the revamped news media . . . now focus more on fashion designers and beauty queens than on the dark realities of a poor and violent country' (Mishra 2000). This slant is often quite subtle. Indeed, the genius of the commercial media system is the general lack of overt censorship. As George Orwell noted in his unpublished introduction to Animal Farm, censorship in free societies is infinitely more sophisticated and thorough than in dictatorships, because 'unpopular ideas can be silenced, and inconvenient facts kept dark, without any need for an official ban'.

Lacking any necessarily conspiratorial intent and acting in their own economic self-interest, media conglomerates exist simply to make money by selling light escapist entertainment. In the words of the late Emilio Azcarraga, the billionaire founder of Mexico's Televisa: 'Mexico is a country of a modest, very fucked class, which will never stop being fucked. Television has the obligation to bring diversion to these people and remove them from their sad reality and difficult future.' The combination of neoliberalism and corporate media culture tends to promote a deep and profound de-politicisation. One need only look at the United States to see the logical endpoint (Perry 2000). But de-politicisation has its limits, as it invariably runs up against the fact that we live in a social world where politics has tremendous influence over the quality of our lives.

Will the Internet Set Us Free?

Finally, a word should be said about the Internet, the two-ton gorilla of global media and communications. The Internet is increasingly becoming a part of our media and telecommunications systems, and a genuine technological convergence is taking place. Accordingly, there has been a wave of mergers between traditional media and telecom firms and each of them with Internet and computer firms. Already companies like Microsoft, AOL-Time Warner, AT&T and Telefonica have become media powerhouses in their own right. It looks like the global media system is in the process of becoming a globally integrated, commercial communications system where six to a dozen 'supercompanies' will rule the roost. The notion that the Internet would 'set us free' and permit anyone to communicate effectively, hence undermining the monopoly power of the media giants, has not materialised. Although the Internet offers extraordinary promise in many regards, it alone cannot slay the power of the media giants. Indeed, no commercially viable media content site has been launched on the Internet, and it would be difficult to find an investor willing to bankroll any additional attempts. To the extent that the Internet becomes part of the commercially viable media system, it looks to be under the thumb of the usual corporate suspects.

For much of the 1990s even those who were alarmed by the anti-democratic implications of the neoliberal global economy tended to be resigned to these developments. The power of capitalism and the profit motive was such that it would inexorably establish a world system based on world markets and unchecked capitals flows. Likewise, the globalisation of the corporate media system was inexorable. As one Swedish journalist noted in 1997, 'Unfortunately, the trends are very clear, moving in the wrong direction on virtually every score, and there is a desperate lack of public discussion of the long-term implications of current developments for democracy and accountability.' It was presented as natural, as inexorable. And for those in power, those who benefited by the new regime, such thinking made their jobs vastly easier.

Conclusions

There is nothing 'natural' about neoliberal globalisation. It requires extensive changes in government policies and an increased role for the state to encourage and protect certain types of activities. The massive and complex negotiations surrounding NAFTA and the WTO provide some idea of how unnatural and constructed the global neoliberal economy is. Or consider copyright, and what has come to be considered intellectual property. There is nothing natural about this. It is a government-granted and enforced monopoly that prevents competition. It leads to higher prices and a shrinking of the marketplace of ideas, but it serves powerful commercial interests tremendously. In the United States, the corporate media lobby has managed to distort copyright so the very notions of the public domain or fair use – so important historically – have been all but obliterated. The US government leads the fight in global forums to see that the corporate-friendly standards of copyright are extended across the planet and to cyperspace. The commitment to copyright monopolies – now granted for ninety-five years to corporations – as the *sine qua non* of the global economy shows its true commitment is to existing corporate power rather than to a mythological free market.

The traditional myth of the relationship of the state to the private sector in US media has become the neoliberal myth on a global scale. The myth now has become transparently a tool of propaganda. The Enron affair – where a huge corporation made billions by paying off politicians to 'deregulate' utility markets and thereby fleece taxpayers, workers and consumers – highlights again how closely intertwined our government is with the largest private corporations. The widespread graft associated with neoliberal privatisations and deregulations – in telecommunications more than anywhere else – has augured in a wave of corruption of world historical proportions. If the market is God and public service is bunk, why on earth would anyone enter government, except to feather their own nest, by any means necessary? For those at the receiving end of neoliberal globalisation – the bulk of humanity – the idea that people need to accept neoliberal globalisation as a given is untenable. For those committed to democracy above neoliberalism, the struggle is to require informed public participation in government policy-making. Specifically, in view of the importance of media, the struggle is to democratise communication policy-making.

In February 2002 in New York City, the World Economic Forum (WEF) held its annual meeting. Designed to gather together the leading visionaries and figures of global capitalism and government leaders eager to serve them, what was striking was the very high number of prominent media figures who participated in their panels. It was an indication of what a prominent role the global corporate media system plays in the new *regime*. Concurrently, several thousand miles to the south, in Porto Alegre, Brazil, the alternative World Social Forum met to pose an alternative view for the global political economy. A central theme there, as well, was media. Much of the attention of the tens of thousands of people from around the world who participated addressed the limitations of the corporate media status quo for democracy, the need for democratic media policy making, and the need to develop viable alternative non-commercial media as the basis of a just and humane society. The overriding spirit at the WEF was that economic and media policies are too important to be trusted to the common people; the attitude in Porto Alegre was the opposite. Indeed, there are indications that progressive political movements around the world are increasingly putting media issues on their political platforms. From Sweden to France and India to Australia, New Zealand and Canada, democratic, generally left-wing political parties and social movements are beginning to make structural media reform – breaking up the big companies, recharging non-profit and non-commercial broadcasting and media – a part of their agenda. They are even finding out that this sometimes can be a successful issue with voters.

There are no simple solutions to the question of how best to organise media and communication to promote a healthy economy and democratic values, just as there is no simple answer to how best to structure the global political economy. Moreover, it is clear that the two debates are very closely related, in view of the significance of media and communication to both capitalism and democracy. That is why it is imperative that the debates on this topic be widespread and conducted in the light of day. If we know one thing from history it is this: if self-interested parties make decisions in relative secrecy, the resulting policies will serve the interests primarily of those who made them. As the old saying goes, 'If you're not at the table, you're not part of the deal.' Our job, as scholars, as citizens, as democrats, is to knock down the door and draw some more chairs up to the table. And when we sit at that table, we have to be armed with the most accurate understanding of what is taking place and what is possible that we can generate.

CHAPTER SUMMARY

- Political economy of communication examines the way media systems interact with capitalism and either promote or undermine democratic values.

- Political economy of communication is particularly concerned with how the profit motive, markets and advertising influence media performance. It provides a necessary context for the examination of most issues concerning media.

- Political economy of communication is premised on the notion that a media system is not natural; it is the result of explicit government policies that create it. In a democratic society, these policies are the result, ideally, of the informed consent of the citizenry.

- A global media system has emerged over the past two decades in conjunction with the global neoliberal capitalist system. The global media system is essential for global capitalism economically and ideologically.

- The global media system is dominated by a small number (8–10) of massive transnational conglomerates. These firms have grown dramatically in the past decade, mostly through mergers and acquisitions. Another 60–80 regional powerhouse firms round out the system. After that you are in the media bush leagues.

- The global media system is dependent upon major changes in media and economic regulations at the national level across the planet.

- The journalism and culture produced by the global media system are highly conducive to the neoliberal political economic order.

CHAPTER 3
Organisation and Production in Alternative Media

Chris Atton

To analyse practices of organisation and production in alternative media is not simply to explore a fascinating and generally overlooked area of media studies: it can also provide insights into mainstream practices. Through their emphasis on widening access to the processes of media production, alternative media practices highlight the limits of mainstream media practices. At the same time they demonstrate how some mainstream production techniques can be appropriated and redeveloped as parts of more inclusive, democratised media projects.

Before we can address questions of organisation and production in alternative media, we must first decide what we mean by 'alternative media'. It is not possible in a single chapter to explore definitions in any depth (Downing 1984, 2001, and Atton, 2002 devote entire chapters to definitions alone). In any case the contemporary case studies and historical examples that make up the bulk of this chapter will tell us more about what alternative media are and what they do by examining their practices in detail. At this stage, then, it is enough to offer some general remarks on definition. John Downing has stated that 'if . . . alternative media have one thing in common, it is that they break somebody's rules, although rarely all of them in every respect' (Downing 2001: xi). We can think of these rules as those governing content, form, organisation and production. In terms of content, Roger Silverstone (1999: 103) affirms that alternative media 'have created new spaces for alternative voices that provide the focus both for specific community interests as well as for the contrary and the subversive'. Regarding form, Silverstone talks of the employment of production techniques borrowed from the mass media 'to pursue a critical or alternative agenda, from the margins, as it were, or from the underbelly of social life' (ibid.). As we shall see though, many alternative media employ techniques that are emphatically not of the mainstream; they often subvert mainstream techniques or abandon them completely.

The rich and diverse history of alternative media practices does not admit of any easy generalisations, yet in the West at least there is a discernible tradition of alternative media that has focused on projects that radically re-form three key aspects of communication: 'skills, capitalisation and controls' (Williams 1980:

54). For the English Radical press (c. 1790–1830) this resulted in papers that were characterised by pauper management, where 'journalists saw themselves as activists rather than as professionals' and where there was an interest 'in expos[ing] the dynamics of power and inequality rather than report[ing] "hard news"' (Curran and Seaton 1997: 15). These features also appear at the heart of contemporary alternative media, as we shall see.

John Downing's (2001) model of alternative media organisation provides a useful framework from which to explore Williams's three foci of skills, capitalisation and controls. First, there is an emphasis on self-management, usually resulting in small-scale, collectively run projects. Second, such media often suggest a 'socialist anarchist angle of vision' which, Downing argues, sets contemporary alternative media apart from their Leninist precursors (still alive, of course, in some forms, as in the *British Socialist Worker* paper). Despite their revolutionary aims and content, Downing finds in the latter an unwelcome emphasis on vanguardism and party 'correctness'. This is not to claim that self-managed media that reject the Leninist, transmission-belt model will easily and unproblematically be freed from concerns over control and correctness. Jo Freeman's (1972) notion of 'the tyranny of structurelessness' reminds us of how even in avowedly non- or anti-hierarchical structures, hierarchies might still develop – an issue we shall explore later. Third, proceeding from this interest in socialist anarchism as an organising principle, alternative media embody 'prefigurative politics, the attempt to practise socialist principles in the present, not merely to imagine them for the future' (Downing 2001: 71). Downing's emphasis here on socialism need not prevent us from applying these core principles to radical media organisations that do not appear to share the socialist aim explicitly. His notion of practising principles in the present does, however, help us understand the reasons behind choosing radical forms of organisation such as the collective, and non-professional approaches (even anti-professional, on occasion) to media production. Taken as a whole, Downing's vision is that of a democratic, non-corporate media network comprising non-hierarchically run, independent groups and individuals horizontally linked, and where whatever organisation and control do take place are necessarily light. We must first understand the range of organisational methods that have been employed by the alternative media.

Organisational Approaches in Alternative Media

Organisational approaches have been a major focus of accounts of the British alternative press (Comedia 1984; Fountain 1988; Minority Press Group 1980; Whitaker 1981), and it is with these that I shall begin, since they offer three clear types of organisational method. First, there is an organisational hierarchy that replicates that of the mainstream press, with an owner and editor overseeing reporters, staff writers and technical production staff. Examples range from the 1960s underground magazine *Oz* to working-class, Party newspapers such as the *Morning Star* and *Socialist Worker*. Second is the non-hierarchical organisation, where individuals have equal control over the publication and where decisions – including editorial ones – are made collectively. In addition to an editorial function, each person will tend to have a specific task (editing, writing, paste-up, printing). Many of the community newspapers described in the Minority Press Group's (1980) overview of the local alternative press are set up in this way. The third type is the loosest of all, where tasks and roles are not fixed, and where everyone is involved in all aspects of production and decisions are made collectively. This is a common organisational form in much contemporary alternative media centred on the new social movements, such as environmentalism and peace, and which privilege activists as editors and writers.

This emphasis on the collective springs from a notion of 'equality . . . interpreted and evaluated in terms of *sharing*' (Landry et al. 1985: 7; emphasis in original). In this instance, 'sharing' emphasises collective organisation without any thought to the size of the collective, or whether it is possible to work collectively regardless of the numbers involved. Furthermore, such sharing rejects the formal, bureaucratic and hierarchical methods of doing business. It often rejects entirely the importance of business and with it the value of individuals taking responsibility, acquiring specific skills and exercising authority (which are seen as autocratic features of despotic hierarchy). The abandonment of business practices as capitalist and reactionary produces, according to Landry et al., an organisation where the quest to be 'maximally democratic' is achieved at the expense of the organisation's 'economic imperatives' (ibid.: 31). This inevitably leads to financial stringency, to a reliance on self-exploited, voluntary labour, cheap materials and even squatted office space; in short, what Landry et al. term 'barefoot economics' (ibid.: 24).

By contrast, we can see how more hierarchical and centralised forms of alternative media have succeeded. The *Big Issue* is an example of an alternative 'advocacy' publication that speaks on behalf of the homeless and through its unique distribution system (the magazine is sold by the homeless on the streets, who each make 45 pence per copy sold) aims to 'help the homeless help themselves'. The *Big Issue* was founded in 1991 and currently has four separate fortnightly editions in London, Scotland, Wales and the north of England. The financial buoyancy of the *Big Issue* is in large part due to the subsidies it received during its first two years. These were provided by businesses, most conspicuously in the form of the Body Shop, whose Gordon Roddick provided half a million pounds to launch the paper. It has successfully sought and retained advertising from a wide range of companies producing consumer products – music and film are prominent (though it does not appear to accept advertising for alcohol or tobacco) – and it runs pages of classified advertisements focusing on jobs in education and social services. Its success is due in large part to its ability to 'sell a good cause', one that, to judge from its circulation (at the time of writing the audited circulation for its Scottish edition is over 40,000 – its London edition is over three times that) reaches far more readers than the 'grassroots' alternative media. This success must also be understood in terms of the magazine's organisation and production. Its structure is similar to that of any mainstream title; it has sizeable editorial, advertising and sales departments; business, finance and personnel managers. Despite being printed on news print (apart from its glossy cover), its liberal use of colour and its layout (reminiscent of a Sunday newspaper's magazine supplement) speaks 'professional' – this is no experimental or amateurish endeavour. Whilst some of its writers might have cut their reporting teeth on alternative grassroots papers such as *SchNEWS* and *Squall*, the *Big Issue* only employs professional writers; the *raison d'être* of the paper – the homeless – contribute only poems and (very) short stories to a 'City Lights' column – they never report on their own circumstances.

By contrast, the organisational methods of grassroots alternative media seek to privilege the role of 'ordinary', unskilled people in their production. What the Minority Press Group (1980) term the British 'radical populist' press of the 1970s attempted to establish regular grassroots alternatives to local community news-papers which, their organisers argued, denied the people in those communities their own voice. The Minority Press Group (1980) and Whitaker (1981) focus on these radical community newspapers and between them offer a range of case studies of radical organisation. It is worth attending to their findings in some detail. For all their diversity of organisational approach, all exhibit similar problems. The *Liverpool Free Press*, examined in Whitaker's account, was headed by a small group that retained the editorial focus throughout the six years of its life, though many others were involved in production and writing work. This group developed open meetings for readers and supporters, though these were held 'for discussions rather than decisions' (Whitaker 1981: 104). Decisions were made by the editorial group through a system of collective responsibility that required unanimity for all decisions. Failure when it came was financial, rather than directly organisational. In the case of the *Aberdeen People's Press*, a truly open method of organisation – an open editorial group that anyone could attend (however temporarily) yet have the same power as a regular attendee – has been shown to be problematic. The paper foundered after only three years, when the open-group method both introduced writers that the core group found distaste-ful (for example, racists) and failed to reconcile each individual's differing commitment to the paper. An attempt to restart the paper with a closed group based on 'clear responsibilities' was proposed, but never materialised (Minority Press Group 1980: 38).

Other papers, such as *Brighton Voice* and the *Islington Gutter Press*, lasted longer than the *Liverpool Free Press*, ostensibly as open collectives, though both collectives note that they were led by a small core group. The *Islington Gutter Press* also found its open meetings too time-consuming and unable to make decisions; these were gradually reduced in frequency and eventually dropped. The main feature of all these cases is the desire to involve as many people as possible in what was, after all, a community initiative, whilst enabling produc-tivity: hence the philosophy of the open meeting and the involvement of people as volunteer writers, layout artists, etc. Only one paper – *Alarm* in Swansea, Wales – operated a full collective throughout its existence: between twelve and thirty people were involved in editorial meetings and ten people in a rota operated the printing press. It lasted less than two years.

These studies bear out the criticisms of Landry et al. to a degree. They show that small groups with clear responsibilities tend to work better than large diffused groups and that papers based on small groups tend to survive longer.

Such small groups are not incompatible with more inclusive methods of discussion and decision-making, as long as flexibility exists. Discussions involving large numbers of people are possible, these case studies show, but decision-making is best left to smaller groups.

In a study of self-managed media that covers two continents, John Downing (1984) offers a more comprehensive survey of the collective approach to alternative media. Within his twenty-odd case studies there is much diversity: collectives that disguised their elitist hierarchy (the triumvirate that ultimately controlled the American *National Guardian* and was the source of an acrimonious split in the paper's collective); collectives that encouraged full discussion involving all staff (and volunteers) and employed majority voting for decision-making (the radical radio station KPFA in Berkeley, California); those who eschewed majority-voting as 'a concession to male power structures' (*Union Wage*; Downing 1984: 100), yet who abandoned consensus decision-making and reverted to majority-voting since the former was exceedingly time-consuming. Interestingly, the only fully successful consensus decision-making in the organisations covered by Downing are in the two Mohawk Nation publications, *Akwesasne Notes* and *Erin Bulletin*, whose success is put down to the 'traditional cultural commitment' to such a practice (ibid.: 109). In some organisations, skills are shared and jobs rotated; others prefer members to develop expertise in a specific area: job 'prestige' is equalised by a standard wage (though often all are unwaged). Downing is not uncritical of the collective approach; he recognises the limitations (especially social and cultural) that different forms of collective activity place on an organisation and that prevent it from operating efficiently and effectively, especially over the entire life of a publication. The Portuguese paper *Republica*, for instance, was only able to remain self-managed for a brief period, due to external political conditions. Others failed in the collective effort because the method was simply not suited to other aspects of doing business in the economic and social contexts in which they found themselves. Downing is critical of those organisations who adopted 'ultra-democratic' forms of organisation for abstract reasons, without tying them to social and political realities (ibid.: 355–6). He notes that the most successful ultra-democratic organisations were those which either had a clear cultural role (such as *Akwesasne Notes* and *Erin Bulletin*) or a highly developed social situation (such as in the Polish underground media of the late 1970s, where editorial group members were already extremely familiar with each other and their working patterns from many years' direct personal experience). In short, Downing's collective, self-managed media is about participation and communication within an alternative public sphere.

Amateur Journalism and Native Reporters

Participation does not only come from being part of the 'management structure' (however loose a structure that might be) of an alternative media project. Alternative media have throughout their history privileged amateur journalists who are writing from a position of engagement with the event or process that is their subject. Here I use the term 'amateur' as Edward Said uses it to describe the amateur intellectual; one who is 'unestablished', that is, with no formal relationship to a profession or institution (Said 1994). 'Amateur' here has everything to say about commitment to radical intellectual and social practices, it has nothing to do with the common notion of the amateur as the ignorant, self-deceived dabbler. These amateur journalists – explicitly partisan – report from the 'front line', from the grassroots, from within the movements and communities they thus come to represent. At this more specific level of journalistic practice, the principles of self-management, organisational and ideological independence, and prefigurative politics are played out in what we can think of as 'native reporting':

> 'Native reporting' can usefully define the activities of alternative journalists working within communities of interest to present news that is relevant to those communities' interests, presented in a manner that is meaningful to them and with their collaboration and support. 'Native-reporter' also evokes those local grassroots journalists of the South by whom Michael Traber sets so much store, whose value lies not in their role of message-creators for a passive audience, but as members of a community whose work enables the entire community to come together, to 'analyse one's historical situation, which transforms consciousness, and leads to the will to change a situation'. [Traber 1985: 3] (Atton 2002: 112–13)

The reporters' active, lived presence within events, whilst no guarantor of impartiality, enables the production of news that tells other stories from those reported in the mainstream: 'our news, not theirs'. This is a radical process of reporting where activists become journalists, and where grassroots reporting and analysis take place within movements and communities. The work of grassroots activists exemplifies the passage of native reporters from participants in a demonstration to activist-journalists, whilst remaining positioned as 'rank and file' within those movements.

The partisan, first-person narratives and commentaries of the native reporter inhabit an uneasy terrain. The sustained first-person narrative in the mainstream is typically the province of the senior reporter or the columnist; partisan commentary will also come from the columnist or the op-ed writer: these are roles of significant status. The native-reporter, by mainstream criteria, is unauthoritative and marginal, at the bottom of the hierarchy of access. Under the radical conditions of alternative media, these reporters become central: the role and function of the journalist are transformed and hybridised. Further, the demotic approach of the native reporter, whether evinced by the gritty camcorder footage shot in the heat of protest or by a 'public-colloquial' style of textual discourse (Fairclough 1995: 72), emphasises a radical populism in visual and written language. Peter Golding (1999: 51) has argued that 'the demotic and casually convivial tone of the popular press [is] rooted in the evolution of a journalism of the market from a more socially anchored journalism of community or movement'. We might consider the radical populism of native reporting as both an acknowledgement of and a return to the roots of popular journalism (say, in the English Radical press), springing from its location and status as a communication technology for communities and protest movements.

Contemporary Case Studies in Organisation and Production

We have seen how the alternative media, or at least that part of them we have called grassroots, are primarily interested in involving a wide range of people in their organisation. Such media appear less interested in the media skills of those people; instead they value them for their experiences, for what stories and perspectives they can bring to issues that concern them in their communities (whether geographic communities or communities of interest). Such people might be activists, involved in demonstrations or protests against, say, the siting of telecommunications masts on school buildings, or trials of genetically modified crops in local fields. They might be involved in the worldwide protest against the nexus of governmental and corporate power evinced at meetings of the World Trade Organization in Seattle (1999) or the G8 summit in Genoa (2001). Such people might also be 'ordinary' people, not actively involved in protest, but certainly interested in what is taking place 'in their name' in their local area, by local or national politicians or by businesses. Whatever their interests or levels of commitment, alternative media are interested in giving a voice to these, perhaps otherwise voiceless, people. In the words of the Glasgow University Media Group (1976: 245), such media seek to invert (even subvert) the 'hierarchy of access' (Glasgow University Media Group 1976: 245) that normally pertains in the mainstream media, where an elite of experts and pundits tends to have easier and more substantial access than do dissidents or protesters to a media platform for their ideas. Writing for the alternative media is less an elitist construct; it is transformed into an egalitarian, devolved communication tool.

How does this work in practice? The rest of this chapter will examine three distinct approaches to organisation and production in contemporary alternative media, in order to explore how such people are able to contribute their experiences, opinions and beliefs, and how they contribute to the production of those media. These three cases will help us understand how different alternative media work in practice. I shall explore a radical newspaper (*Counter Information*), an activist video magazine (*Undercurrents*) and a radical Internet project (*Indymedia*). Each case focuses on a different aspect of organisation and production: the study of *Counter Information* emphasises the role of the collective and the multi-skilled nature of its participants (as reporters, editors and layout artists) throughout the production cycle of a typical issue. With *Undercurrents* I examine the role of the native reporter as both broadcaster and technician, and highlight the necessity for the centralisation of some of the professional aspects of production. My examination of *Indymedia* aims to explore the global reach of a radical Internet project which can offer unlimited, largely unedited creative space to activists across the world. My overall focus in this section is on the radical, grassroots media, since they offer both a striking contrast to established, hierarchical approaches (as in the *Big Issue* or in any mainstream media) as well as a variety of approaches to production within themselves. There is not space to offer a detailed historical or geographical survey here. These examples do, however, demonstrate a wide variety of organisational and production features which, whilst being far from exhaustive, do at least demonstrate the ingenuity and creativity (and the limits) of alternative media projects.

Counter Information

Counter Information calls itself a 'class struggle anarchist' news-sheet which has as its primary aim 'social change towards a more egalitarian society'. It was founded in Edinburgh, Scotland, in 1984 to provide a news digest of the national miners' strike of that year, based on information from the miners themselves and 'collated as a service by anarchists and revolutionaries from Edinburgh and Clydeside'. Within a year its aim had broadened to include reports of 'workers' resistance'. The role of the activist as providing 'personal accounts of resistance to this rotten system' (*Counter Information* 6, July 1985) is stressed.

The format of *Counter Information* has remained largely constant, each an A4 news-sheet of 2–4 pages, appearing only quarterly. Its circulation fluctuates at around 12,000, which is high for this kind of publication, though evidence suggests that this figure represents instead a fluctuating print run, determined by available financial resources (the paper frequently asks for donations to keep afloat). Finance is also one determinant of its frequency – the others are time and a shortage of volunteer staff – which is very low for a publication dealing with 'news'.

The writing, editing and production of a quarterly issue of *Counter Information* typically take six weeks. This period is punctuated by three editorial meetings and one layout meeting. All meetings are open to all members of the collective but out of a collective of ten, there is a core of half who attend most meetings. Since all decisions are taken collectively and consensus is sought on all matters, such a reduction in size facilitates those processes. The first meeting is held at the beginning of the six-week period. Here material that has been received since the last issue went to press is assessed for inclusion in the forthcoming issue. That is, a month-and-a-half to two months of material is assessed. The sources of this material are many: primary sources will typically include reports from other revolutionary and alternative papers; some small articles from the mainstream press (which may be followed up by contact with those directly involved); the occasional unsolicited article.

The assessment of the sources is twofold. First, this meeting enables the editorial collective to identify what it calls the main 'struggles' and events taking place that are significant in the wider (national and international) context. Significance is measured in terms of amount of material received on a particular struggle and in terms of (the lack of) coverage the struggle has received in the mainstream press. To this end, specific individuals hold a watching brief on the mass media. Second, the material is assessed for currency. Since *Counter Information* appears only quarterly and is only four pages in extent, items must be chosen that are not only deemed to be significant to a wide audience but which also, it is hoped, will retain their significance in the months to come. A local story is not necessarily out of the question, but it must demonstrate wider relevance or be part of a wider phenomenon (for example, the many local protests against road-building), but must also be ongoing. A protest that is just being planned might not have generated enough material, whilst one on the point of winding-up might already have been 'done to death' in other sources.

Once the main 'struggles' have been identified, these will form the basis of the longer articles in the paper (there are two to four of these in each issue; each can be anything between 350 and 500 words). The length of each article will also be decided at this first meeting. These will be written up, based on the information received, by a member of the collective who has 'a deep knowledge of the field or who is directly involved in the event, struggle or action' (all quotations in this section are taken from an interview with a member of the editorial collective, conducted by the author). Where there is no expertise within the collective, the collective will 'commission' (though no money changes hands) a first-hand account of the struggle or action from another group already known to them. This first meeting will result in the commissioning of such articles and the allocation of other articles to members of the collective, who will write most of the articles in any issue.

The second meeting, usually two weeks later, is considered a 'progress meeting'. Occasionally the main articles are ready for this meeting, but that rarely happens. Here the number and type of smaller articles are decided, and with these the collective is able to be more precise about word lengths across the range of articles. Any new information and reports received since the first meeting are also reviewed, and decisions made on how (if at all) such news needs to be covered. The third and final editorial meeting (held two weeks after the second) has one aim: that all articles agreed upon should be written, typed and copied to the collective for editing. Once again, new information and reports are examined. Changes in length, perspective and content are suggested and agreed for all articles under consideration. The main articles are discussed in most depth; the rest are only examined in any depth if a member of the collective 'feels strongly about an article going in or not going in'. Typically, individuals leave this meeting with the task of cutting articles or changing their content. After a further two weeks, the layout meeting takes place. 'Theoretically, this shouldn't involve editorial discussions, but in practice it does', because articles are often not ready for the final editorial meeting. Consequently, the first couple of hours of the layout meeting is a last-minute editorial meeting. The rest is layout proper, 'a marathon' usually lasting twelve hours ('from 1 pm to 1 am'; other meetings, by contrast, last between two and three hours); some material is even written during this time, if promised copy fails to turn up, for instance. The layout is undertaken by three members of the collective only, though others often stay around or come and go, inevitably contributing to the process. The organisation of *Counter Information* exhibits similar interests to those we have met in the radical community press of the 1970s. The preference for a small editorial group is noticeable and there is clearly an interest in developing a close-knit group of trusted editors and contributors. Whilst the collective appears comfortable with its size, it is willing to admit new members as long as they are prepared to get involved and develop the necessary skills.

Undercurrents

Undercurrents is a video magazine produced by activists across the world involved in campaigns that include environmentalism, the peace movement, human rights campaigns, anti-capitalism protests, squatting and coverage of other alternative media projects. Or rather, this is what it was – its final, tenth issue was produced in 1999 and it is unlikely to resume production, unless, as its editors state in the liner notes to that issue, 'we find a way to clone ourselves and survive without sleep or financial support'. This is evidence indeed of the unsustainable pressures on alternative media projects brought on by self-exploited labour and 'barefoot economics'. The magazine was founded in 1994 by Small World Media, 'a film production company specialising in environmental and political features' (Malyon 1995: 24), from whose commercial activities *Undercurrents* was subsidised. We should note the presence of professional film-makers in this activist undertaking. Whilst the unedited reports are all shot by amateurs, the jobs of editing, production and distribution are undertaken centrally by a small group of professionals based in London.

This hybrid model of alternative media production differs from those we have already encountered. This organisational model is in large part forced on the project through the necessity for professional editing facilities; most grassroots groups would not have access to such facilities and even if they did, would be unlikely to have the skills to use them. Moreover, even if local groups could afford the services of a local, professional editing suite, they might well find their amateurish efforts deemed unfit for editing; for example, whilst Hi8 video stock is broadcast quality, VHS or Video 8 is not. A professional studio specialising in broadcast work might well reject poorer-quality video stock. In addition, such a studio might find the unprofessional nature of the footage shot – or indeed its content and perspective – unacceptable. *Undercurrents* requires a sympathetic editing team, sympathetic to both the variable standards of film stock and techniques employed, and to the aims and ideologies of the activists themselves. In Small World Media activists were able to find both, for its members are both professionals and activists. The organisation also offered training to activists: 'Britain's only dedicated training programme to those who want to produce their own news and use video as tool to bring about real change' (liner notes to issue ten).

Undercurrents edited and presented the work of international activists to a largely British audience; the content of its ten alternative news videos were all shot by amateurs – activists, native reporters – from their side of the story. Unlike the bulk of mainstream news television footage, these are not shot from behind police lines; instead they graphically show a version of events from the other side, and do not flinch from presenting elite groups (politicians, police) as violent, unreasonable or inequitable. They also demonstrate vividly both the imagination and commitment of protesters, at the same time as they show those protesters as vulnerable, as both oppressed and activist. Camera operators and reporters alike celebrate the vast differences in production and news values from the mainstream. Thomas Harding, a founding member of the *Undercurrents* editorial collective, has emphasised these aspects of 'native production' as central to the aims of the magazine. It is not enough for activists to display their attitude towards an issue, to the oppressive relations of the situation; their work will be all the more powerful when they show the work's position within those relations (Benjamin 1982 [1934]). Walter Benjamin's notion of the 'author as producer' is a valuable way to understand this process. He argued that the political position of content alone is not enough. To mobilise others to join with you, and to encourage them to produce their own dissenting work, you must show how the form of the medium may be radicalised. In the case of *Undercurrents*, this is to encourage the amateur video-maker to use the domestic camcorder to record their own experiences and their attitude towards oppressive relations, using techniques that critique those relations. As Harding emphasises, this can mean eschewing professional standards. Activist video can accrue power through 'underproduction':

> Keep those long shots. Don't worry if it's a bit wobbly; it will feel more authentic. In general, turn your weaknesses (few resources, little experience) to an advantage by keeping your feature simple but powerful. (Harding 1997: 149)

In her study of AIDS video activism, Alexander Juhasz (1995) argues for the employment of mainstream media forms such as the documentary to claim authority over the radical content of a programme, content that would never be thus presented through mainstream channels. Like Harding, though, she emphasises production processes that involve members of the communities for which (and in which) the video is being produced:

> Alternative AIDS media . . . actively situates itself *within* the object of study . . . to look is to see and know *yourself*, not the other – an entirely different route to pleasure and power. (Juhasz 1995: 138; original emphases)

The video activist should also present herself against the dominant frames of the mainstream representation of protesters and reporters. As in all grassroots alternative media, these two roles are combined in *Undercurrents*. In an exploration of one such native reporter ('Jen'), I showed how she positions herself as both activist and reporter in her feature on the British government's contradictory attitude in its human rights policy and its promotion of the British arms trade:

> In a little over seven minutes Jen moves from conventional reporter to activist, throughout representing herself not as a simple professional, not even as a simple activist, but as a vulnerable, brave individual, situated in the everyday yet capable of remarkable actions, whether interviewing a senior politician or taking direct action against the military-industrial complex. She is oppressed and activist; witness and critic. Her words and actions are, in the end, those of her audience, her movement through identities and relationships in this brief feature as complex as any in everyday life. (Atton 2002: 115–116)

This stress on the everyday, on situating oneself and one's media work within the complexities and multiple identities we all adopt in everyday life, is central to an understanding of the production mechanisms of alternative media.

Indymedia

The network of Independent Media Centres has become a highly visible feature of the media landscape of the global anti-capitalism movement at the turn of the millennium. The Independent Media Centres (IMC) or *Indymedia* network came to prominence during the demonstrations in the American city of Seattle against the World Trade Organization summit meeting there on 30 November 1999. The Seattle IMC acted as an independent media focus for the broad coalition of social justice groups, trade unions, anarchists, socialists, communists, environmental groups and others – a coalition that has come to be known as the anti-capitalist movement. In Seattle the Centre had both a physical and a virtual presence. Its virtual presence on the Web enabled its small core staff to distribute streaming audio and video footage of the demonstrations, as well as written reports, across the world. Technically this was achieved through the use of open publishing software, where any independent journalist (any activist, for that matter, though the two were often the same) could upload their reports using a pro-forma on the IMC website. No prior approval was needed from the core group; nor was that group responsible for editing the content of reports in any way. Hundreds of hours of audio and video footage and hundreds of thousands of eyewitness reports, analyses and commentary became available to activists, supporters, detractors – to 'global citizens' at large.

Since Seattle, the *Indymedia* network has expanded. There are currently seventy-eight IMCs in thirty-one countries. The concentration remains greatest in the US (thirty-six) and Europe (one in each of seventeen countries, with two in the UK). Other regions are far less well represented. There is one IMC in India and only two in Africa (Nigeria and South Africa). The Seattle IMC remains the network's de facto centre, and it is from its collective that the bulk of technical information about uploading comes, as well as proposals for managing the substantial flow of information the network generates. For example, the network now operates a unique form of editorial control. Whilst reports may be uploaded from or by any source, the editorial group reserves the right to remove contributions judged unsuitable. The 'Publish' page of *Indymedia* (http://www.indymedia.org/publish.php3) states that 'The Independent Media Center is a collectively run media outlet for the creation of radical, *accurate*, and passionate tellings of the truth' (author's emphasis). Towards this aim the collective states that 'while we struggle to maintain the news wire as a completely open forum we do monitor it and remove posts'. The large majority of these posts are removed for 'being comments, not news, duplicate posts, obviously false or libelous posts, or inappropriate content [such as hate speech]'. *Indymedia* do, however, still make these posts available in a separate page titled 'hidden stories' (http://www.indymedia.org/search-process.php3?hidden=true). Whilst editing does take place, it does not prevent voices from being heard, nor prevent users from accessing that content. Neither does this quasi-editorial function of the core group extend to the editing of individual pieces of work: if they do not breach the criteria set out above, then pieces will remain on the 'open' pages of the site. These limitations apart, IMC/*Indymedia* enables any activists to contribute their work. The use of open source software bypasses the need for an editor or webmaster to upload contributions: writer and producers may do this themselves, using the pro-forma on the 'Publish' page. The effectiveness of this method has been shown most recently by its approach to the coverage of the events of September 11 and the ensuing Operation Enduring Freedom. '9–11: Peace & Justice' is the title of a feature page on the Seattle site (http://www.indymedia.org/peace) that links to news, analysis and comment posted to many of the sixty-four IMCs, as well as providing links to news and features appearing on other independent media organisations. These include local radio stations offering streaming audio and independent media monitoring projects such as Fairness and Accuracy in Reporting (FAIR).

Indymedia connects local work to a global struggle, and it is from within this global context that the movement perceives itself. Despite the presence of some editorial control, open source programming erodes any centralisation of *Indymedia* that might otherwise occur. From the perspective of both producers and consumers (often the same people when we are talking about activists), *Indymedia* functions as a content aggregator of independent journalism, organised by country, issue and medium (text, audio, video, multimedia). Not only do journalists place original, previously unpublished work there, but IMCs themselves will often link to already broadcast or published reports. To consider *Indymedia* as an organisation is to consider a network of independent, collectively run 'nodes' through which independent journalists may circulate their work, largely unimpeded by the gatekeeping of those collectives. It is not only the scale (in terms of geographical spread, global reach and volume of material) that makes the *Indymedia* network an interesting moment for the study of alternative media; it is the most thorough working-out on the Internet of the conditions and processes of alternative media projects.

Conclusion

From the examples above, we have seen how different alternative media (print, video, Internet) have radicalised Raymond Williams's three core aspects of communication: skills, capitalisation and controls. In the case of skills, we have seen how the native reporter can bring a radical, personal perspective to both the content of their work and the style in which it is produced (as in the case of *Undercurrents*). We have seen how many alternative media projects are poorly financed, relying largely on donations and voluntary, unpaid labour to survive – a restraint that is only overcome by the advocacy media, such as the *Big Issue*, which is better placed to attract prominent financial backers through its promotion of an issue that is less radical, through a medium that is more professionally produced. Organisationally, the controls on advocacy media resemble those of the mainstream media. By contrast, the grassroots media prefer radical forms of organisation, particularly the collective, the better to meet their political aims (broadly speaking, socialist) and to practise those aims in the present – what John Downing terms 'prefigurative politics'. These practices come at a cost however: collective methods of organisation and production are often unwieldy;

they can make decision-making very difficult and often lead to the collapse of alternative media projects. From our case studies, we have seen that those grassroots alternative media projects that flourish tend to be the ones with a small, committed collective that is responsible for the day-to-day running and planning of the publication, leaving a larger pool of contributors free from this administrative burden. Where technological expertise is required (as in *Undercurrents*), this core collective might well include people with a high level of professional training.

Finally, *Indymedia*'s diffuse, decentralised network suggests a significant future for alternative media projects. Lightly organised by a small collective that privileges the creative freedom of its contributors, *Indymedia*'s non-hierarchical methods of organisation and its democratisation of production techniques encourage thousands of contributors, all taking responsibility for their own work. This global network of native reporters has only become possible through the radical deployment of Internet technology. It has become a largely self-sustaining medium, one that appears to have successfully overcome the economies of scale that have for so long bedevilled print-based alternative media projects.

CHAPTER SUMMARY

- Alternative media encourage self-management. A wide range of 'ordinary', non-professional people will be in charge of organisation and production, as managers, editors, designers.

- There is an emphasis on collective organisation, in order to involve as many people as are willing to contribute. Collective organisation, though, is not without its difficulties – a large, unwieldy collective can prevent the efficient organisation of production.

- The most effective form of organisation tends to be a small collective, but where individual contributors still have creative freedom.

- To achieve this egalitarian aim of involving a wide range of people, alternative media radically redefine the organisational and writing skills necessary to produce a publication.

- 'Amateur', non-professional writers ('native reporters') can subvert the hierarchy of access to media by foregrounding themselves as activists and developing reporting techniques that demonstrate not only a radical attitude to 'oppressive relations' but also radical forms of production.

- In alternative media that require a professional understanding of production techniques (e.g., video), there will still be a role for professionals. These people also tend to be activists, sympathetic to and working with the 'amateur' staff of the organisation.

- Through these practices, alternative media are able to 'give voice to the voiceless', that is, to give media access to those who find themselves under-represented in mainstream media (whether those people are in local communities or part of a community of interest, for example, a protest movement).

- Organisation and production practices within alternative media highlight the limits of mainstream media practices. They demonstrate how mainstream production techniques can be radically redeployed to serve more inclusive aims.

PART III

CORPORATE CHANGE AND ORGANISATIONAL CULTURES

CHAPTER 4

Strategising Technological Innovation: The Case of News Corporation

Timothy Marjoribanks

The digital age will not herald the end of print. Far from it. Print remains a very good business for News Corporation and the Company will continue to prosper in it. Despite the proliferation of new delivery systems, content remains king. The managerial skills needed to run a top newspaper company – strong editorial skills, creation of compelling and original content, the ability to build brands and read the market – will be as relevant in the 21st Century as they are today. (Murdoch 1997)

Experiences of work, and relations in the workplace, are currently undergoing profound processes of transformation around the world, linked intimately to developments in information and communications technologies and globalisation (Castells 2000). The global dispersal of information and communication technologies is not only creating new industries and new categories of work, but is also challenging the types of tasks carried out in existing industries, the products that are produced, and the relations between workplace participants (Dow and Parker 2001; James et al. 1997). The world of the media is critically linked to these processes of transformation in many ways. New media technologies, now available globally, are making possible new forms of content and delivery, while also fundamentally impacting on media production processes and organisational relations. In particular, information technologies are having a dramatic effect on the organisation of global media workplace relations (Marjoribanks 2000a; Pavlik 1996).

It is the interaction between processes of global technological innovation and the reorganisation of relations in the local media workplace that is the focus of this chapter. Specifically, I develop a theoretically informed qualitative case study of the relationship between technological innovation and workplace reorganisation in the newspaper holdings of News Corporation. In so doing, I argue that this type of study is crucial, not only for increasing our understanding of the current state of the newspaper industry, but also because it allows us to address the following key questions which are challenging contemporary workplace production and organisational processes across all media forms:

- Who controls technological innovation in the workplace?

- Who benefits from the introduction of technology into the workplace?

- How is technologically inspired workplace reorganisation influenced by institutional and societal relations?

Answering such questions will also provide insights into the politics and power struggles that occur around workplace reorganisation. I shall show that the introduction of technologies into the media workplace is the result of inter-actions between the experiences of workplace actors, the history of the local workplace, and national and global institutional and social contexts.

Technology and the Newspaper
Workplace: Experiences and a Theoretical Framework

Transformations in workplace experiences and relations in the newspaper industry are occurring in the context of broader processes of global restructuring of work. For much of the twentieth century, work was based on mass production principles, in which standardised goods were mass produced, and in which work organisation and production were hierarchically organised, routine and a collective experience. Crucial to this model of work, at least from 1945 to the early 1970s, was the acceptance by workplace actors that the terms and conditions of employment would be regulated to varying degrees by the state, employers and trade unions. This model of work came to be known as Fordism (Marglin and Schor 1990). Since the 1970s, however, this model of work has been challenged, economically and politically, as unsuitable for a technologically dynamic, market-based global society. In its place has arisen a post-Fordist model of work, in which work is proclaimed to be more flexible for management and employees, less hierarchical, and individualised. In practice, this newly emerging model of work has also been associated with a political agenda of reducing both the regulatory role of the state, and the legitimacy of unions as the collective organisational representatives of workers, with terms and conditions of work being decided at the level of the individual employee and employer. While such trends are emerging in societies around the world, debates continue around such questions as who is benefiting from such transformations, and how such transformations are impacting on experiences of work (Campbell and Pedersen 2001; Hollingsworth and Boyer 1997; Schor and You 1995).

Within these broad transformation processes, some vital areas of investigation for understanding transformations in work, organisations and production processes are the relationships between, and experiences of, technological inno-vation and workplace reorganisation. Existing research on these relationships suggests that technological innovation is experienced unevenly at the level of the local workplace, where it impacts directly on the lives of people in relation to issues such as employment status and quality of work-life (Fagan and Webber 1994; Freeman et al. 1995).

The contradictory effects of new technologies have been experienced in the newspaper workplace. Traditionally, production work in the newspaper industry has been the subject of strict demarcations, or divisions, between the tasks that people fulfilled. Skilled craft workers undertook specific production jobs with titles such as linotype setter, proofreader and compositor, and controlled the knowledge needed to perform those tasks. Through this control over key aspects of the print production process, print workers were able to exercise a high level of influence within the workplace, especially associated with the existence of strong craft-based unions. For example, industrial action including strikes and stop-work meetings undertaken by print workers could prevent the publication of newspapers, even if journalists or editors continued to write stories. Journalists have historically occupied an ambivalent position within the newspaper workplace. While they have organised in unions, on an individual basis they have also seen themselves as professionals who have at times resented and actively opposed the capacity of print workers to stop production. Nevertheless, the capacity of newspaper unions to control important elements of the work production process put them in a powerful position relative to newspaper owners and managers, who have been characterised as having given up control of important elements of the workplace in the pre-computer production era (Picard and Brody 1997; Tunstall 1996).

The advent of computerisation and other information technologies has had a revolutionary effect on workplace relations in the newspaper industry. Most dramatically, computerisation has brought with it the possibility of deskilling or even removing altogether many of the traditional crafts associated with the print production process. Computerisation has also impacted on the place of journalists in the production process. Whereas previously journalists were responsible for writing stories, the development of processes such as electronic pagination and desk-top publishing means that they can now assume responsibility for much of the production process as well. This has provided journalists with more flexibility, and more control, over the production process, but it has also intensified the content of their work. To give just one example, in many newspapers journalists are now responsible for the proofreading and layout of their own stories, where once these were specialised production tasks. In these ways, technology has also provided an opening for owners and managers to re-establish control over the production process (Nieman Reports 1999, 2000).

These experiences of new technology in the newspaper industry provide a specific example of some of the broader trends occurring in the contemporary work organisation. Just as there is the potential for greater flexibility within production as newspaper employees develop skills across the range of production processes, so too there is the potential for greater individualisation of the workplace experience as solidarities based on the possession of specialised skills are replaced. These variations in the newspaper industry raise vital questions about the negotiation processes involved in the introduction of new technologies into the workplace, in particular around who controls the process of innovation and reorganisation, and how this control is exercised.

Questions such as these have been central to theoretical debates within sociology around the relationship between technological innovation and workplace organisation. One important set of approaches is characterised by determinism, in which structures of technology or social relations predetermine workplace organisation. In relation to media workplace organisations, an approach emphasising the determining influence of technology suggests that similar organisational forms and workplace relations will emerge in all work-places in which the same technology is introduced. By contrast, social choice approaches emphasise the agency of organisations, and more particularly of key actors in organisations, in choosing their own technologies and workplace structures. This approach suggests that the study of the relationship between technological innovation and newspaper workplace organisation should proceed on an individual, case-by-case basis, and that workplace transformations are shaped ultimately by the choices of actors in specific workplace contexts. While these broad frameworks provide valuable insights into technology and processes of workplace reorganisation, ultimately they do not provide an adequate analysis of the interactions between actors and their contexts (Thomas 1994; Tolliday and Zeitlin 1991).

In contrast to these approaches, this chapter adopts the approach of historical institutionalism (Immergut 1998; Locke and Thelen 1995; Sabel 1982; Sabel and Zeitlin 1997; Tolliday and Zeitlin 1991). Historical institutionalism is an approach that is at once responsive to the constraints of institutional and social contexts, including the technological environment and the relations among workplace organisations and workplace actors, while also allowing scope for the operation of choice on the part of workplace actors. Historical institutionalism seeks to achieve this integration of agency and structure by emphasising the significance of the interaction of the worldviews of workplace actors, their social and institutional contexts and historical contingency in explaining transforma-tions in workplace relations. While workplace actors can influence the outcomes of reorganisation processes through their activities, their actions are simul-taneously constrained by their context. Central to the social and institutional context of the media are the discourses and practices of the state, and the relations between media corporations, the state and unions.

The historical institutional approach suggests the following propositions for studying the relationship between technological innovation and workplace reorganisation:

- Workplace relations are shaped by the interaction of actors' worldviews, their choices of action, and the institutional and societal context.

- Technological innovation is an ongoing process which unfolds over time.

- State policies and administrative decisions, legislation and judicial rulings, and the struggles between politicians and political parties constitute part of the context in which technological innovation and workplace reorganisation occurs.

- The manner in which technology is introduced into the workplace, and the associated reorganisation of workplace relations, are the outcome of historically developed workplace relations. These relations may also be influenced by the manner in which other organisations in the same industry have previously introduced new technology.

The last point is important to the focus of this chapter on News Corporation as a global media organisation. In particular, it suggests that while grounded research of specific workplaces is required, it is also vital to analyse the relations and interactions between workplaces if we are to understand how technology is introduced into the workplace, and the effects of technological innovation.

News Corporation as a Case Study

The focus of this chapter is on the relationship between technological innovation and workplace reorganisation at newspaper holdings of News Corporation in the UK, Australia and the US. Specifically, I develop a multi-site comparative case study of this relationship as it has unfolded at newspapers owned by News Corporation at Wapping in London, which include *The Times* and the *Sunday Times*, the *Sun*, and the *News of the World*; the *Advertiser* in Adelaide, Australia; and the *New York Post* in the US.

In an age where much of the attention on issues of production and organisation in the media is focused on newly emerging Internet-based technologies, an immediate question that arises is: why develop a case study of newspapers? A fundamental reason for focusing on newspapers as a research site is that they continue to constitute an important sector of the media, not only for News Corporation, but for the media industry as a whole, financially and in terms of prestige and potential political and social impact (Tunstall 1996). In addition, as discussed earlier, newspapers have experienced the full force of the contradictory impacts of developments in information and communications technologies. The way in which newspapers handle such contradictions provides an important study into the impacts of new technologies. Further, with many media organisations now owning a variety of media forms, experiences in the newspaper industry may well be applied to other media.

To explore these issues, a series of interrelated qualitative case studies of newspaper sites was developed, based on interviews, field observations and document analysis. This approach allows for exploration of the relationship between technological innovation and the reorganisation of the newspaper workplace through the perceptions, experiences and understandings of the participants themselves (Hansen et al. 1998; Hodson 2001). Such a research strategy is suggested as suitable by the analytic framework of historical institutionalism, which indicates that to analyse processes of workplace restructuring, we need to understand the worldviews and choices that media workers make at particular moments and over time.

This chapter also adopts an international and comparative approach (Frenkel et al. 1999). In the case of News Corporation, the justification for a comparative approach is that it allows for an examination of convergences and differences in practices of workplace reorganisation, in a context in which the same path-breaking media organisation is introducing similar technology across geographically dispersed sites. Through such an analysis, we should be able to understand not only the processes of transformation, but also the reasons for transformation. Adopting a multi-site approach within the same organisation across international boundaries will also allow us to explore the ways in which understandings of, and practices related to, negotiations around technological innovation, and processes of organisational restructuring, are transmitted between organisational sites (Marcus 1995). Indeed, an analysis of News Corporation soon makes it evident that while specific newspapers operate as individual entities in terms of day-to-day publishing, they are very closely connected – or networked – through processes such as inter-organisational implementation of, and learning about, production technologies.

News Corporation, Global Strategies

News Corporation began to emerge under the leadership of the Australian-born Rupert Murdoch in the 1950s, when he took control of the *News*, an afternoon newspaper in Adelaide, South Australia. The company soon expanded into other states in Australia, and then into the UK when Murdoch purchased the *News of the World* in 1969, to be followed soon after by the purchase of the *Sun*. The re-creation of the *Sun* as a major player in the UK newspaper industry can now be seen as one of the early indicators of the rise to international prominence of the company. By the early 2000s, News Corporation has become a major media player on the world scene, with interests not only in newspapers, but also in book publishing, broadcast, cable and satellite television, magazines and movies. These interests are located primarily in the US, the UK and Australia, but at various times in the 1990s and 2000s the company has had interests in countries as diverse as New Zealand, Fiji, China and Hungary. While News Corporation is the parent company, its UK newspapers operate within News International, its Australian newspapers within News Limited, and the *New York Post* simply as the *New York Post*, but previously News America Publishing.

While operating in a diverse range of media markets and media formats, newspapers continue to remain central to the corporate strategy, and the very identity, of News Corporation. In the 1998 Annual Report of the company, for example, it was commented that: 'Newspapers are the backbone on which News Corporation – financially and culturally – was founded. Their importance and strategic role remain key in all the geographic regions in which the company operates'. The 2001 Annual Report of News Corporation gives a further indication of the scope of their newspaper holdings, reporting that: 'With operations on four continents, hundreds of mastheads and some 15,000 employees worldwide, News Corporation's newspaper business is unmatched by any other English-language publisher'. The 2001 Annual Report goes on to indicate that 70 per cent of all British adults read a News International newspaper; that circulation has remained strong in all of its Australian newspapers; and that the *New York Post* had become 'the only daily metropolitan newspaper in the nation [the US] to achieve seven years of circulation growth'. Such self-reported data suggest that newspapers do indeed retain a key strategic place in the operations of News Corporation.

In seeking to identify the key characteristics of News Corporation, Eric Louw, Senior Lecturer in Communication at the University of Queensland, has drawn on the work of sociologist Manuel Castells to argue that News Corporation captures the essential elements of a newly emerging model of global network organisation. That is, in a globally diverse company such as News Corporation,

> We find multiple (and proliferating) styles of control and decision-making being tolerated in different parts of the network, so long as those at the centre of the web can gain some benefit from allowing a particular practice and/or organisational arrangement to exist in a part of their networked 'empire'. (Louw 2001: 64)

While Rupert Murdoch sits at the centre of the networked News Corporation, the different parts of the 'empire' operate in multiple and sometimes autonomous ways. According to Louw, Murdoch's 'power derives not from top-down control of each niche of his empire, but rather from the accumulative influence of reaching into so many different spheres. Allowing for "difference" becomes a source of strength' (Louw 2001: 10). This analysis of News Corporation is supported by the perspectives of those involved at senior levels within the newspaper interests of News Corporation. Rupert Murdoch himself has been quoted to the effect that:

> Day to day, I trust the executives on the spot to get on with it [i.e. running newspapers]. They should solve the problems themselves. The executive on the spot really is the boss; they don't refer to me as the boss, I hope. . . . You've got to let your people manage and let your people edit too . . . I fly into a crisis that's blown up, or a crisis that I've more or less precipitated myself. (Murdoch, quoted in Coleridge 1993: 31)

Andrew Neil, editor of the *Sunday Times* for over a decade from the 1980s to the early 1990s, characterised the organisational structure and managerial practice of News in a similar fashion, although his comments also suggest that Murdoch has a greater influence as an individual than he acknowledges. In his autobiography, Neil wrote:

> When I took the job of *Sunday Times* editor I imagined a short honeymoon period before I would feel his wrath. In fact, he left me alone for most of the decade, keeping a wary eye on my progress from a distance, intervening only when he felt strongly about something. . . .
>
> Editorial freedom, however, has its limits: Rupert has an uncanny knack of being there even when he is not. When I did not hear from him and I knew his attention was elsewhere, he was still uppermost in my mind. When we did talk he would always let me know what he liked and what he did not, where he stood on an issue of the time and what

he thought of a politician in the news. Such is the force of his personality that you feel obliged to take such views carefully into account. And why not? He is, after all, the proprietor. (Neil 1997: 202, 203)

The picture that emerges of News Corporation, from these perspectives and from other analyses (Auletta 1997; Chenoweth 2001) is of an organisation in which enormous influence is held by Murdoch as chief executive, but also in which there is at least some degree of autonomy granted to specific organisations within the corporation. At the same time, Murdoch is a constant presence, even when not on site at a specific newspaper.

Having established the broad organisational model of News Corporation, we can turn our attention to the more specific issue of how News has developed its global strategy. Murdoch himself has at times downplayed the idea that the organisation has developed any formal global goals. In the 1980s, Murdoch was reported as saying:

It is our policy to be very reserved with regard to global media. There is no such thing as a 'global village'. Most media are rooted in their national and local cultures. (Koschnick 1989: 102)

By the 1990s and into the 2000s, however, the company was more explicit in its recognition of the importance of the global features of contemporary media. By the late 1990s, the company was proclaiming that 75 per cent of the world's population would soon have access to its content, while it was also much more aggressively seeking entry into huge markets such as India and China. The company also makes much of the fact that in contrast to many of its major competitors which tend to be US focused (as in the case of AOL-Time Warner) or European focused (as with Bertlesmann in Germany), News Corporation is truly international. This is evident not only through their global distribution of content, but also in the global flow of managers through the company, and in the international composition of the company's managerial staff. Murdoch has also been reported as thinking of News Corporation as a 'loose network', in which content is globally syndicated within the organisation, and in which there is global movement of personnel, at least at the managerial level (Coleridge 1993: 485). As an example, when News Corporation bought the *New York Post*, News Corporation personnel from London and Sydney were brought in to restructure the newspaper (ibid.: 500). More recently, the newly appointed editor in chief of the *New York Post*, Col Allan, had experience in charge of News Limited newspapers in Sydney, and brought with him an 'Aussie invasion' of staff (Case 2001).

As well as such global movements in personnel and content, it is possible to identify an attempt to develop global strategies in relation to technological innovation within News Corporation. As these developments are explored in the remainder of this chapter, I shall also argue that attempts to develop a global strategy must engage with, and are frequently modified by, local and national contexts.

Local Transformation: Technological Innovation and Workplace Reorganisation

While it is clear that there are vital global dimensions to News Corporation, ultimately the people who constitute the organisation experience transformation at the level of the local workplace. To understand the relationship between global technological innovation and workplace reorganisation, therefore, we must turn our attention to specific workplaces. In this section, I shall analyse News Corporation newspapers that have been subject to dramatic processes of reorganisation related to global technological innovation, then explore the similarities and variations in the subsequent experiences of workplace reorganisation.

Technological Innovation

The approach of News Corporation to technological innovation became a matter of international significance with the Fleet Street revolution of the 1980s. Until the 1980s, newspaper production in Britain was synonymous with Fleet Street, in London. Fleet Street was not only the home of some of the most famous titles and names in British newspaper production, but also the site of powerful national newspaper union organisations and their chapels, or local workplace branches, which had succeeded in securing considerable influence over the production process. For proprietors such as Murdoch, the unions were a fetter on the profit-making potential of newspapers, as exemplified by their ability to challenge the processes by which management wished to introduce new computerised technologies. For News International, matters ultimately came to a head after a prolonged series of negotiations between management and unions in the mid-1980s related to the proposed introduction of computer technology into the newspaper production process. The company ultimately rejected a series of union concessions, and decided to relocate to Wapping in the Docklands area of London. News International then dismissed 5,500 workers, leading to a year-long dispute, notable for mass pickets, high police presence and the creation of a fortress-like mentality at Wapping. The end result was the establishment of a non-union workplace at the new site at Wapping in 1986. A new non-union workforce of electrical and non-craft workers was employed and trained on-site to produce newspapers, while sufficient numbers of journalists were enticed by the company to cross the picket lines. By the late 1990s, Wapping was the largest newspaper printing works in Europe (Marjoribanks 2000a; Tunstall 1996).

The impact of Wapping was soon to spread, not only to other UK newspapers such as the *Financial Times* (Marjoribanks 2000b), but also to newspapers owned by News Corporation in other countries. The *Advertiser*, in Australia, for example, had been undergoing processes of computerised technological transformation since the 1960s. By the mid-1980s, production of the *Advertiser* was occurring by electronic means, and in 1985, an announcement was made that a new publishing and printing plant would be established in a suburb of Adelaide. These plans took off with the takeover of the newspaper by News

Limited in 1987. As an integral part of A$1 billion to be invested by News Limited in its newspapers, the *Advertiser* was to become part of the most expansive development in the history of Australian newspapers. As such, it was also part of a unique group of newspapers, with News Limited's newspapers being the first in the world to be fully paginated and output either digitally or to film. Significantly, the *Advertiser* was the last of the News Limited newspapers to introduce electronic pagination, and as a result local management was able to build on the experiences of newspapers in Sydney, Melbourne and Brisbane. In stark contrast to the Wapping experience, as we shall see later in this chapter, these processes of technological innovation occurred in the context of negotiations between management and the unions (Marjoribanks 2000a).

For News Corporation, the United States has become increasingly central to its operations, and now provides its largest source of revenues. While much of this is derived from various modes of television and film media, newspapers have been central to the experience of News in the US. While News has been associated with a number of newspapers in the US, it is perhaps most closely identified with the *New York Post*. As with London in the UK context, owning a New York paper has given News Corporation a critical voice in the US media market. Its history of ownership of the *New York Post* has been volatile, related in part to regulations around owning different media forms in the same city, and also because of the company's perceptions about the role of the unions. Despite major concession bargaining between management and unions in the 1970s and 1980s, Murdoch argued in the late 1980s that the New York newspaper unions were a source of loss for the company, in particular through their capacity to save jobs that Murdoch believed could be mechanised through the introduction of new technologies. After being required to sell the *Post* in 1988 because of legal restrictions on media ownership, Murdoch was allowed to repurchase the newspaper in 1993, when it was ruled that it was the only way to save the financially struggling newspaper. Murdoch would only agree to purchase the paper, however, if the unions agreed to major concessions. Despite winning major financial concessions, the newspaper was shut down in late 1993 when the Newspaper Guild, the union representing journalists, took strike action in response to management's further demand that they be allowed the right to fire members at will. While the print unions soon returned to work, Guild members were required to reapply for their jobs, and only 35 of the 270 who had gone on strike were rehired (Kurtz 1994). The Guild was derecognised, and even into the 2000s, the New York Guild was seeking unsuccessfully to have the sacked strikers legally reinstated. While all this was going on through the 1990s, the *Post* also established a new production plant in the Bronx for US$250 million, and was engaging in price wars with other New York newspapers, in particular the *New York Daily News*.

Workplace Reorganisation

Having outlined the experiences of technological innovation at key newspapers owned by News Corporation, we are now in a position to explore the similarities and variations in the subsequent transformation of workplace relations as a means of furthering our understanding of the negotiation processes at work.

Similarities across the Cases

A key similarity across the cases is the technologies that were introduced into each of the workplaces. In processes of technological innovation stretching back over many years at the newspaper holdings of News Corporation, traditional hot metal print production techniques have been replaced by computerised pre-press and production systems. Such systems have provided opportunities for greatly improved quality of production, for example through flexible page setting and the use of colour, while also allowing for rapid global transmission of information. Wherever such systems were introduced, there also occurred a fundamental reorganisation in the types of skills required to produce a news-paper. Almost overnight, there was at least the potential to remove pre-existing job demarcations based on factors such as craft specialisation, and where possible, management at News has acted to remove these demarcations, and to replace craft labour with non-craft labour. From the perspective of management, such reorganisation has allowed for the creation of a more flexible workforce, in which employees are expected to be multi-skilled. In addition, the introduction of new technologies has also been accompanied by a shift in physical location, at least of the production processes if not of journalists. While such relocations are in part related to questions of space, at least in London it was also related to a perception on the part of management that physical relocation was required to escape the influence of the unions.

There has also been a common tendency towards heightened managerial control of workplace practices across the sites. This has essentially involved using new technologies as a means of moving from a workplace context in which unions could control the labour supply to a context in which, even where unions are recognised, non-craft labour is central to the labour process. Thus, even in times of dispute with parts of the workforce, newspapers can still be produced. This constitutes a major shift in workplace relations in the newspaper industry, with technological transformation contributing to a context in which it is not possible for the workforce to control knowledge about the production process in the same way as when craft-based workers were central to newspaper production.

While these similarities exist across the cases, there are also crucial variations between the cases, particularly in the extent to which intensification of managerial control in processes of workplace reorganisation has been realised. I argue that these variations are related fundamentally to the pre-existing workplace relations, and to national and global institutional and social relations.

The Local Context

At the local workplace, there were important historical differences between the newspapers in the development of relations between owners, managers, unions and employees, and these differences impacted on what the workplace actors perceived to be possible in terms of workplace reorganisation. A key variation, especially when the UK and US newspapers are contrasted with the Australian newspapers, concerns the negotiation processes around the introduction of new technology.

In London, management was firmly of the view that the unions were resolutely and inflexibly opposed to the introduction of new technology. While the unions involved in negotiations over technological innovation in the 1980s sought to overcome this perception on the part of management, they were unsuccessful. The resulting de-recognition of unions in the shift to Wapping has had a long-term impact, being referred to by both employers and the unions as a turning point for the British newspaper industry. In addition to the mass layoffs that occurred with the shift to Wapping, workplace relations were individualised with the introduction of personal contracts and the ending of collective bargaining. Ultimately, the move to Wapping created a 'constraint-free environment' (Oram 1987: 89), in which management had the flexibility to operate as it saw fit. More recently, the News International Staff Association has been created, not as an independent union but as an in-house staff representative body, and in 2000 conducted the first formal collective negotiations with management at the company for fifteen years. Despite this shift, it appears that management is still opposed to the presence of unions at Wapping, at least from the perspective of the union movement (Foster 1999).

As in London, relations between management and the unions in New York have also been marked by antagonism, with the unions perceived by management to be unresponsive in the face of emerging technological and organisational innovations. This antagonism has frequently expressed itself in disputes around the introduction of new technology, and this has continued under the ownership of News Corporation. At the extreme, this has manifested itself in the de-recognition in the early 1990s of the Newspaper Guild, and while other unions continue to operate, they do so in a context of institutional weakness after many years of concession bargaining.

In contrast to the local workplace relations in London and New York, workplace relations at the *Advertiser* have been characterised as a form of co-operative paternalism, in which there was an assumption that management and employees could work around reorganisation processes in a harmonious manner (Patrickson 1986; MacIntosh 1984). In the context of technological innovation, this assumption translated into a perception that unions would accommodate transformation, and that the appropriate way to proceed was through negotiations between management and unions. One important outcome of these processes, and a significant contrast with Wapping, is that job reduction at the *Advertiser* has occurred through negotiated voluntary redundancies.

Also vital to the process of workplace reorganisation at the *Advertiser* in Adelaide was that it occurred in the aftermath of the events at Wapping in the 1980s. Members of the *Advertiser* were clearly aware of those developments, but did not want a similar scenario to unfold there. The history of the relationship between the parties at the *Advertiser* was important in ensuring that it did not become a 'Wapping South'. Nevertheless, decision-making power at the *Advertiser* has been perceived in particular by employees to have shifted from local management to News Corporation management based in Sydney. This has resulted in some employees commenting that the *Advertiser* has lost its unique family feel, to become just another part of the global News Corporation empire.

These local workplace relations are an important part of the story of the relationship between technological innovation and workplace reorganisation. In particular, the relations between management and unions that emerged over time impacted on the perceptions of workplace actors about what was possible, and about how to go about the process of transformation. The history of workplace relations in London and New York made management determined to wrest control from the unions, if necessary through de-recognition. Once this control was achieved, management was not about to pass back any influence to the remaining unions. By contrast, change has occurred at the *Advertiser* through negotiation. Also vital, however, are the national and global contexts in which these local workplaces are located.

The National Context

Common to all three sites under analysis is that they are located in countries that have been experiencing major transformations in the relations between the state and market since the end of the 'golden age of capitalism' in the early 1970s. In the UK and the US from the late 1970s, in particular, a powerful backlash against the regulatory role of the state was experienced with the emergence of neo-liberalism as a political ideology emphasising the market. Central to this ideology were the related ideas that workplace relations should be regulated by management without 'interference' from the state, and that unions were not legitimate workplace actors. Crucial to the experience in the workplace, however, was the fact that this ideology was translated into institutional practice, with the governments in both countries enacting legislation and developing policy intended to diminish the influence of unions. For example, a series of Employment Acts in the UK enacted in the 1980s and 1990s had the impact of weakening the institutionalised place of unions, and of collective bargaining as the appropriate process for workplace negotiation. In the US, decisions of state institutions including the Supreme Court and the National Labor Relations Board had a similar impact. These government actions then created a context in which corporate managers could act to diminish or even remove the influence of unions from the workplace.

For companies such as News Corporation, which had felt constrained by what they perceived to be excessive union influence, the new national context provided an opportunity to transform the organisation of production which they seized. Even into the 1990s, when governments more sympathetic to labour were in office in both the US and the UK, the national-level institutional shifts that had occurred in the 1970s and 1980s left an institutional legacy that had shifted the ground of debate around workplace relations. For example, while Fairness at Work legislation has been recently enacted in the UK to provide a framework for unions to regain recognition, at workplaces such as Wapping a generation of workers have not experienced union representation and management expects to manage without unions (Foster 1999).

In contrast to the UK and US experiences, in the 1980s and early 1990s, Australia had a Labor Party government in office that, while committed to undertaking major economic reorganisation, also recognised a role for trade unions in such processes. This recognition was most visibly expressed with the establishment of the Accord, an agreement between the governing Australian Labor Party and the Australian Council of Trade Unions, the main union body, to bring about economic and employment growth through negotiation between the state, unions and employers (McEachern 1991). While the Accord process has been subjected to a number of important critiques (McEachern 1991), at least at a formal institutional level it did provide a context in which unions were considered to be legitimate actors. Also vital to the continued recognition of unions as legitimate was the Australian Industrial Relations Commission, a state institution with the role of regulating employment. As one example of its impact in this period, in its 1983 Termination, Change and Redundancy decision, the Commission ruled that employers needed to provide employees with all relevant information about major changes in technology. Through such decisions, unions in Australia were operating in a very different context to their counterparts in the UK and the US. With the election of the conservative Liberal Party to national office in 1996, however, this system was to undergo major transformations. The Accord was immediately done away with, and a much more aggressive stance was taken towards the union movement, in effect mirroring many of the initiatives that had already occurred in the UK and the US. But at the crucial time when major technological innovation was occurring, unions in the Australian context were operating in a context in which they remained recognised as legitimate actors.

The Global Context

A number of global developments have also been important in influencing the relationship between workplace reorganisation and technological innovation. As noted earlier, current managerial practice is notable for the development of networks of relations, and for News Corporation this has been especially the case in terms of inter-organisational learning, but also in terms of the global movement of media content and managerial staff. For example, the process of introducing specific technologies at the *Advertiser* was modelled on the progress made at Wapping. Morever, when the experiments in Australia proved success-ful, it was anticipated that these further developments would be introduced at Wapping. New technologies have also allowed for more syndication of stories throughout the global holdings of the company. Not only have these processes allowed the company to improve the print quality of its newspaper product, they have also created a situation in which the company has been able to reduce the size of its workforce.

There are also important manifestations of a more international outlook on the part of workplace participants themselves, and an awareness of the need to take into account events occurring in other parts of the News Corporation organisation. As we have seen, for example, unions and management at the *Advertiser* were well aware of the events that had occurred at Wapping, while Murdoch's goal of reorganising the workplace at the *New York Post* also drew direct parallels with the experience of Wapping. Through such processes, we can identify a global dimension to the workplace transformations under analysis as similar technologies are spread, and as loosely networked organisations learn from the experiences of one another.

Conclusion

This multi-site case study of newspapers owned by News Corporation offers important insights into the relationships between technological innovation and workplace reorganisation in the contemporary newspaper industry. In particular, it is vital to study the perspectives of the participants in the context of the individual workplace, and the connections between workplaces and their national and global institutional and social contexts. In this way, the chapter provides support for historical institutionalism as a framework for analysing the transformation processes in the newspaper industry. In particular, the current case study allows us to draw a number of conclusions.

First, the perceptions of workplace actors, as captured by their worldviews and previous experiences, have been vital to the transformation processes at the newspaper holdings of News Corporation. These perceptions operated in London to limit the possible approaches towards workplace reorganisation. Workplace relations in Fleet Street had developed to such a point that, from the perspective of management, the only possible way to introduce technology was to relocate and to remove the unions as a workplace influence. The transformation at Wapping then had an impact on perceptions of the possibility of change in both New York and Adelaide. In particular, events at Wapping revealed that the skills and organisational capacities possessed by craft workers would no longer necessarily be a source of strength that would guarantee them a place in processes of organisational transformation. At the same time, workplace actors were active in constructing their own context for transformation, and this process was tied to the history of workplace relations at specific sites. For example, participants in Adelaide were aware of the Wapping experience, but were equally aware that they did not want to pursue that path.

Second, the case study also indicates that technological innovation is an ongoing process. While there are identifiable moments, such as the dispute at Wapping, that often highlight the tremendous impact of technology on the workplace, technological innovation goes on beyond these flashpoints, and continues to have effects for many years and in diverse ways.

Third, government action was vital in setting the social and institutional context for workplace reorganisation. The contrast between the processes of reorganisation in the UK and the US on the one hand, and in Australia on the other, show the importance of government and other state actors to the processes of transformation.

Fourth, there have clearly been processes of inter-workplace learning occurring. For an organisation such as News, an important element of this inter-workplace learning occurs at a global level as personnel and knowledge about technology move from one site to another.

Returning to the questions raised at the beginning of this chapter, the case study of News Corporation suggests that there has been a profound reorganisation of the relations between management and the workforce in the newspaper production process, and that control of strategies for technological innovation has shifted to management. The benefits of such transformations have also tended to flow to management, and from the perspective of management, one of the key benefits has been a major reduction in the role of unions in workplace negotiation processes. Despite these broad trends, the chapter has also illustrated that it is only through studies of individual work sites, as located within national and global contexts, that we can understand the processes by which strategies for innovation have been implemented, and have impacted in specific ways on workplace relations and experiences.

CHAPTER SUMMARY

- Developments in information and communications technologies, and processes of globalisation, have had a profound impact on production and organisational processes in the newspaper industry, challenging the tasks carried out, the type of product, and workplace relations.

- A multi-site comparative and qualitative approach, in which newspapers owned by News Corporation in the UK, Australia and the US are examined, allows us to identify not only processes of workplace reorganisation, but also the reasons for convergences and divergences in such processes.

- Analysis of the experiences of News Corporation suggests that it has developed a global strategy of technological innovation, in which different organisational sites in the company are able to benefit from the experiences of one another.

- Important similarities in the processes of workplace reorganisation across News Corporation include the global dispersal of similar technologies and an intensification of managerial control of production processes.

- Significant differences in the processes by which workplace reorganisation has developed are related to the specific histories of individual organisational sites, including the perceptions of workplace actors, and to the national and global social and institutional contexts in which those sites are located.

- Workplace relations in the newspaper industry are shaped by the interaction of actors' worldviews, the history of the workplace, and the national and global context. In the case of News Corporation, the interaction of these relations has resulted in management being the primary beneficiary of technological innovation, in particular through increased control over negotiation processes.

CHAPTER 5
Organisational Culture inside the BBC and CNN

Lucy Küng-Shankleman

This chapter provides a glimpse inside two of the world's leading media organisations during a period of turbulent environmental change. The BBC and CNN have very different histories, remits and identities, but both must now compete to provide news in a media environment shaped by increasing competition, globalisation, digitalisation and convergence. The focus of this chapter is corporate culture, and the unique role this plays in media organisations. Culture is a potent influence in any organisation, but particularly so in media ones. It can act as a powerful constraint, limiting acceptance of new products and processes, but it can also be a motivator, an enabler, a liberator of organisational energy. For both the BBC and CNN, their core capabilities and competitive strengths are deeply rooted in their cultures; in some senses they could be said to spring from their cultures. Their cultures are the emotional engines of their strategic successes. CNN would not be the world's best-known news organisation without a culture dedicated to producing the best news programming; nor would the BBC have maintained its exceptional programme quality during a decade of organisational turmoil were there not a deep cultural commitment to its professional standards and public service ethos, whatever disruption the environment (or management) might throw up.

But corporate culture, although a frequently used term, can also be a rather fuzzy and ill-defined concept. Within this context, Edgar Schein, Professor Emeritus at the Sloan School of Management at MIT, offers a definition that is both comprehensive and concise, and this was used as the basis for the empirical research described here. Schein defines culture as:

> a pattern of shared basic assumptions that a group learned as it solved its problems of external adaptation and internal integration, that has worked well enough to be considered valid, and therefore is taught to new members of the group as the correct way to perceive, think and feel in relation to those problems. (Schein 1992: 12)

This chapter therefore presents the cultures of the BBC and CNN in terms of a paradigm of interrelated assumptions, or unconscious beliefs, about the meaning, function and purpose of their professional activities shared by those working in these organisations. The style of presentation is as follows: in each case the paradigm is presented in its entirety, followed by discussion of the four individual assumptions that make up each paradigm. Assumptions are, according to Schein's definition, unconscious, and those presented here therefore represent an amalgamation and synthesis of interviewees' *underlying sentiments*, not actual, overt comments. However a selection of direct quotes taken from the interviews have been included after each assumption to provide readers with a sense of the sentiments abroad in these companies and of their strength.

The in-company research underpinning this analysis was conducted between 1994 and 1995. The primary research tool was issue-focused long interviews conducted with senior managers in each company (twenty-five at the BBC and thirteen at CNN), the majority of whom were interviewed twice, one for data-gathering and a second time for feedback.

The BBC's Culture in its Own Words

Figure 5.1   The BBC's cultural paradigm

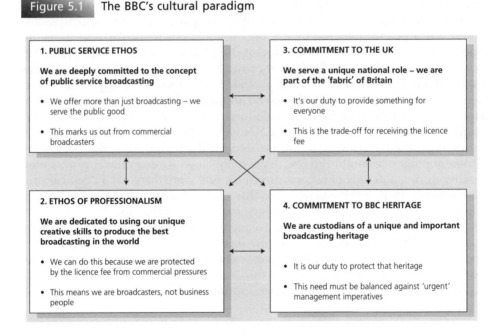

1. **PUBLIC SERVICE ETHOS**

We are deeply committed to the concept of public service broadcasting

- We offer more than just broadcasting – we serve the public good
- This marks us out from commercial broadcasters

3. **COMMITMENT TO THE UK**

We serve a unique national role – we are part of the 'fabric' of Britain

- It's our duty to provide something for everyone
- This is the trade-off for receiving the licence fee

2. **ETHOS OF PROFESSIONALISM**

We are dedicated to using our unique creative skills to produce the best broadcasting in the world

- We can do this because we are protected by the licence fee from commercial pressures
- This means we are broadcasters, not business people

4. **COMMITMENT TO BBC HERITAGE**

We are custodians of a unique and important broadcasting heritage

- It is our duty to protect that heritage
- This need must be balanced against 'urgent' management imperatives

BBC Assumption 1: 'Public funding makes us different'

● The BBC is special, different and important because of its public service status.

● It's in the public good that we exist, it's good for the nation.

- This means we are not 'just' broadcasters, and our public service goals must be viewed as superior to financial or commercial priorities.

- This marks us out from our commercial peers – and makes us a special case.

This assumption derived from the public service ethos that has been present in the organisation since its earliest days (Burns 1977). It concerned a definition of broadcasting conceived in terms of the public good, of public betterment and had a number of consequences. The first is a sense of higher purpose, a profound conviction that the BBC makes an important contribution to the nation; that its programming does not just fill empty hours in the audience's evening, but, to echo Lord Reith's views, *enriches* the viewer's life. As one BBC manager expressed it in an interview:

> Our aim is to provide entertainment that is morally sound and has a bit of the Reithian extra about it. Television producers are like doctors, good producers make good moral judgements as well as good programmes, I think it's as important as in medicine.

The commitment to serving the public good, of bettering the lives of the public, embodied in this assumption, acted as a powerful intrinsic motivator:

> It's in the public good that the BBC exists culturally, politically; it's good for the fabric of the nation. . . . I get fantastically frustrated . . . and say 'Let's go back to basic principles' and 'Why am I here?' And it's because I believe in public broadcasting. . . . That's the thing about this organisation; it's got that capacity in the end to motivate you because you believe in this great good that you're contributing to.

BBC Assumption 2: 'The best in the business'

- The BBC sets the standards. Our journalistic, artistic and technical skills are second to none. Given the scope, we produce the best broadcasting in the world.

- We can do this because we are licence-fee funded: this protects us from commercial pressures and gives us the space to be creative and produce original, high-quality programming.

- We are broadcasters, not businesspeople, and our focus should be on the skills of broadcasting, not of business.

This assumption related to an ethos of professionalism, a striving to offer broadcasting of the highest possible quality. This strand of BBC culture was the 'motor' behind the organisation's tradition of excellence in programme-making:

> We've been a Rolls-Royce organisation, everything has been done very well. I would argue, if you were looking for best practice in broadcasting around the world, you'd probably find quite a lot of it here, in terms of product, in terms of the level of service that has sustained that product.

However, a more complex aspect of this assumption is that many saw its programme-making excellence as being inextricably linked to licence-fee funding. Certainly many within the organisation believed that the two elements combined to create a 'virtuous circle' whereby guaranteed funding from the licence fee has enabled creativity and professionalism to flourish, and a critical creative mass to develop, which enabled the BBC to raise public service broadcasting to the highest standards possible, which in turn created a discerning and demanding viewing public, which is then prepared to finance the organisation on an ongoing basis. Threats to the licence fee, or proposals to alter the organisation's financial basis, were construed as threats to the organisation's fundamental activities and, as such, highly emotive:

> I think . . . in a way the corporate culture is driven by the guarantee of income, because in terms of taking risk and thinking for tomorrow rather than just for today, you create a kind of creative culture, in which people thrive, and have energy and so forth. And that is the corporate culture if you like, the two things sort of come together. And I think it is crucially this issue of funding.

The organisation displayed great belief in its creative and professional skills. Some, however, were concerned that pride, taken to an extreme, could mutate into arrogance and complacency:

> Certainly it's one of great self-belief, enormous pride . . . the downside of that is smugness and arrogance, but the upside is a real self-driven belief, even when you might be irritated, cross, angry you're still doing everything possible to produce the best possible programme . . . but you'll also not like anyone else to disagree.

And just as employees worried that pride could turn to arrogance, so too were some concerned that elitism could lead to insularity: that because the BBC has set the standards for worldwide television for so long, its employees would see little reason to look outside, to consider what others in the field might be doing:

> I believe the organisation is at almost all levels deeply introspective, and I think there's a certain culture of, and attitude 'we're just better than the other guys, always have been and always will be'.

Ironically, however, the downside of the profound commitment to broadcasting excellence was a certain disdain for non-broadcasting activities. BBC employees prized broadcasting rather than business skills, and status accrued with creativity, with programme-making prowess. Senior management positions often went to those who had won their spurs in creative areas, from production to scheduling. Some felt that this impoverished standards of management:

> Essentially, the BBC is an organisation in which people care passionately about output and genuinely debate and think through in a very rigorous way how to make that output the best it can possibly be. . . . Where they are poor is in using traditional management tools to increase the effectiveness of their activity.

BBC Assumption 3: 'Part of the British way of life'

- We serve a unique national role, we are part of the fabric of Britain.

- Our primary duty is to service the British public – this is the trade-off for receiving the licence fee.

- This means giving them the very best programming we can (and as experts we probably know better than they do what is best).

This third assumption concerned the BBC's view of its national role. BBC conceived of its role as being far, far, more than simply supplying television and radio programmes. It was not simply in service of the nation but a fundamental part of the nation:

> As everything else fragments around you and becomes multinational, international, satellite and all the rest of it, the BBC remains a sort of touchstone for the identity of the nation.

The cultural conviction about the importance of the national role played by the BBC had deep roots, extending back to Reith's view of public service broadcasting, and generated a strong sense of responsibility:

> This is the great thing with the BBC . . . the sense of acting on behalf of the nation, the BBC as a unifying culture – I'm sorry these are grandiose words but these are really what, if you talk to people in some areas of the BBC . . . they believe in.

But the BBC's sense of fulfilling a unique national role also had negative connotations. Like the pride associated with Assumption 2, there was concern that a sense of responsibility could easily mutate into self-importance, and then into arrogance:

There's a sort of 'Auntie knows best', condescending, patriarchal, matriarchal: 'We'll look after you' old-fashioned welfare state public service and a more sophisticated, 'We're aware of your needs', 'We're in tune with the nation', 'We're part of the nation and we can enrich it'.

BBC Assumption 4: 'Defending a great heritage'

● We are custodians of a unique and important broadcasting heritage.

● It is everybody's personal duty to protect that heritage.

● This obligation must be weighed against urgent management imperatives.

Just as children of famous parents have difficulty shrugging off the expectations of their heritage, so too is the current-day BBC to some extent weighed down by the organisation's extraordinary track record of power, influence and broadcasting success. For many, the BBC represented the pinnacle of televisual achievement, and that achievement was made possible by the rigorous values instilled by Lord Reith.

> I think that one of the tensions of the BBC is that the staff see themselves in a way as the custodians of the Reithian ethos . . . I think the tension arises not that the people at the very top don't see that, but that they see changes are necessary. . . . Whatever else people feel about the BBC, they feel a very strong sense of identity with it. They may dislike a huge number of things about the changes, but they feel extremely strongly, and therefore extremely possessively, about this thing called the BBC. . . . It's an enormously conceived commitment and it's an area of enormous strength, but it can also be an area of great tension, if the BBC, in the shape of its chief executives . . . or the senior team around those entities, wish to do something different, or something which the staff consider runs against the true interest which they feel they represent.

For BBC staff, its heritage was part of what made the organisation – and by extension, its employees – special. It was a great source of motivation:

> It is a great privilege to me to work for an organisation that has such a heritage, that has made the greatest radio and television programming in the world for so long . . . and still produces world-beating output. Even though competitors have come along and they are increasingly well-funded, we can still beat the rest of the world.

The motivation appeared to be intimately connected with perceptions of Reith's unique contribution to the history of broadcasting, and could explain the latter's curious longevity and appeal. Reith left the organisation over sixty years ago in 1938, but none the less his name was still regularly invoked by staff members, although at times somewhat cynically:

Reithianism died thirty years ago; it's curiously more alive in television than in radio. The basic principle was leading public taste. . . . Reith was a boring old fart actually, he thought he could give people a bit of variety to keep them quiet, and then get the good journalism and the opera. What people mean when they talk about Reithianism goes back to the late 1950s . . . which was the sense that you could lead people from one thing to another and stretch them gently. But also the BBC in the 1950s started to tap into a rich vein of entertainment, of drama, so I think when people talk about Reithianism, they are talking about that. A lot of people talking about Reithianism have never read John Reith, but it's become a phrase. . . . He's a useful fiction for the BBC.

However, problems can arise when the exigencies of the environment dictate a strategy that threatens to compromise the organisation's heritage, to force it off the Reithian path. There was concern that employees see themselves in the role of impoverished scions of a once wealthy family, battling to save the family treasures from the auction houses.

This is a deeply conservative organisation that hates change of any kind and fights it in every possible way . . . I think that view of the heritage is . . . part of an excuse or weapon used in the argument to stop change . . . heritage is used as a kind of emotional argument.

Figure 5.2   The BBC's assumption and attitude 'map'

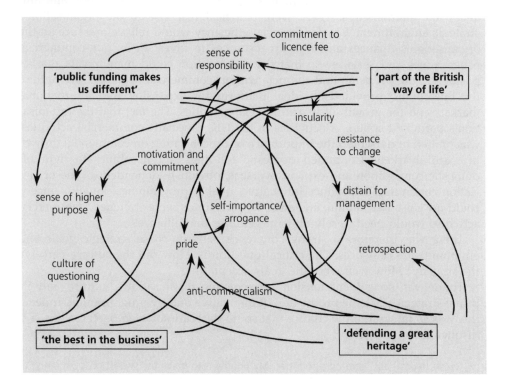

Summary: New Strategic Directions versus Old Cultural Values at the BBC

Having explored the BBC's culture, with its distinctly Reithian overtones, the next question is how did this respond to the ambitious programme of organisational and strategic change initiated during the director generalship of John Birt? At this point in its history, the BBC's strategy was seeking to respond to three specific issues in its wider environment:

- the squeeze on the organisation's financial resources, arising from 'flat' income and rising costs;

- increasing and better-funded competition;

- instability and uncertainty – the combined implications of convergence, digitisation and unclear intentions on the part of the UK government towards the organisation.

In response to these factors, and the government's requirement that it become a global player in the media field, the BBC developed a five-pronged strategy: innovative quality programming (including new non-commercial services such as BBC Online), efficiency, commercial activities, world development, and alliances and partnerships. These were a logical response to the organisation's strategic environment. Greater financial efficiency would relieve pressure on the organisation's finances and free up resources to invest in its non-commercial programmes and services, so that the organisation could maintain its market position in the UK better and compete with its commercial peers. The strength of the BBC brand provided an ideal platform for expansion into international markets and the growth of its commercial activities. The fact that the organisation's permitted sphere of activities in the UK, especially commercial activities, was limited underscored the importance of concentrating on commercial growth in world markets. Continued domestic funding, and its ability to fight off domestic competition and expand overseas, obviously depended on the organisation continuing to produce innovative, quality programmes. Finally, since it could not raise risk capital, and since its own funds were stretched, commercial activities would need to rely on joint ventures and alliances.

There was therefore a strong coherence between these strategic goals and environmental pressures. The critical question is: How did the culture perceive the strategy? How well were the goals accepted?

There was no evident tension between the organisation's culture and its prime strategic goal, the production of innovative quality programming. Indeed, this was so integral to the culture that some staff did not even perceive this as a distinct strategic priority:

> I've stuffed the BBC strategic priorities. My priority is to make the widest possible range of high-quality drama in the knowledge that if we don't get drama right on BBC1 – and we are

the defining factor on BBC1 – then BBC1 will be sunk. If BBC1 is sunk, then that in the public perception probably means the BBC. BBC2 is irrelevant. The radio stations, the symphony orchestras also in that context, only in that context, are also irrelevant. So it's the survival of BBC1 with a substantial audience loyalty, and an audience out there that believes they get things they don't get anywhere else that is important, and if you then focus down, well what can you do about this? You can't mend the BBC, you can mend bits of it, and in mending bits of it you might mend the BBC.

The second strategic goal was greater efficiency. This too appeared to pose no conflict for the culture:

The audience is who we serve, programming is how we serve it, and efficiency is how we fund it.

The third, fourth and fifth strategic priorities can be considered together. All concern commercial activities, focusing on world development to be achieved via joint ventures and alliances. Here the BBC's public service ethos, its commitment to serving the British public and the low priority given to business activities generated tension between strategy and culture:

There's a lot of cynicism within the publicly funded part of the BBC about our commercial activities. I think there's a natural snobbery about anything to do with business generally . . . In some areas people are rather cynical about the calibre of the personalities and the projects involved. It's very much a sense that Worldwide has to prove itself, demonstrate . . . that it's a first-class commercial media organisation.

 **Figure 5.3**   The 'fit' between the BBC's environment, strategy and culture

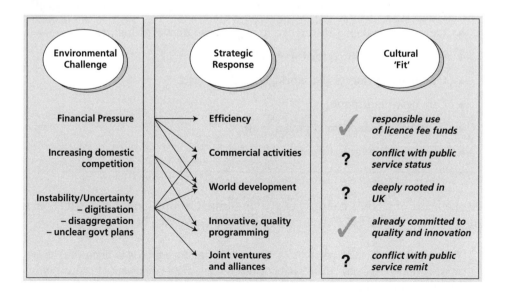

CNN's Culture in its Own Words

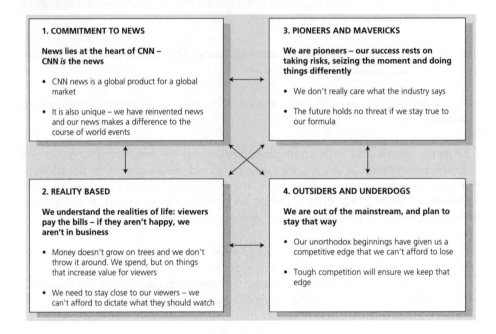

Figure 5.4 CNN's cultural paradigm

1. COMMITMENT TO NEWS

News lies at the heart of CNN – CNN *is* the news

- CNN news is a global product for a global market

- It is also unique – we have reinvented news and our news makes a difference to the course of world events

3. PIONEERS AND MAVERICKS

We are pioneers – our success rests on taking risks, seizing the moment and doing things differently

- We don't really care what the industry says

- The future holds no threat if we stay true to our formula

2. REALITY BASED

We understand the realities of life: viewers pay the bills – if they aren't happy, we aren't in business

- Money doesn't grow on trees and we don't throw it around. We spend, but on things that increase value for viewers

- We need to stay close to our viewers – we can't afford to dictate what they should watch

4. OUTSIDERS AND UNDERDOGS

We are out of the mainstream, and plan to stay that way

- Our unorthodox beginnings have given us a competitive edge that we can't afford to lose

- Tough competition will ensure we keep that edge

CNN Assumption 1: 'News lies at the heart of CNN – CNN *is* the news'

- Our news makes a difference to the course of world history.

- Our news is a force for the good.

- Our news connects the world with the world.

- Our news is unique.

- A global product for a global market.

- We have reinvented news.

At the heart of CNN's culture lay a commitment to breaking news, which is as fundamental as the BBC's commitment to public service broadcasting:

> What we do that's really special that nobody else does like we do is to bring you the live breaking story of the day. There's nobody quicker and more competent at bringing the breaking event than CNN.

Underlying this assumption was a deeply held, and deeply motivating, belief that CNN's news makes a difference to the course of world events. CNN believed that its news can change the course of world history and be a force for the good, perhaps even one that unites a fragmented planet:

> It's utterly brilliant at moving quickly to cover real-time events and organise those real-time events into some coherent strand of oral history.

CNN therefore saw itself as a 'news missionary', bringing news to and from far-flung reaches of the globe. A global perspective was as critical to its news formula:

> The overall mission of CNN is to produce live news coverage . . . the quickest and the best . . . and to broadcast it to the world.

It was felt that this global outlook contributed to making the organisation unique:

> We've redefined the borders. . . . We're as relevant to a sheikh in Saudi Arabia as we are to somebody in Detroit.

CNN's philosophy, regarded as eccentric by domestic peers, has been reinforced by the organisational triumphs (the Gulf War, Tianenman Square) which have resulted from it. The organisation also made a deliberate effort to avoid ethno-centrism and to diminish the 'Atlanta perspective' that could inhibit consumer acceptance:

> To a very large extent we've tried to make CNN International place and country of origin neutral. . . . There's a fixation on . . . well, on not sounding like an American. We've tried to make it place-neutral and we've tried to take a kind of androgynous perspective on what constitutes news.

CNN Assumption 2: 'We understand the realities of life'

- Viewers pay the bills: if they aren't watching, we aren't in business.

- Of course, we want to do a good journalistic job, but keeping advertisers and viewers happy is part of that.

- Serving the public does not mean getting high-handed and deciding what they need – at CNN the *viewers* dictate, not the producers.

- It's not our job to tell people what they should think.

- Money doesn't grow on trees and we don't throw it around. We spend – a lot if necessary – but only on things that increase value for our viewers.

This assumption was rooted in a deeply pragmatic attitude towards the activity of broadcasting: 'Our mission is to cover the biggest stories in the globe, in a way that people want to watch them.' CNN existed, like the BBC, to serve its public, but the balance of power was different: Viewers have the upper hand, they dictate, they know best – even if programme-makers personally hold different views:

> You are in the business of providing news and information to people, the theory being that if you are doing it well, you will have lots of people watching. If you don't have lots of people watching, maybe you should examine how you are providing it.

This assumption also reflects a deep financial pragmatism, which led to an extreme cost-consciousness:

> I think that no company watches money the way that we watch money – they account for everything – and what is interesting is that the journalists do. In other news organisations it is a problem for accountants. We go out and we do the story and the accountants will take care of it, but we will pour in the resources that we need to do it. I believe that Turner looks at the resources and says 'These are the resources. What can we do with those resources? And in doing that, what will give us the cutting edge?' And that's why you've got people who are willing to work all hours and will continue, because there is also something about being on air and progressing a story, and you keep going with it.

Interestingly, such cost awareness was not demotivating. It simply served to underline CNN's unique and special character:

> You could even be unflattering about it. It's very money conscious. Which can get very wearing sometimes. On your less flattering days you call it a cheap environment . . . I've never gotten a bonus, which is one thing in this culture which won't change – but I get all these cheesy stupid Christmas gifts, you know, a really ugly bad clock, a Goofy . . . by corporate American standards these little things are . . . a joke. But I make fun of it and make a joke of it. I can connect this all back to Ted and I know I work for Ted, and ultimately Ted is the driving identity.

CNN Assumption 3: 'CNN the pioneer – the dissident – the iconoclast'

- We've redrawn the rules, redefined the game.

- We do it differently – we are where we are today because we can think outside the box.

- We like risk, we like change, we like challenge. We know how to handle it. We are where we are today also because we know how to seize the moment.

- To hell with the industry, and the future for that matter. We will triumph, somehow – we always have.

CNN saw itself as a crusading pioneer, its success rooted in taking risks, doing things differently, ignoring received industry wisdom. In part this had been driven by necessity: for many years CNN could not afford to follow standard industry practices. Later it made a virtue out of necessity (and many of its practices – the VJ system, its affiliate network – were eventually adopted by its one-time detractors). This iconoclasm developed into a near official policy of disregarding convention:

> It's an edge that we have because we started off as nothing fifteen years ago and people made fun of us, and nobody thought Ted knew anything about the news, so why was he starting a news network? . . . And that's an important edge to keep, whether you call it underdog or whether you call it the lean and mean machine.

Because, for CNN, success rests on breaking moulds, disregarding received wisdom: 'I'd say we question what the industry says: we have proved that it pays to question what the industry does.'

CNN's history is one of experimenting with unexpected approaches to broadcasting – satellite technology, repurposing – being ridiculed for such activities, and finally of being copied. This generated an opportunistic approach to decision-making, where the real challenge was not a changing world outside, but ensuring they keep an open mind:

> When you think your way is the only way, what a trap. In fact our mothers and our fathers told us that when you think you know it all, that's when you stop learning. You're not listening any more, you don't know when the change happened, but you're still fighting it. You have no clue the winds have changed, that it's a new day, a new order, a new way of looking at things, people are marching to a different drum. . . . But you don't even know that's a drum playing, it's noise to you.

This 'official' opportunism was rooted in Turner's founding of the business:

> The Ted Turner genius is to see an odd view of the utilisation or impact of a technology without necessarily understanding or giving a damn about the technology itself in the short run. Ted's genius was to comprehend that the arrival in 1975 of satellites that could transmit television signals meant one guy could get his signal out to lots of places in the country without the extraordinary cost of individual wires connecting them all together. . . . But Ted didn't go 'Wow' and say 'That's fabulous technology'. He said, 'I got this little itty bitty TV station in Atlanta that doesn't have an audience and I've bought a bunch of programmes for it. If I put those programmes on a satellite and gave them to cable systems all over the US I'd get a ton of viewers I don't have and I could raise my ad rates!' He said, 'I need an audience to pay my bills, we're broke, we don't have any money!'

CNN Assumption 4: 'We are the underdogs and outsiders of US broadcasting – and proud of it'

- Our unorthodox beginnings have given us a competitive edge that we can't afford to lose.

- Tough competition is good – it will ensure we stay lean, mean and on our toes.
- Risk is good; without risk there's no progress.

The concept that CNN was an underdog, a battling outsider in a hostile industry, was central to its cultural paradigm and linked many of its beliefs:

> This place grew up with a cultural inferiority by being in Atlanta and with a total underdog mentality by virtue of being on cable when cable wasn't chi-chi. As a result it has been driven by a desire to get as big as its competitors. At the same time it's a cash-poor, capital-poor, betting-the-farm-on-the-next-acquisition kind of place. . . . The corporate goal was never high throughput in productivity; the corporate goal was to be bigger than we were because we were too small.

Interestingly, CNN was also a physical outsider:

> We're the outsiders . . . we're still outsiders . . . because we're not in New York. . . . We're just not in the same ball game. We're not in that little New York–Washington power corridor.

CNN's pioneering culture led to a bias for action, for hands-on activity:

> This is the 'do it' school of business here. You have an idea, you get it approved by the hierarchy, and then you do it and nobody tells you how to do it.

For the underdog, the pioneer, survival is a battle, and CNN's view of the outside world was highly combative and spiked with military terminology:

> We used to say: 'You want to be an overdog, then you wanna behave like an underdog'. No matter how good you are, you want to wake up every morning figuring there's somebody smarter, crazier, luckier than you are out there who's gonna reinvent something and then you're in trouble.

Unsurprisingly, pugnacity was partnered with a strong stomach for risk:

> We wouldn't be here if we were afraid of risk. In young companies . . . you have to be risk-takers. . . . If you're not willing to take a risk, you'll be gone. Because there's always somebody smart. Nobody owns these ideas.

And also by an allowance for the occasional associated failure:

> If you foster the notion that it's better to make fifty decisions and fuck up a few than make three and never make a mistake. . . . We're not gonna penalise you for making a mistake, we're gonna penalise you for not making an effort to do something terrific.

Figure 5.5   CNN's assumption and attitude map

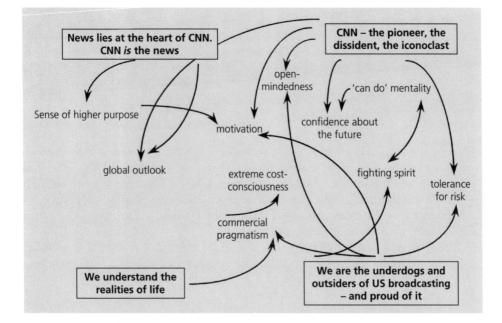

Summary: Culture's Impact on Strategic Options at CNN

As with the BBC, having examined CNN's culture, the next stage is to explore how well this fitted with CNN's broad organisational goals. The first key observation is that CNN and its culture were products of environmental change. Perhaps as a result there was little evidence of cultural 'tension' about environmental upheaval. Culture and environment seemed broadly in alignment, and there appeared to be a widespread understanding of the environmental pressures shaping its strategic direction.

An interesting facet of the impact of CNN's culture was that it predisposed the organisation to disregard formal strategic planning (an activity which it happily left to its parent). This could have stemmed from its desire to break moulds and do things differently, from its immersion in the world of news, which means a concurrent focus on real time, on action rather than analysis and on short-time horizons. Whatever the root, it promoted flexibility in the organisation:

> There is a certain impermanence that comes [when] the environment keeps changing. You've no guarantee that whatever you've built yesterday is workable tomorrow. That's been a part of our thinking and our attitude.

CNN felt no need to create a facade of strategic rationality. This freed it to respond vigorously and laterally, should the need arise. Such an opportunistic approach has a long heritage within the organisation:

Consider if you will the brilliance of Turner, which was to go into cable television as a programmer in 1976 and then in 1980 with CNN, at a time when there were about 18 million cable homes in the United States. Today there are about 63 million. The sheer growth of subscribers was likely to throw off lots of revenue. Consider the brilliance of a rapidly expanding business . . . a 400 per cent increase in size in a fifteen-year period, not too shabby. At the same time the universe of channels, while it went up significantly from twelve to thirty-six or from twenty to forty, didn't go from twenty to two hundred. So while the cable universe is exploding, the number of people who could compete with you by creating new channels, and the distribution problem of getting global distribution, is a significant inhibition on competition.

During the research period, CNN's strategy sought to address two environmental threats. The first was increased domestic competition (at least four organisations announced plans to challenge CNN's supremacy in news). The second was industry instability (convergence between media, telephony and computing was at a more advanced stage in the US than in Europe). In response, CNN developed three strategic priorities.

The first was further global expansion. This offered a means to consolidate existing strengths and was also a logical extension of existing competencies – newsgathering on a global basis and repurposing. Unsurprisingly, there was little conflict with cultural assumptions.

Programmes like *World Report* establish the value of our connections with the *World Report* contributors, from whom we get news, which helps fill our airtime and supplies us with pieces of the world in terms of news-gathering capabilities.

The second strategic priority was to develop new business areas. Equally, this strategic goal posed little conflict. CNN's achievements had long been rooted in exploiting new developments. Its associations with new technology are positive. Like its host nation, CNN's culture embraces the new, and the organisation tackles challenges with the customary underdog mentality and fighting spirit:

They're talking about in this country in five or ten years' time there'll be 500 channels. . . . So if we as a company say, 'Okay, we've got our five networks right now, we're ready, we're in a good position', that would be naïve, because even if these other channels get only a few people to watch, they're still going to break down our total numbers of viewers. So we will make a conscious decision that . . . we need as many networks or stations as we can. . . . In other words, if somebody is going to take away viewers from CNN, it might as well be us.

The third strategic goal was increasing the amount of scheduled programming broadcast. This certainly offered the potential for tension, because the cultural commitment to news militated in many ways against appointment-based broadcasting:

Again, we have to be careful we don't ever lose track of what it is we do, and that is cover the news, that's our responsibility.

Figure 5.6   The 'fit' between CNN's environment, strategy and culture

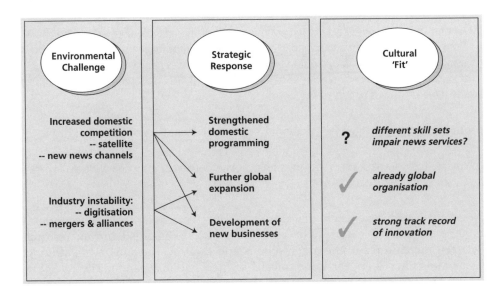

Conclusions

This exploration of the corporate cultures of the BBC and CNN concludes by examining four broader issues that emerge from this analysis. The first concerns the role of the founder. A striking aspect of these findings is the pervasive and long-lasting influence of the founder of the organisation, and indeed the surprising similarity in the roles of these two individuals, despite the fact that they were active in very different historical periods. The personal beliefs of John Reith and Ted Turner are perpetuated in the current-day organisations to a surprising degree. In both cases, these individuals' vision and foresight created path-breaking organisations which have made a unique contribution to the development of broadcasting. However, whereas the cultural values inherited from Turner are strategically enabling, those deriving from Lord Reith are, in the context of the organisation's current competitive environment, more problematic. Although a powerful and unifying motivator, they were a constraining influence on strategic thinking:

> You can't imagine that's the kind of thing that worries Rupert Murdoch. When he gets out of the bathtub in the morning he doesn't say, 'Jesus, I can't throw the shop away, what will they say? I'll be the man who ruined Reith's ideal', which must go through the minds of successive director generals. Whereas Rupert Murdoch gets out and says 'Who am I going to eat today?' It's a very different view of the universe.

Just as many aspects of the BBC culture – commitment to public service, commitment to the UK – derive clearly from Reith, so too can many aspects of CNN's cultural paradigm be traced back to Ted Turner. These include its maverick, outsider, underdog philosophy, and its appetite for risk and opportunism:

> All of it ultimately goes back to Ted, who was sort of the ultimate under-dog who came from behind and fought and scrapped and was made fun of for years, because he had this risky idea, initially, that turned out to be not nearly as risky as people thought it would be. I think we take that mentality with us, that we are sort of still an outsider compared to, say, the three broadcast networks.

From this came an intensely personal – and emotional – commitment:

> I mean, Ted's a whack job, he's a crazy man. But he's *our* crazy man, and we love him! He's our crazy mother-fucker, okay?

A second broad conclusion concerns the strong correlation between organisational and national culture. The similarities, which emerged during research between the cultures of the organisations and their host nations, were striking. Corporate cultures appear to be fractals of their national parent. The BBC, like the UK, is struggling to come to terms with the end of an empire, the passing of a golden age, and seeking perhaps to play a larger role than its resources allow. CNN's culture is pure 'frontier spirit' and reflects the differentiated individualism, free speech and proactivity that are central values in US management. Its attitude to change echoes that of the US as a whole; change is normally associated with improvement and is therefore to be welcomed. CNN, it could be argued, is seeking to conquer new geographic frontiers and spread the gospel of independence, just as the American pioneers did centuries ago.

A third finding concerns culture's *effect on how audience needs are defined*. Both of the organisations investigated for this study claim the same mission: to serve the public. However, an identical mission was interpreted in different ways. For CNN, 'serving the public' meant giving the public what they want, even if this didn't quite reflect the tastes of broadcasting professionals – the public, after all, knows best and viewers are the ultimate arbiter. The organisation saw its core task as catering for the existing public appetite for news, and in the process maximising audiences and thereby revenues. To do this it needed to make its news as attractive as possible – which in the context of CNN has traditionally meant more immediate, more global, more 'live'. In organisational terms, this places a priority on the ability to react fast, on good audience feedback, on rapid production turnaround (even if production values are a bit rough and ready), and on quick communications, internal and external. For the BBC, imbued with the Reithian ethos, 'serving the public' meant at times 'leading' public taste, if necessary stimulating an appetite for its programming.

The final broad point to be drawn concerns the wider role of culture in broadcasting organisations. The distinct cultural beliefs held by CNN and the BBC – about broadcasting's fundamental purpose, about the nature of competition, about viewers, about the relationship between competition and quality – drive those organisation's products, performance and strategic options. Their cultural beliefs have laid the foundations for each organisation's striking current and past successes, and will also determine how these organisations respond to the coming media revolution, and perhaps also their ability to survive it.

CHAPTER SUMMARY

- Corporate culture, in the form of shared unconscious assumptions, plays a unique and important role in broadcasting organisations. For both the BBC and CNN, their core products and competitive strengths are deeply rooted in the inner beliefs common to those working there.

- However, corporate culture also plays an important role in determining how broadcasting organisation's wider strategies are perceived and accepted. This research showed that at both organisations the cultural assumptions, while being a source of strength, were also in conflict with some of those organisation's strategic priorities, raising questions about whether those goals were achievable.

- The founder of a broadcasting organisation plays a disproportionate role in shaping its subsequent culture. The personal beliefs of Lord Reith, who founded the BBC in the 1920s, and Ted Turner, who founded CNN in the 1980s, are perpetuated in the current-day organisation to a surprising degree.

- There are strong similarities between the culture of an organisation and that of its 'host' nation. CNN's culture reflects the 'frontier spirit', individualism and proactivity, which are strong values in American culture. The BBC, like the UK, is struggling to come to terms with the end of an empire, and perhaps seeking to fulfil a role larger than resources will allow.

- Culture can affect how audience needs are defined. Both the BBC and CNN claim the same mission: to serve the public, however, an identical mission was interpreted in different ways. For CNN, 'serving the public' meant giving the public what they want, even if this didn't quite reflect the tastes of broadcasting professionals. For the BBC, 'serving the public' meant at times 'leading' public taste, if necessary stimulating an appetite for its programming.

- The BBC's culture has four core common assumptions: a belief that public funding makes the organisation special, different and important; a belief that the BBC is 'the best in the business' and that given appropriate resource, scope and opportunity, is capable of producing the best broadcasting in the world; a belief that the BBC serves a unique national role and is part of the fabric of Britain; and a belief that those working at the BBC are custodians of a unique and important broadcasting heritage.

- CNN's culture also has four basic beliefs. The first, that news lies at the heart of CNN, that CNN in some senses '*is* the news'. Second is a belief that viewers 'pay the bills', and unless they watch, the organisation can't function. Third is a belief that CNN is a pioneer and dissident, that it has redrawn the rules of news broadcasting. Fourth, CNN views itself as the underdog and outsider of US broadcasting, and that its unorthodox beginnings have given it a competitive edge that it can't afford to lose.

Note

The content of this chapter is based on, with permission, Lucy Küng-Shankleman, *Inside the BBC and CNN: Managing Media Organisations*, London: Routledge, 2000.

PART IV

PRODUCERS, PRACTICES AND THE PRODUCTION OF CULTURAL FORMS

CHAPTER 6

The *Brains Trust*: A Historical Study of the Management of Liveness on Radio

Paddy Scannell

We study the past in order to understand the present. What today is familiar and taken for granted once was not so. There was a time when radio and television did not exist. When these new social technologies of communication began their historical, institutional life, those involved were faced with the task of finding immediate, practical solutions to the question of how to 'do' broadcasting across the whole range of an emerging programme output. What is radio news? What is television news? In each case, starting from scratch, answers had to be found to such basic questions by those who pioneered what we now simply take for granted. Today everyone *knows* what broadcast news is, by virtue of routine broadcast practices that produce it as such. In this chapter I engage with another fundamental problem for broadcasters, from the beginning through to today, namely the management of liveness, perhaps the most basic characteristic of radio and television. I want to show what the problems of live broadcasting are and, at the same time, how they can be dealt with successfully so that the effects of liveness are precisely what audiences respond to and enjoy. I shall focus this issue in terms of the management of spontaneous, unscripted, live-to-air discussion on radio, something by now so utterly familiar that it is hard to see what the problems with it might be. In order to do so, we must go back to a time when such talk was not the norm on radio and try to uncover what prompted moves in the direction of live, unscripted discussion for listeners and how it was done.

I first tell the story of the production of a single wartime BBC radio programme, the *Brains Trust*. Although it is, I think, an interesting story in its own right, it serves to illuminate some of the most enduring characteristics of radio as a broadcast medium, and is meant as a contribution to our understanding of radio today. My account is based on primary sources drawn from the BBC's written and sound archives and from contemporary accounts by those most intimately involved in the programme. But the methodological focus of this chapter is not on the history of the BBC, nor on how to do historical research (Scannell 2002). It is rather on the pre-history of programmes-as-broadcast; the whole complex, hidden process of coming up with an idea for a programme and its subsequent development from concept to realisation as a transmitted broadcast. At the heart of my discussion is a concern with the communicative intentionality of this process and how that is inscribed, in the form and content of the end-product, the programme-as-broadcast, in such ways that audiences can find it there. In order to explore this question, I draw upon a number of approaches from sociology, pragmatics and phenomenology which I have found helpful. I try, in the course of my discussion, to make clear the relevance of these different disciplines to an understanding of both production and product and how the former is, in hidden ways, embedded in the latter.

The *Brains Trust*

The *Brains Trust* was the first live, unscripted discussion programme on British radio in which the speakers responded spontaneously and without foreknowledge of them, to questions sent in by listeners.[1] It began in response to a request by the planners of the Forces Programme, in the autumn of 1940, for something that would alleviate the boredom of the troops in their billets and at the same time respond to an identified need for information and discussion in the most general sense. This particular programme request could have gone to any one of three production departments for development: Talks, Features or Variety. Each had a quite different internal culture, with a different ethos in relation to their common task of making programmes. In short, if the programme went to Talks, its defining communicative characteristic would be 'intellectual'; if it went to Features, it would be 'artistic'; and if it went to Variety it would be 'entertaining'. It was therefore a crucial decision to send it to Variety, thereby prefiguring the decisive communicative form the programme would take. But even then, within any production centre there are different producers with different attitudes and styles towards the common task of producing, in the case of Variety, entertainment. Thus, it was significant (it made a difference to the subsequent history of the programme) that the Head of Variety, John Watt, chose to delegate its development to the good genius of Howard Thomas. Individuals can and do make a difference within the corporate culture of production in the BBC, which Thomas had joined in 1940, from a career until then in advertising and commercial radio.

The brief Thomas received from Watt was succinct: to create an informational programme that was 'serious in intention, light in character'. The form that the programme eventually took was 'no sudden inspiration. Like most good and simple ideas it was hammered out during weeks of hard thinking' (Thomas 1944: 13). Thomas wanted a programme with 'mass appeal', to bring listeners into 'personal' contact with some of the best brains of the day in the most friendly and informal way. They had of course been heard on radio before. Indeed, the mission of the Talks Department before the war had been precisely that. Yet if the idea had been developed by Talks, so Thomas argued, it would have put enlightenment before entertainment whereas he put a premium on the latter. The kind of talk that Thomas wanted to capture was something like table-talk, the lively after-dinner conversation of the educated intelligentsia. 'Spontaneous answers by interesting people, that was it'. The key to securing the effect of liveliness and spontaneity was to have a panel of speakers and a Question Master (Howard coined the term) to introduce the speakers, to set them the questions and to control and manage the talk that went out over the air.

Thomas put up his ideas for a programme he originally thought of calling *Any Questions* in a seven-page memorandum (26 November 1940. WAC 51/23/1).[2] It was accepted and he now began the task of transforming ideas into reality. Questions were invited, on air, and they came in, at first in a trickle then a torrent. By the time its fame was established, the programme received two and a half thousand questions a week, rising to a peak of just under four thousand. To deal with such a volume of mail took two staff two full days each week. Many letter writers wanted further information on topics discussed the previous week, and they were supplied (where appropriate) with suggestions for further reading. Questions suitable for the programme were classified into broad topic areas and then selected both for variety of subject and in relation to the interests and personalities of the speakers. Thomas would then go home with a bundle of about a hundred possible candidate questions and whittle them down to a dozen or fifteen. These were then typed up and passed to Basil Nicolls for final approval.

The vetting of the question list was partly to do with the circumstances of wartime broadcasting, but as much to do with the internal culture of the BBC, where 'referral up' by producers on matters that might have policy implications was by now deeply engrained in the institutional culture. Until the end of 1942 Nicolls, as controller of programmes, was solely responsible for vetting the programme. On one occasion he wrote to the producer instructing him to avoid 'all questions involving religion, political philosophy or vague generalities about life'. He routinely weeded out anything that he thought might cause 'irritation in Parliament'. At the beginning of 1943 the Board of Governors relieved Nicolls of his task only to take it upon themselves. They solemnly debated whether or not a question on the profit motive should have been allowed (in their view it should not) and it was they who dealt with a request from the Archbishop of Canterbury that there should be at least one regular member of the programme who spoke for Christian opinion.

All this interference from above came to be deeply irksome for the regular speakers and for Howard Thomas. But back at the start his main concern, as the questions began to come in, was to pick the right speakers and then find the way to bring out the best in them at the microphone. He found a perfect mix in the balance between the characters and performances of the three regular panellists. There was Huxley, the scientist: knowledgeable and factual, perhaps rather dry and occasionally irritable, but whose solidity and seriousness formed the back-bone of the programme. Then there was Joad: never short of an opinion, widely read, a fluent and occasionally brilliant speaker who, even if he didn't know what he was talking about, was never dull. He and Huxley were perfect foils: 'Their disrespect for each other's views and their willingness to "mix it" brought a clash that attracted millions.' These two, though very different, were clearly 'brains'. The last in the original triumvirate was not, but Thomas insisted on him, overriding Cleverdon's objections and arguing that it was essential to have a link between the professors and the listeners who had never heard a professor. Campbell, an ex-navy man, was widely travelled with a colourful turn of speech and an attractive broadcasting manner. His no-nonsense, common-sense views could bring the talk down to earth again after the lofty flights of Joad. Campbell was relished by listeners for his curious bits of information and odd facts. He once declared on the programme, in all seriousness, that he knew a man so allergic to marmalade that whenever he ate it for breakfast, steam came out of his head. Like the other two, he was a natural performer. Thomas did not create, or even develop their radio characters, but he did carefully choose them as a combination. What they stood for seemed, to him, the right blend; the cool brain, the ready tongue, the voice of experience (Thomas 1977: 74).

The programme was recorded each week on Friday afternoon, either on film or tape, in the BBC's Maida Vale studios. It was recorded 'live', in one continuous take, as the discussion unfolded in the studio.[3] Although there was sporadic behind-the-scenes discussion about whether the programme should be trans-mitted live-to-air, recording was preferred for a number of reasons. In the early years of the war, all programmes were scripted for security reasons, and it was to overcome this considerable handicap to its spontaneity that Thomas decided to record it each week (Thomas 1944: 82). There were further advantages. It gave time-flexibility to broadcasters and performers, allowing the programme to be recorded at a time convenient for the panellists and freeing them from the obligation to be in a BBC studio each week at the time of the programme's transmission. Moreover it gave the possibility of repeats (the programme was broadcast twice weekly) and for transmission in the BBC's rapidly expanding wartime overseas services.

Before the weekly recording session Thomas first took the weekly panellists out to lunch at the BBC's expense. A drink or two – no more – lest excess should dull their subsequent performance, was allowed to the participants. Both food and drink, as legitimate programme costs, had to be wrung from an unwilling BBC administration, but Thomas defended the expense as a necessary pre-liminary to getting the best out of the speakers. It helped them to relax, it introduced guests to the regulars, it created familiarity, it loosened tongues. In short, a good lunch accompanied (hopefully) by good table-talk was the best way to begin to loosen up the participants for the talk-to-come. Once in the studio they were seated at a table with a microphone in the middle. Every session began with a ten-minute warm-up with a couple of unrecorded questions put to the panel by McCullough. This preliminary was essential in a number of ways. It was indispensable for newcomers, allowing Howard Thomas to spot their idiosyn-crasies and, where possible, to correct them. Some, when speaking, would turn to the person next to them, thus deflecting their voice from the microphone. Others would talk at the table, holding their heads down as they spoke. Others covered their mouths. There was the occasional over-emphatic table-thumper. Some could not keep still, leaning forwards then stretching backwards, twisting and turning their heads – the result, as heard by listeners, was an unpleasant series of gushes and fades as their voices came and went. While Thomas attended to such matters, the sound engineers attended to the properties of the speakers' voices in relation to the microphone. Pitch and volume had to be adjusted and balanced to produce an even-sounding programme for absent ears. Shouters could be softened, whisperers coaxed to increase their volume. Naturally loud voices were placed at the corners of the table, at an angle to the microphone. Quiet voices were placed full on to it. As a rule this was where women were positioned to stop them raising their voices and sounding shrill. Joad and Huxley were always placed opposite each other to allow them to spar more easily.

After the warm-up the programme quickly slipped into the real thing. The green light came on. The programme was now 'on record' and McCullough deftly introduced each participant before sailing into the first question. Thomas himself always sat in on the sessions. Positioned slightly behind McCullough and away from the table he tried, from moment to moment, to hear the talk with an ear for the listener. When he felt a discussion was getting too wordy, he would pass a note to the question master telling him to wrap it up. Thomas was always keenly sensitive to the programme's pace, tempo and balance. To maintain tempo he would, if necessary, switch the order of questions. If, for instance, Joad had discoursed at length on a philosophical question, he would tell McCullough to bring forward a question on snakes for Huxley.

It was extraordinarily hard to convince listeners that the talk was completely unrehearsed. The BBC publicly guaranteed the questions were not known in advance by any of the panel. Thomas would point out how it was virtually impossible to read a prepared script in the completely natural manner that characterised the *Brains Trust*. If speakers knew the questions ahead of their replies, their answers would be duller, longer, less provoking. It was the spontaneity, the slips, the verbal clutchings in mid-air and the occasional flooring of the speakers that listeners enjoyed. Spontaneity, as an achieved effect-in-public, as an effect-for-others, never simply happens. It must be planned and worked for. If it is to be achieved, it must be so effortlessly. The programme's format was a device for producing talk-in-public as an art, the art of conversation.

The Management of Talk

The study of talk has developed from the philosophy of ordinary language or 'speech act theory' as it is now commonly called (Austin 1962; Searle 1969) and from pragmatics, a recently established field of enquiry into language-in-use, which has its roots in philosophy, linguistics and sociology (Levinson 1982). Pragmatics is related to, but not the same as, Conversation Analysis (CA). CA is a distinctive branch of ethnomethodology that was pioneered by Harvey Sacks in the 1960s and which treats naturally occurring talk as a fundamental kind of social interaction (Sacks 1992). A cardinal distinction made by CA is between institutional and non-institutional forms of talk. CA began by studying 'ordinary, plain talk' as it showed up in everyday contexts; telephone conversations, for instance family talk at mealtimes. Later it moved on to the study of the kinds of talk produced in institutional settings (in the law courts, a doctor's surgery, a classroom or seminar room, a radio or television studio). It showed that such talk has certain basic differences from 'ordinary' talk which is crucially to do with how the talk is 'managed'. It is a core assumption of ethnomethodology that even the most seemingly natural and spontaneous social phenomena have nevertheless to be 'done'; that is, they have to be performed (enacted) in recognisable ways in recognisable social settings (Garfinkel 1984). CA brings this perspective to bear on seemingly 'natural' and 'spontaneous' talk, showing in fine detail how it is indeed managed by the co-participants in any conversation. Thus, CA has examined how talk is initiated, how it is developed (the negotiation of topic changes, for instance) and how it is closed down. How to get into a conversation, how to keep it going and, finally, how to get out of it are issues that, on a moment's reflection, we can all recognise as dilemmas that we do indeed face and deal with in our talk with others. It is the great virtue of CA to show how talk-as-interaction is, in fact, routinely and matter-of-factly accomplished by human beings as accomplished social actors.

In non-institutional settings the management of talk is a task that is jointly negotiated throughout by its co-participants. But this is not the case in institutional settings, where conversational tasks are pre-allocated according to specific roles assigned to different speakers. In particular, what tends to be predetermined is who will ask questions and who will answer them. Thus, in broadcasting, the interview (a by now staple kind of talk-as-interaction on radio and TV, but one that had nevertheless to be invented as a broadcasting technique) consists of an interviewer who asks questions and an interviewee who answers them. It is the responsibility of the interviewer to open up the talk, to establish, maintain and change the conversational topics that are the focus of the interview and, finally, to bring it to a close. In this respect talk on radio and television is structurally similar to talk in other institutional settings. But there is one unique institutional feature of the design of broadcast talk, namely that it is produced not for the participants in the talk as broadcast, but for absent listeners or viewers. Participants in on-air talk are collaborating (or not) in the production of an interaction which, while it is between them, is not ultimately for them. It is designed to be listened to by absent others. This is the double problematic at the heart of all broadcast talk: its institutional production and management in institutionally controlled settings for unseen absent listeners and viewers who are elsewhere.

Broadcasting's audiences are not co-present. This means that while the broadcasters do, in fact, manage, regulate and control the broadcast performance which they produce in an institutional setting (typically the radio or television studio), they have no control over the behaviours of their audience simply because they are not there. It took some time for the broadcasters to realise this. By the late 1920s the BBC was regularly providing musical concerts and drama on radio, and listeners were expected to prepare for such occasions as if they were in the theatre or concert hall. They were advised, in the *Radio Times*, to turn the lights down, get rid of distractions (settle the baby, put the cat out) and thus create an atmosphere suited to the occasion (Scannell and Cardiff 1991: 371). But no one did. Gradually policy- and programme-makers began to appreciate that instead of expecting their absent listeners to behave as *they* wished, they must adjust their programmes to fit in with the actual circumstances in which listening took place.

Thus, in respect of talk, it became clear that listeners did not want to hear sermons, or lectures or political speeches, the prevalent forms of *talk-in-public* at the time (Mattheson 1933). Listening to radio was a leisure activity, a pastime located in the contexts of ordinary, daily, domestic life. Radio talk, for it to become effective, had to learn to move from existing forms of public talk towards the usual forms of talk-in-private: conversation, chat, ordinary plain talk, the talk that goes on at home, on the buses or in the playground between families, friends or work colleagues. This transformation has been traced by David Cardiff in the efforts of the BBC Talks Department to find forms of talk that worked on radio in the course of the 1930s (Scannell and Cardiff 1991: 153–80). A crucial problem they faced was the management of liveness. The most basic characteristic of radio and television, as time-based media, is that they are live to air and in real time. In live, real-time broadcasting there is no interval between the production, transmission and reception of programmes, and in the early years of radio and, later, television, *all* broadcasting was live and in real time.

Perhaps the primary problem posed by live broadcasting is negative. Any live situation is inherently fragile. There is always the possibility, at any moment, that things could go wrong and hence there is an ever-present imperative to avoid cock-ups, for if things *do* go wrong, this is immediately and unavoidably visible to the audience. It can be a painfully embarrassing experience, for instance, when actors forget their lines on stage. The hidden prompter, who is following the script of the play, is there to provide a cue and thus to rescue the situation, but even so this back-up system cannot disguise the momentary failure or break-down of the performance. Consider then, the management problems of live-to-air talk on radio. On the one hand, there are various problems to do with technical failure and human error (which still occur occasionally today). On the other hand, there are issues to do with the performance of talk at the microphone; how is it to be done in ways that maximise its effectiveness and minimise its potential to fail? But what is effective radio talk? I have indicated that it was gradually discovered that radio talk should try to be like ordinary conversation. But the key difference between such talk and radio talk for the first twenty years or so of the BBC's activities is that all talk on radio was scripted in advance and read to air in live transmission.

Not the least of the benefits of scripted talk, from the BBC's point of view, was that it allowed complete institutional control over what could be said at the microphone. In other words it was, potentially, a form of censorship. Offensive, libellous or politically dangerous remarks could be (and were) pencilled out of the scripts submitted in advance to the Talks Department by those invited to speak at the microphone. So long as speakers stuck to the script, and they invariably did, there was no danger of their saying the wrong thing. There is no doubt that the control of live talk on radio through the requirement that it be scripted served, in part, as a useful way of eliminating in advance the possibility of something untoward or unacceptable being said on air. But it also dealt effectively with the terrors of unscripted live performance, and the very real fear of making a fool of yourself in public. What if, when it came to it, you had nothing to say about the question put to you? Or if you lost the threads of what you were saying? Or began to repeat yourself? Or did not know when or how to stop? Or if you tried to be amusing and failed? Performing in public is an intrinsically risky business that is, from moment to moment, fraught with the possibility of performative collapse. Stage fright is something experienced by all who place themselves in the public eye. Spontaneous verbal fluency, being able to express yourself immediately on any subject at a moment's notice, is a rare skill that requires not merely training and practice, but confidence and courage.

The success of the *Brains Trust* was the result of two carefully considered factors: first, the selection of speakers who could produce the sought-for talk-as-interaction at the microphone and, second, the management of that talk as it unfolded, live, from moment to moment. I have considered the management of liveness thus far in negative terms, as a problem that needs to be controlled in order to avoid technical failure and human error or deviation. But this does not begin to explain why the production of live talk at the microphone should be such a desirable thing, nor why, when done well, it should meet with such instant acclaim as the *Brains Trust* did. For all its advantages in terms of control, the basic problem with scripted talk is that it is boring. Everyone can immediately hear the difference between scripted and unscripted talk. To our ears scripted talk sounds flat, dull, lacking in spontaneity and immediacy in comparison with what we take to be the *real* thing: spontaneous, natural and, essentially, *live* talk. Pre-war talk on radio almost always meant a talk written and presented by an authority or expert of some sort; talk as monologue. Talk as conversation – people talking between themselves in the studio, the objective of the *Brains Trust* – scarcely existed. The programme's immediate impact testifies to the pleasure of hearing real live talk, live on radio.

The Management of Liveness

We thus must consider the management of live-to-air talk on radio in positive terms; how and why it works as such. In most general terms, the transition to unscripted talk in the BBC indicates its gradual awareness of the need to take its listeners into account in the design of programmes. And if we ask why this was not (as might be expected) a cardinal consideration from the start, two answers suggest themselves. First, there is the social composition of the broadcasters. From the beginning through to the present, the BBC has been predominantly staffed, in its senior levels (of policy and programme-making) by a middle-class, professional, male intelligentsia. This now is recognised as an issue by the corporation, but before the war (and for many years after) it seemed quite unproblematic. Thus the ethos of public service, as it came to be articulated before the war, took it as a given that the task of broadcasting was one of cultural enrichment and that, moreover, the broadcasters knew what that meant and required without needing to take its audiences into account. Whereas the logic of commercial broadcasting impels those concerned to consider what their audiences might want, the logic of public service broadcasting as a state-regulated monopoly has no such inner compulsion. The 'brute force' of the monopoly was the second crucial factor that delayed the impact of audience needs upon the collective corporate consciousness of the BBC.

I have indicated that the relationship between broadcasters and their audiences is an unforced one, because it is unenforceable. Broadcasters cannot make their audience listen in the ways they would wish because, unlike performers in a church or theatre, they have no sanctions against them. But audiences do have one very powerful sanction against the broadcasters if they do not like what they are getting: they can immediately switch to another service. In monopoly conditions, however, the only alternative was to switch off. Minimally, it could be argued, the BBC's services were better than nothing. The brute force of the monopoly gave the broadcasters the power to impose their vision of what broadcasting should be upon their audiences without consultation or consideration of what they might want, because there were no internal or external pressures to do so. What has propelled the BBC in the direction of popularising its services has, historically, often been linked to the 'threat' of competition, most notably when commercial television was introduced in 1954. In 1940 the exigencies of total war immediately compelled a quite new attention to listeners and a desire to involve them more in programmes. Audience participation, through the simple device of inviting listeners to send in questions, was as much a novelty as unscripted discussion.

All the key management decisions taken about the *Brains Trust* (including the recognition by the programme planners of the Forces Programme of the need for such a programme) must be understood as driven by the wartime imperative to connect with audiences in the interests of national morale, for that was the crucial mission of the BBC on the 'home front'. The Forces Programme reversed, at a stroke, the thinking of the pre-war BBC. It was, from the start, thought of from the point of view of its listeners (in the first place the troops and, after Dunkirk, the home-land audience of Britain) and what they might want, rather than from the point of view of the broadcasters and what they thought they should provide for listeners. The programme planners of this radically new service took into account the circumstances of listening and what listeners might want to hear from the beginning.

The emphasis on entertainment is indicative of this changing attitude to listeners and prompted the key decision (unthinkable before the war) to give the task of developing the programme to Variety (responsible for entertainment) rather than Talks. The choice of Howard Thomas was equally extraordinary. Howard Thomas was not an insider. He did not share the corporate ethos, the values of the production culture of the BBC at that time. It is hard, indeed, to imagine someone like him being recruited into the BBC other than in the exceptional circumstances of war.[4] Thomas was a pioneer programme-maker for commercial radio in the late 1930s. He worked in the London office of J. Walter Thompson, one of the largest American advertising agencies, and made variety programmes sponsored by the manufacturers of brand-name goods. His shows were recorded on disc in JWT's own radio studio, for transmission back to Britain from mainland Europe by Radio Luxembourg. The culture of commercial radio in the 1930s was very different from that of the BBC. It was populist and popular, and built round star performers – band leaders, singers and entertainers (Thomas 1977: 32-44). Before the war the BBC had tried at first to crush Radio Luxembourg and then grudgingly to compete with it (Scannell and Cardiff 1991: 230–2). When war broke out Radio Luxembourg closed down immediately, and the BBC now recruited one of its leading producers. It is not surprising that two of the most successful wartime programmes – the *Brains Trust* and *Sincerely Yours, Vera Lynn* – were produced in the BBC by an outsider from commercial radio.

The key to the programme's success was the production of live-to-air unscripted, unpremeditated talk-as-interaction. Let us see how it was managed, bearing in mind that the key design consideration is that this talk should be something that listeners would want to listen to. This means that it must somehow show, in the design of the talk, that it is managed with listeners in mind; that listeners can recognise that the talk produced on radio is, in the first place, *for* them. The radio audience is not an overhearing audience. To overhear means to listen to something not meant (intended, designed) for the overhearer. If you tap into a crossed line on the phone, you are eavesdropping on talk between two people producing talk with and for each other, but not for you, the absent third party. Is radio talk like that? Are listeners sneakily tapping into talk that is essentially a private conversation between those involved in it, and somehow accidentally broadcast? And if not, must it not be the case that talk-on-radio should somehow be hearably, evidently, *meant* to be listened to by listeners? How then, does it show up, as a hearable aspect of the talk itself, that it is designed for receipt by an audience? How is this an achieved and accomplished fact about the *Brains Trust* as broadcast?

In an essay on 'Conversation' written a decade or so before broadcasting began in Britain, A. C. Benson suggested that what was most needed in social gatherings was 'a kind of moderator of the talk, an informal president':

> The perfect moderator should have a large stock of subjects of general interest. He should, so to speak, kick off. And then he should either feel, or at least artfully simulate, an interest in other people's point of view. He should ask questions, reply to arguments, encourage, elicit expressions of opinions. He should not desire to steer his own course, but follow the line that the talk happens to take. (Benson undated, c.1910: 67)

Such was the role of the *Brains Trust*'s question master, Donald McCullough, whose assigned task was to moderate the talk produced in the studio in the interests of absent listeners. McCullough, at all points in the broadcast, acted as the intermediary between the live interaction in the studio and those for whom it was enacted. He introduced the programme and brought it to a close. He nominated the topics and who should address them and in what order. The rules of engagement were few but vital. When McCullough read out the question, anyone who wished to speak could raise their hand but not speak until he had identified them by name. This served two purposes: it made it clear, for listeners, who was speaking and, at the same time, it prevented overlapping talk.

In test trials of the programme, a *laissez-faire*, speak-as-you-like policy was adopted. Such 'high involvement' talk may be exciting for participants but off-putting for audiences since it becomes hard to follow who is saying what or what is being said. The simple system of one-at-a-time was adopted in the interests of listeners, though at the possible expense, Thomas noted, of lively debate and discussion. It was a delicate task to find the right balance between encouraging spontaneity while, at the same time, ensuring that it did not become *too* spontaneous, with the speakers becoming so involved in the discussion that they forgot the primary consideration of absent listeners for whom they were, first and last, performing.

This was Howard Thomas's overriding concern. In attending to the voices of speakers, to how they sat at the table, to whether they spoke too quickly, or gesticulated too much, or talked too long (McCullough would be prompted to noiselessly signal that they should wrap up their turn); in considering the tempo of the talk as it unfolded, in occasionally changing the sequence of questions for greater balance and variety – in all these ways Thomas showed his practical understanding and mastery of what was at stake in the production of live-to-air discussion on radio as something whose communicative intention was that it should be found to be entertaining by its designated absent audience. If audiences did indeed find that it was an entertaining programme then, as I have tried to show, it was no accident. It was rather the intended outcome of a wide-ranging set of considerations and stratagems which combined to produce talk-on-radio as something to be listened to by them. For audiences, and indeed for most academic analysts of broadcast output, what was attended to in the first place by the programme's producer and, in the second place by this production-oriented account and analysis, has a 'seen but unnoticed' character. It is presumed, but seldom taken into account, in assessments and evaluations of programmes. The virtue of making explicit the underlying significance of prac-tical considerations and decisions in the production process is that it begins to account for how programmes do, as a matter of fact, work as that which they are found to be by broadcast audiences.

Conclusions

In a famous chapter in *Capital* on 'The fetishism of the commodity and its secret', Marx observes that every product of labour is 'a social hieroglyphic' which does not have its meaning branded on its forehead (Marx 1976 [1867]: 167). The task he set himself in his monumental work was precisely to decode the enigmatic character of commodities through a detailed study of how they were made. His complex analysis of the relations of production revealed how surplus value was created in the workplace but realised in exchange. For Marx the secret of the commodity was the hidden exploitation of the labour that went into its making. The kind of analysis I have sketched above tells us something different about what lies hidden in human products. One thing that shows up clearly in the narrative of the production of the *Brains Trust* is all the thought, effort and concern – in short, the *care* – that went into its making. What this historical account has disclosed is the *care structure* of a particular programme.[5] The subsequent analysis attempted to show how that care is there in the programme-as-broadcast in seen-but-unnoticed ways so that listeners could find that the programme was indeed what it aspired to be, namely entertaining. Any human practice has a care structure, which is formally indicative of all the involvements that come together in the articulated and accomplished practice to deliver it as it is manifestly intended to be for others.[6]

But why should care be hidden in things? Why does it not reveal itself? I have shown the crucial contribution of Howard Thomas to the working success of the *Brains Trust*. In all sorts of ways it was 'his' programme. Yet one of the most frequent questions sent in by listeners was: 'Why, if the programme is spontaneous, does it need a producer?' This back-handed compliment suggests that, for listeners, its producer had vanished so completely into the programme that it seemed to be a self-replicating phenomenon, standing as if it were the author of itself and knew no other kin. Any practice is independent of those who make or produce it. The care structure is impersonal and anonymous. To recover the individual human inputs into past broadcast programmes is of course, in part, to honour the dead, to redeem them from the silences of history. But it serves, fundamentally, to underline the objective character of human practices which stand, uncoupled from their creators, in the common light of day for all to use and enjoy (or not) as they see fit. The non-reciprocity of practices is the mark of their disinterested generosity. They present themselves to others with no strings attached, and without soliciting acknowledgement or thanks.[7]

To analyse the care structure of a practice is to make explicit the conditions of its intelligibility. In the case of broadcasting, it is always the most obvious things that need most explaining. If a programme is found by audiences to be entertaining, how are the conditions of its recognition *as such* there in the programme? It cannot be the case that the 'entertainingness' of programmes amounts to no more than the subjective projections upon them of individual listeners or viewers. The disclosedness of things,[8] the ways in which they reveal themselves as what they are, in terms of what and who they are for (the *Brains Trust* is *for* the enjoyment of listeners), indicates that their meaning is immanently *in* them in such ways as to be discoverable by anyone. But the immanent meaning of any humanly made thing (including radio programmes) is there only by virtue of all the forethought involved in its production, right through from the initial concept to the realised end-product. It is a distinctive feature of humanly made things considered as *pragmata* (as things-for-use), that they by and large actually do work as they were intended to do – otherwise they are not much use. If the exploitative aspects of labour are concealed in things, so too is the care and concern involved in their making. The one does not preclude the other.

The fascination of the study of production, for this author at least, is to uncover what we all, naturally, take for granted; namely the self-evident facticity of the world which is, at one and the same time, disclosed and yet concealed in any worldly thing or practice (Heidegger 1962, 1999). Whenever we turn on the radio or television today we most likely will encounter, in any non-fictional programme, people in various situations producing unscripted, spontaneous talk of some kind or other. We are seldom aware that this talk is something that has to be managed in ways that are specific to radio and television, because broadcast programmes do not, on the whole, reveal the conditions of their production. We are even less aware that broadcast practices have a history; that there was once a time (now long gone) when all broadcast talk was scripted. The particular value of a historical approach to broadcast production practices is that it can make explicit what is at stake in the actual discovery and working out of a practice at the point of its origination. Practices have their histories. Their recovery helps us understand that how broadcasting works is the outcome of accumulated knowledge and know-how, worked out as practical solutions to immediate issues in its own day, and subsequently routinised and projected forward into a future, which in turn becomes the today that we, the living, inhabit. The management of liveness, which I have considered here as an issue for radio broadcasting is not, of course, a matter of concern just for broadcasters or academics. Fundamentally it concerns the ways in which we the living, in any today, confront and cope with liveness, being alive, the management of the foregiven conditions of our existence. Something of this is the hidden pearl in *any* human practice.

CHAPTER SUMMARY

- The particular value of a historical approach to broadcast production practices is that it can make explicit what is at stake in the actual discovery and working out of a practice at the point of its origination.

- The discussion of the *Brains Trust*, an early live radio discussion programme, offers an opportunity to consider how programme producers managed spontaneous, unscripted live-to-air talk – a programme form that is now often taken for granted.

- At the heart of this discussion, and drawing on theoretical ideas of pragmatics, phenomenology and sociology, is the concept of 'communicative intentionality'. This is inscribed by the producers into the form and content of their end-product, the programme-as-broadcast.

- The analysis of the production of the *Brains Trust* documents the effort, time and care of the producers that went into its making. This 'care structure' is there in the programme as broadcast and is heard but unnoticed by listeners in that it achieved what it aspired to be for them, namely entertaining.

- To analyse the care structure of a practice can therefore help to make explicit the conditions of its intelligibility. In the case of broadcasting, it is always the most obvious things that most need explaining.

• Practices have their history. Their recovery helps us to understand that broadcasting works as the outcome of accumulated knowledge and know-how, worked out as practical solutions to immediate issues in its own day.

Notes

1   What follows is mainly drawn from Howard Thomas's accounts of the programme (Thomas 1944, 1977), which he treats as very much his own creation. The production files in the BBC Written Archives at Caversham (WAC) show that this claim, which Thomas vigorously asserted (demanding that the programme be billed as 'originated by Howard Thomas') was disputed within the Corporation partly because the original demand for a question/answer programme was handed to the production departments from programme planning, partly because Douglas Cleverdon was, from the beginning, the programme's co-producer and partly because of a corporate culture of anonymity. There was much conflict about all this at the time, but there is no doubt that the *Brains Trust* was Thomas's brainchild.

2   A programme of this name began on West Region, on 12 October 1948. The title was conceived quite independently, but it was based on the *Brains Trust* format, and invited questions on current political issues from a live audience to be answered by a panel of four (of whom two at least were always MPs) through the programme's host (or Question Master). *Any Questions* is still running on BBC Radio 4 today, more than half a century later. Its companion programme on Radio 4 is *Any Answers*, in which listeners respond on air to the issues raised each week in *Any Questions*. The format transferred to television in the 1970s and *Question Time* (BBC1) remains the BBC's long-running flagship programme for the weekly discussion of current affairs. Thus a concept developed over sixty years ago is still in use today as the BBC's preferred format for the discussion of politics on both radio and television.

3   Liveness should not be confused with immediacy. A programme, in order to be 'live', does not necessarily have to be transmitted in the moment of its production (i.e. in real time). The effect of liveness is preserved in recording in a number of ways (Bourdon 2000), but most simply by recording in one continuous unbroken take. Continuity editing, very common today, procures the same effect. I have found no evidence of post-production interventions to tidy up, for whatever reason, the original 'live' recordings of the *Brains Trust*.

4   He didn't last long, handing in his three months' notice of resignation in November 1943 because of 'irksome restrictions' on his work. His name was then immediately withdrawn from the billings of the *Brains Trust*, even though he continued to produce it while he worked out his contract. At this Thomas went public, denouncing the petty-mindedness of the BBC and declaring that he was the original and only begetter of the programme. Details in WAC Press Cuttings, Forces Programme 1944 (2): 200.

5   Heidegger (1962: 225–73). A useful gloss on the care structure can be found in Dreyfus (1991: 238–46).

6   The BBC's Listener Research Department ran an annual check on audience reactions to the *Brains Trust*. Their findings confirm that the vast majority of listeners recognised 'that the essence of the Brains Trust is discussion, but it is also widely maintained that the occasional "matter of fact" question makes good listening' (WAC Listener Research Report, 'The Brains Trust 1944–5', LR/3657).

7   On broadcasting considered as a disinterested, non-reciprocal communicative practice, see John Peters' discussion of the Parable of the Sower (Peters 1999: 51–62).

8   Heidegger (1962: 104 and *passim*) and, for further discussion, Dreyfus (1991: 102–7, 270–273); Haugeland (1992: 27–44).

CHAPTER 7

Journalists with a Difference: Producing Music Journalism

Eamonn Forde

The academic study of popular music journalists in particular, and arts critics in general, has been limited. This chapter focuses on popular music journalists. Running through the chapter is the core argument that music journalists, despite having a number of important similarities with mainstream 'hard news' journalists, must be singled out and considered as a unique case. The profession simultaneously exists both inside and outside the traditional journalistic sphere, and therefore theoretical models and findings derived from news production studies (for example, White 1950; Breed 1955; Tunstall 1971; Chibnall 1977; Schlesinger 1978/1980) are of limited use for understanding this unique and under-researched field of music journalism (see Table 7.1).

Music journalists have their own distinct professional tradition, employment conditions, goal definitions, newsroom power structures, position within corporate publishing organisations, and sources and source relations. Tellingly, music journalists on both dedicated music titles and on broadsheet newspapers often describe themselves not as 'journalists' but rather as 'writers', 'reviewers', 'music critics' or '*music* journalists'. In doing so, they mark out a clear ideological, cultural and professional distinction between their world and that of the traditional journalist. The socio-cultural and professional dynamics of these two 'worlds' are defined by music journalists not in terms of opposition or antagonism but in terms of necessary difference. They are, as English (1979: 20) suggests, 'journalists with a difference'.

This chapter presents a discussion of the music press in the UK, with a specific focus on the period 1997–2002. This was a turbulent time for the overall music magazine market, characterised by both publisher and journalistic uncertainty about the direction in which the sector was moving. The chapter traces the major publishers' attempts to come to terms with a fragmenting market and declining sales. It follows the corporate reactions to market forces through redesigns, closures and (in the case of IPC) corporate buyouts. This discussion of the changing political economy of the publishing industry is then followed by a more detailed discussion of how this impacted at the level of the newsroom and the music journalism profession.

Table 7.1	'Hard' news and music journalism compared

Hard news journalism	Music journalism
Requires National Council for the Training of Journalists qualifications	No formal journalistic training required except in the case of the news editor. Editors feel formal journalistic training to be a hindrance
Deals mainly with analysis of factual information	Deals mainly with textual interpretation
Emphasis on objectivity	Emphasis on subjectivity
Information-led	Product-led
Descriptive	Evaluative
Reporters	Critics
Long-term career path	Short-term career path leading to high turnover of writers
Higher level of career stability	Higher level of career instability
Working life and social life tend to be separate	Working life and social life inseparable
Readership demographic is broad	Readership demographic is niche
Readers tend to be 'readers for life'	Readers tend to remain with the title for finite period determined by age
Poly-thematic/broad range of topics covered	Mono-thematic/narrow range of topics covered
Age not necessarily a key issue in ensuring cultural proximity with readers	Age a key issue in ensuring cultural proximity with readers
Not necessarily the 'ideal readers' of the titles they write for	Are the 'ideal readers' of the titles they work for
Work for standalone titles	Tend to work for magazines that are part of wider portfolio of titles
Can work across a number of (competing) titles	Cannot, in the main, work for competing titles/publishers
Relative stability in readership demographics courted	Continual revision of the readership demographics courted
Professional distance, for the most part, from sources and subjects seen as essential to their job	Lack of professional distance from sources and subjects seen as essential to their job

Context: The Political Economy of Music Magazine Publishing

It is important, at the level of political economy, to understand first the organisational and financial structures within which music magazines are structured, redesigned, launched and folded. Music magazine publishing must be approached as a distinct and unique wing of the publishing sector. The discussion focuses on the two main publishing organisations whose virtual duopoly within the market means that all music magazines must, for the most part, work around the agenda they set. International Publishing Corporation (IPC) through its IPC Ignite! division produces *New Music Express* (hereafter referred to as *NME*), *Muzik* and *Uncut*. It also published the rock/alternative weekly *Melody Maker* (*MM*) until 2000 when it was folded. East Midland Allied Press (Emap) through its Emap Performance division produces *Smash Hits*, *Kerrang!*, *Mixmag*, *Q* and *Mojo*. It also published the rock/alternative monthly *Select* until 2000 when it too was folded (see Table 7.2).

Both tabloid and broadsheet newspapers have explicitly used pop coverage to draw in younger readers since the 1980s (Rimmer 1985). Their belief was that popular music consumption patterns are finite and determined by age, with a sharp fall-off point in the mid-to-late-20s (Negus 1992). Newspaper readers tend to display life-long title and brand loyalty (Tunstall 1983: 157–8). Music magazines, however, tend only to hold readers for a limited number of years

Table 7.2   Sales figures of music magazine titles (January–June 2002)

Title	Frequency	Publisher	Sales	Main type of coverage
Top of the Pops	Monthly	BBC	235,007	Teen-pop
Smash Hits	Fortnightly	Emap	190,177	Teen-pop
Q	Every 4 weeks	Emap	180,168	Rock
CD:UK	Monthly	Attic Futura	138,122	Teen-pop
Mixmag	Monthly	Emap	100,336	Dance
Mojo	Monthly	Emap	100,138	Current and classic rock, blues, world, jazz
Kerrang!	Weekly	Emap	83,988	Hard rock, heavy metal
Uncut	Monthly	IPC	83,478	Current and classic rock, film
NME	Weekly	IPC	72,057	Alternative rock
Ministry	Monthly	Ministry of Sound	65,030	Dance
Metal Hammer	Monthly	Future	44,070	Hard rock
Muzik	Monthly	IPC	36,018	Dance

until their taste patterns and media consumption patterns shift. The magazine *Q*, for example, was launched with this in mind and positioned in a chain to follow on from *Smash Hits*. Such 'temporality of consumption' is best defined through Bourdieu's (1993: 96) contention that the critics as 'cultural intermediaries' should be the 'ideal reader' of the paper they write for, working from a position of direct cultural, aesthetic and intellectual empathy with their readership. 'To each position there correspond presuppositions, a doxa, and the homology between the producers' position and their clients' is the precondition for this complicity' (ibid.). This cultural and aesthetic homology is, as noted above, temporal. As writers evolve and their tastes shift, so too do their readerships. In the case of the music press, this dynamic is at its most pronounced, and clearly marks it out from the traditional press.

Music journalists and their readers pass through an intensely symbiotic development process, but one that is entirely conditional. As new and, more importantly, younger writers and readers come to the title, so the title's agenda and appeal are slowly revised. Within this revision, there exists an insidious process of cultural exclusion and repositioning slowly edging the long-standing writers and readers on to other (older) titles. There is here a simultaneous migration in terms of both employment and consumption and this can be considered in terms of a 'transferable and evolving homology', where accumulated 'cultural capital' (Bourdieu 1993: 44–5) is carried over to a new title which better suits the writers' professional needs and the readers' consumption needs.

Spanning the Generations: From the Cradle to the Grave

The music press is visibly divided along generational lines that determine and continually revise the market demographic they court, as well as the employment and talent bases they draw on. Emap's earliest successes with *Smash Hits* (1980) and *Q* (1986) in many ways reveal this generational dynamic and niched demographic targeting in motion. Their market impact revealed the presence of fecund publishing strands outside of the remit of the then dominant alternative rock weeklies. They represented – at the time of *Q*'s launch – opposite ends of a publishing spectrum (teenage girls and 25+ males). The ground between and beyond these two demographic groupings was eventually carved up by genre-specific niche titles all owned and developed by Emap as part of their 'cradle-to-the-grave' publishing philosophy.

This publishing approach is based upon straightforward corporate portfolio management where companies break their operations down into 'strategic business units' (Negus 1999: 46). Each operational unit is assigned a particular budget and set of middle managers accountable for the overall market success of their portfolios. By breaking the company's activities down in this manner, the owners and directors develop a corporate strategy for the organisation as a whole. This allows close monitoring of the corporate activities and market penetration of each portfolio and title as a means of maximising profits while minimising waste and expense (Purcell 1993). In introducing new titles into the market aimed at new, or previously ignored, 'taste publics', there are wider repercussions for the market structure and the agendas of the existing magazines as a whole.

Bourdieu (1993: 108) suggests that any structural transformations within the 'field' and market of cultural production will lead to the 'displacement of the structure of tastes, i.e. of the symbolic distinction between groups'. By this, he suggests that when a new producer (in this case Emap), a new product (or range of products as evidenced in Emap's broad portfolio structuring) and a new system of tastes (i.e. in the subsequent fragmentation of the market into sub-niches and tastes cultures) are brought or forced into the market, those existing producers (IPC), products (rock weeklies) and systems of taste (male students) are sidelined or become moribund.

The corporate logic underpinning Emap's approach was that the diversity of their portfolio served to attract a wide demographic of readers, ensuring that their future purchasing habits stayed within their range of magazines, thereby keeping all profits and advertising revenue within the company. The approach recognised that readers of music titles are seldom readers for life. Each title within the Emap music portfolio is carefully niched so that it does not cannibalise the readership of the magazines either before it or after it in the chain. Each title should, as far as possible, be hermetically sealed and exist as a stepping-stone, logically following on from the remit and aesthetic of the title before it in the chain and lead, at the upper end of its readership, into the next title.

Titles are carefully visually branded to ensure stylistic crossover and symmetry between all their titles so that they can be identified as a 'family' of magazines. As Tony Herrington, publisher of left-field music monthly *The Wire* observed, Emap

> get [readers] for life. Start out with *Smash Hits*, then you go through *Select* [while it still existed], then you go through *Q* and then into *Mojo*. So they've got you for life . . . Emap have been the most successful publishing house certainly in culture titles . . . [and] other publishing houses look to Emap and try and emulate what they do.

Emap's titles are defined through their 'niche statements'. These should make clear in economic and corporate terms the following:

- the scale of their operational market;
- the needs of their readership;
- their readership's purchasing power;
- the size of the total market and their share of that market;
- who their direct and their peripheral competition are;
- the format and the appearance of the title;
- its strengths and characteristics; and,
- how it slots into and contributes to the company's overall portfolio.

Publishers' Successes and Failures

IPC ultimately embraced this publishing paradigm, although its success has not been on the scale of Emap's model. In 1995/96 the general consensus within the company was that the 'Britpop' commercial crossover had been something of a hollow victory for the rock weeklies; their sales did not benefit greatly from the mainstream success of acts such as Pulp, Blur and Oasis. The alternative acts they once had the monopoly on were being written about in the tabloids and broadsheets. As sales for the rock weeklies continued to slide throughout the 1990s, IPC re-evaluated the market positions and roles of their weekly titles as market trends suggested the growth of the glossy monthly sector was directly proportional to the decline of the weeklies.

Alan Lewis (then editor in chief of IPC music titles) stated in 1999 that the general bureaucratic feeling within IPC was that *MM* should be repositioned towards a younger readership so that it did not directly compete with the *NME*. He said:

> We felt it [*MM*] was really too close to *NME*. That didn't matter when the scene was healthy . . . But as the scene became less healthy and there was less advertising about, people began to wonder why we were publishing two titles which essentially had the same agenda – i.e. indie rock.

The paper was to operate as a bridging paper between *Smash Hits* and the *NME* (Sullivan 1998), and aimed to lure readers away from Emap titles and to court a younger demographic. As *MM*'s news editor, Carol Clerk, noted during the period of repositioning: 'The editorial policy is more to get these younger readers, not just catch them when they're leaving *Smash Hits*, but get them while they're at *Smash Hits*.'

The final stage of *MM*'s market repositioning came in late 1999, when the paper changed from an A3 'inkie' to an A4 glossy. Beyond losing its core readership, the paper's redesign also lost the title (and IPC) key advertising revenue. An anonymous *MM* section editor claimed that, before Mark Sutherland took over as editor, quarterly advertising revenue in the paper had never dropped below £500,000 and within one year of his editorship it had slipped to £100,000. This was, according to the section editor, because technical and equipment advertisers were not happy to be associated with the paper's new direction. The industry's overall lack of faith in the redesign was summed up by (former *Mojo* editor) Mat Snow: 'Put it this way, they identified a niche in that market, but is there a market in that niche?' As it turned out, in IPC's eyes there was neither a sustainable nor a profitable market in the niche.

Corporate Reactions to Falling Sales: Branding, Brand Extensions and Acquisitions

The reaction of publishers to the oversaturation and fragmentation of the music press market has been to shift the emphasis away from journalists and journalism by 'de-politicising' the profession. On a more corporate level there has been a dual movement towards niche orientation and title branding. The importance of branding and brand extensions increases exponentially when the marketplace becomes oversaturated by operating as an important buffer zone around the central product (Nilson 1998: 8). This is primarily because, 'as the tangible aspects of the product or service . . . [become] . . . more similar, the intangible aspects, the abstract values . . . [increase] in importance' (ibid.). Steve Sutherland (former *NME* editor and subsequent *NME* brand director), when interviewed in 1998, indicated the direction in which both IPC and Emap would develop their portfolio of titles in the following years. He said that his most important role as editor was to 'take care of the *NME* brand and . . . also explore opportunities for that brand to expand'. What this meant was heavy IPC investment in a programme of pan-media branding, including the existing *NME* website (www.nme.com), sponsorship and TV coverage for their annual awards ceremony and (in conjunction with Virgin Radio) the launch of a digital and Internet radio (www.nmeradio.com) (Hodgson 2001).

This movement by the *NME* into pan-media and new technologies branding opportunities (e.g. Internet, Internet radio, masthead television) is typical of the activities of all the mainstream titles. Each branded title must present unique and distinct core values to raise its profile above rival titles as well as supporting its sister titles and their branding activities. The larger publishers present a portfolio of titles and, hence, a portfolio of brands. Therefore, 'each brand needs to be managed separately, but they also need to be managed together to avoid sub-optimisation' (Randall 1997: 138). Publishers draw on 'category management' (ibid.: 139) in order to develop a strategy for the category as a whole rather than for any single branded title. Indeed, the 'first duty of each magazine's branded identity is to contribute to and support the branded identity of the portfolio of which it is but one part' (Forde 2001: 31).

All this represents a corporate loss of faith in a market for uni-functional and mono-thematic cultural products, prompted undoubtedly by the success of general interest male lifestyle and eclectic media culture titles such as *FHM*, *Loaded* and *Heat*. Music magazines are increasingly expected to cover other cultural areas (film and fashion being the most obvious). This mirrors the corporate shift and series of mergers in the 1980s which saw the global record companies becoming absorbed into wider 'entertainment corporations' with interests in cinema, television and book publishing (Negus 1992). Previously, music magazines were organisationally distinct from the music industry (Stratton 1982). The trend towards 'entertainment corporation' mergers reached a fascinating peak in July 2001 when IPC was bought out by AOL-Time Warner for £1.15 bn, which effectively means that a portfolio of music magazines are now owned by a company that also produces records.

While the press is not wholly reliant on the music industry for advertising revenue (as 'lifestyle' advertising becomes increasingly important to their generated revenue), they must be seen by their readers to be detached otherwise they lose their credibility as 'mediators or cultural brokers' (Stratton 1982: 272). They cannot be seen to be aligned/aligning with the industry as it is 'their perceived independence of the [record] companies which legitimates their position and which, correspondingly, gives a taken for granted credibility to what they write or say' (ibid.). The impact on these titles' autonomy from the Warner labels has yet to be felt. However, the precedent set in the US in 1967–68 when *Rolling Stone* was kept afloat with a $100,000 loan from WEA and help with distribution and administration from CBS (Frith 1983) would suggest an uneasy relationship of compromise. What is now happening is a shift from the music press/music industry relationship of fluid 'mutual dependency' (Negus 1992) towards one of total structural and organisational dependency.

Cultural Intermediaries, Professionalism and Socio-cultural Dynamics

Having considered the structural and politico-economic contexts within which music magazines are produced and run in the UK, it is important to consider how the journalists and editors themselves work both within and around these power structures by adopting a 'professional-organisational' (McNair 1999) approach. Indeed, in the limited studies into the music journalism profession, the tendency has been to consider structural and organisational issues, thereby excluding the individual from the debates (Frith 1978, 1983; Chapple and Garofalo 1980; Negus 1992). As argued above, music journalists are unlike traditional journalists for a number of reasons, most notably in terms of qualifications and entry routes, their position (in the main) as critics rather than reporters or correspondents and their self-evaluation of their socio-cultural function. Indeed, all *types* of critic must be considered outside of the dominant models of news production. The remainder of this chapter will consider the relationships between the different professional and organisational roles: primarily how occupational goals are identified and pursued (both individually and collectively); how power structures within the newsroom impact on production; and how the 'culture' of the newsroom both encourages and negates reflexive change in the title/readership homology. By using the concept of the 'cultural intermediary' (Bourdieu 1993), the chapter will break from the traditional studies of news production and existing studies of the music press. It will offer an alternative interpretative framework to clarify the differences between 'journalists' and 'music journalists' and mark out the music journalism profession as unique and particular.

One of the most interesting facts about the music press (and, indeed, journalism in general) is that magazines are run on a daily basis by a small number of full-time staff (occupying the key editorial and design/layout posts) of between seven and ten. Within the major publishing organisations, the employment trend has increasingly been towards the 'casualisation' of the labour force as writers (and even certain section editors, who are employed for a specified number of days on a 'shift' rate [Niblock 1996]). Increasingly they are employed on 'de-democratising', short-term, freelance contracts (paid on a printed word rate), resulting in an explicit and irreconcilable power imbalance between the majority of employees and the publishing executives (Forde 2001).

In terms of the political topography of the newsroom, the majority of music title section editors (see role breakdown below) sit in close proximity to each other (often around the same set of desks). This has a number of important ramifications for the manner in which the titles are assembled and freelancers treated. While most offices are open-plan, a number of titles (notably *MM* while it still existed, *Uncut* and *NME*) have a separate and enclosed office for the editor, and this topographical separation does impact on the socio-professional culture of the title. In enforcing both a spatial and an occupational distanciation between the editor and the rest of the staff, a particular hierarchical order is subtly imposed. As a result, the circulation of ideas and decisions (and the opportunities open to freelancers and staffers to participate in this circulation) is clearly different from those magazines produced in open-plan offices. There is, of course, an explicit hierarchical structure within all organisations in that they all have clear boundaries, a normative order, clear levels of authority and are oriented around the achievement of explicit goals (Smith 1977). Yet it is the manner in which the organisational and hierarchical structure is imposed which is of crucial importance here because the dynamics of the 'professional' and the 'social' are at their most inseparable within the music journalism profession.

Zelizer (1993), in a break from the sociological notions of 'routinisation' in the newsroom (Tunstall 1971; Schlesinger 1978), has discussed how journalism can be approached in terms of both 'performance' (regarding it as fluid, varying across different situations) and 'ritual' (considering how an organisational collective results in patterned behaviour). As a model, this applies particularly well to the unique case of the music press. The cycles of production are typically weekly (*NME*, *Kerrang!*), fortnightly (*Smash Hits*, *DJ*), and monthly (*Q*, *Uncut*, *The Wire*, *Mixmag*, etc.) and so the 'stopwatch culture' of the dailies applies in characteristically different ways. The deadline stretches over the weekly/fortnightly/monthly production cycle within which the whole title is put together, with particular sections being finished before others and sent in advance to the printers.

There is no *single collective deadline* around which all editorial and production activities are geared, but rather a staggered set of deadlines. This has important ramifications for the manner in which the different section editors relate to one another in socio-professional terms, how they position themselves within the production model and how they synchronise content. The frequency of these different production cycles determines the emphasis given over to formal editorial meetings. *NME* typically holds editorials on Tuesday afternoons when initial copies of the paper are delivered from the printers. These editorials have a dual function: to evaluate reflexively that week's coverage and discuss advance planning (usually up to five weeks in advance). In sharp contrast, monthly titles such as *Q*, *Uncut* and *Mojo* do not hold such formal editorials. Rather, the editors of all these titles argued that 'editorial meetings' were conducted on an ad hoc basis, seeing fixed editorials as synonymous with their title being in a state of crisis or in need of a radical overhaul. The regular editorial meetings in hard news journalism (Tunstall 1971; McNair 1999) are key in explicitly laying out the power hierarchy to ensure professional unity between posts, yet in the music press this power structure is more typically mercurial and difficult to determine as it is simultaneously united and disjointed.

Freelancers do not attend fixed editorials on a regular basis and their geographical exclusion from the newsroom (particularly regional stringers) means they are excluded from the decision-making and policy-shaping that takes place informally during the ad hoc editorial discussions. It is equally important to note that the working culture of music magazines is by no means confined spatially to the office; important professional and social dynamics do take place outside the office, primarily in the local pubs and at gigs. The social is the professional and the professional is the social. Certain editors would make a point of taking their staff to the pub at the end of the production cycle. Their belief was that such personal interaction was essential for strong professional interaction. Often informal editorial meetings would take place there, representing a more fluid and organic (rather than an inert and hierarchically inscribed) management system, very much in keeping with the flexibility described in models of new wave management (du Gay 2000).

There is the related danger of this social interaction excluding contributors who are spatially outside the office. A former *NME* freelancer suggested that because the key section editors (assistant editor, features editor, album editor and live editor) all sat in close proximity, they generated a closed loop of opinion which impacted on the dynamic of the whole office and the aesthetic of the title. The professional ideology of the paper was shaped here, he felt, as staffers censored and moulded copy to fit the agenda of the key processors in what Mortensen and Svendsen (1980: 175) call 'internal, explicit control' typical of most media systems. While 'production is a collective enterprise' (Bourdieu 1993: 23), the terms and conditions of entering this 'collective' in the music press are complex and professional: organisational and personal factors will operate to dictate both inclusion and exclusion.

Because critics work, socialise, flat-share and occasionally have relationships with other critics, press officers and artists, the 'field of cultural production' is affected in particular and important ways. There is not the same sense of professional distance that exists in the relationships between hard news journalists, their sources and their subjects (except possibly in the case of crime correspondents [Chibnall 1977]). Therefore the analysis of professional dynamics both inside and outside the newsroom, and the consideration of behavioural and occupational patterns in different environments, are crucial for an understanding of the total profession (Schlesinger 1980). Bourdieu marks out the need to separate 'critics' from studies of 'journalists' when he argues:

> No one has ever completely extracted all the implications of the fact that the writer, the artist or even the scientist writes not only for a public, but for a public of equals who are also competitors. Few people depend as much as artists and intellectuals do for their self-image upon the image others, and particularly other writers and artists, have of them. (Bourdieu 1993: 116)

Indeed, it can be argued that music writers write, primarily, for other music journalists (rather than a readership) and their analysis is shaped accordingly

(Gleason, in English 1979). A former *MM* freelancer stated that in the early 1990s, writers on the paper generated a small and closed field of opinion and used their reviews to try and impress or out-do their colleagues through references to esoteric artists as a game of cultural one-upmanship. Their social and professional world is so small that they end up influencing each other (English 1979) and even writers on rival titles and from rival publishers will socialise in the same places. The entire profession is underscored entirely by self-referential discourses. These incestuous social networks serve to forge a common critical consensus to a point where the same ideas and buzz-acts are circulated quickly within the 'community'. This 'sort of game of mirrors reflecting one another produces a formidable effect of mental closure' (Bourdieu 1993: 24), leading into a form of 'metacriticism' narrowly defining itself and its parameters either alongside or against existing criticism (Farber 1976). It is the intensity of this self-referential nature of music journalism that marks the profession out as one that must be approached outside of the dominant paradigms.

Roles, Goals and Structural Co-dependence

In order fully to understand the operational activities of an organisation, it is essential to consider the different levels of activity through analysis of the behaviour of the individual, the behaviour of the small group and finally inter-group behaviour (Smith 1977). Academically, it is essential to move beyond structuralist notions of the organisations as impersonal spheres and consider the professional and socio-cultural dynamics within them in order to understand both how individuals are 'processed by organisations' (ibid.: 78) and how they contribute to the culture of organisations. The remainder of this chapter will consider in turn the key roles within music titles and the manner in which they co-exist and co-depend. For reasons of space, the focus will not consider the role of the sub-editor, the art editor or the photographer, except to note that their layout and visual/'cosmetic' functions are generally outlined from 'above' by the editor, the features editor or the reviews editor to accord with their aesthetic and ideological slant for the title.

The Editor in Chief

This post is generally occupied by an individual with a proven editorial track record and exists at the mid-point between 'executives' and 'staffers' (Breed 1955). They liaise between the management, advertising departments and the editorial teams across a portfolio of titles and are responsible for the overall market success of these titles (Niblock 1996). Purcell (1993) notes that the corporate office (of which the editor in chief is a key component) fulfils four distinct roles that impact on resource management:

(1) the development and implementation of corporate strategy;
(2) the monitoring of the performances of the various divisions within a company/portfolio;

(3)   the handling and location of capital within the company; and

(4)   the managing of links with external capital (through links with advertisers, the development of brand extensions, corporate sponsorship and so forth).

The editor in chief performs a key function as a mediator between the economically driven sphere of publishing management and the more culturally oriented sphere of music journalism. These two worlds are often mutually contradictory and, at times, antagonistic. The editor in chief is seen by editors, because they will have worked as editors themselves, as much more approachable than other senior managers and can, in times of crisis, help reconcile the editor's journalistic needs and the publisher's economic needs. However, the editor in chief is both professionally and culturally closer to the middle managers and, ultimately, it is their interests they will most strongly represent and promote in both their routine and crisis meetings with editors.

The Editor

In terms of the day-to-day activities within the newsroom, the editor is the single most important individual because they give 'the magazine its character' (Davis 1988: 14). Unlike the era of the autocratic 'press baron' (Curran and Seaton 1997), editorial power is increasingly restricted and conditional in the modern corporate environment as editors are accountable to their publishers and directors (Davis 1988). In the music press, the distribution of newsroom power is mercurial and, as such, subject to delegation and negotiation between the other hierarchical positions within the title, although certain editors do not regard the newsroom structure as a truly collective enterprise. Mat Snow – interestingly echoing Tunstall (1971: 42–9) – suggests that the editor has three interrelated roles, defined along editorial and administrative lines:

(1)   the journalistic (commissioning, processing and layout);

(2)   the financial (budgeting and working with the advertising department); and

(3)   the managerial (ensuring healthy socio-cultural and professional dynamics).

Most editors (unless they launch a new title) 'inherit' their staff from the previous editor and, following their appointment, there is a (sometimes turbulent) period of transition as they replace certain staff members. Within the music press, the appointment of a new editor is a reasonably regular occurrence, as a title's homology with its readers must shift to attract a new generation of readers at the bottom end. This is generally achieved through the appointment of a new (younger) editor and a subsequent recruitment drive for new writers with closer cultural proximity to the desired new readership demographic. Indeed, John Harris (on leaving the Select editorship) suggested that if an editor stays on 'for longer than four years, it's to the detriment of the title' (quoted in Addicott 1999). The turnover of editors on music titles is necessarily much higher than in the traditional press, as age plays as much a role in the aesthetic evolution of a title as bureaucratic professionalism and market performance.

The Features Editor

Despite features being the least-read part of the music press (Frith 1985), the music industry regards them (particularly cover features) as central to their promotional activities (Negus 1992). Indeed, editors and publishers see cover features as powerful tools that attract 'promiscuous' readers in an over-saturated magazine market. As such, their high position within the newsroom hierarchy means they play a central role in shaping the title's homology with its readers. They represent an important 'gate' into the music press for the industry as well as a principal power-centre within the newsroom, particularly in terms of free-lancers progressing up the career ladder. Cover stories and features have often been dismissed as almost exclusively promotional and symbolic of a passive music press. While features are negotiated between the press officer, the features editor and the editor to coincide with a new release or tour, it does not follow that there is a top-down relationship of press dependency and press officer power. Complex criteria of inclusion and exclusion operate (at times idio-syncratically) within each magazine and it is erroneous to view this flow as linear or predictable.

Music magazines need to be understood not simply in terms of their rela-tionship to the music industry. They also need to be understood as social and cultural organisations in their own right as well as an economic and structural part of a larger commercial publishing infrastructure. The features editor exists at the meeting point of these various commercial and occupational forces, and features and cover stories are necessarily generated within and arise out of this complex interchange. The features editor must plan furthest in advance to ensure (occasionally exclusive) access to major artists and, in bureaucratic terms of 'cradle-to-grave' publishing, must present their planned features to avoid inter-title cannibalism. Such complex structural positioning and planning are factors that features editors on traditional news titles do not have to navigate to the same extent (if at all). They must work around not only what the other section editors within their titles are covering (to avoid unnecessary overlap on a particular act in the same issue) but also what the other editors in their portfolio are covering.

The Reviews Editor

While the features editor can perhaps be regarded as the most important gate in the music press for established and becoming-established acts and writers, the reviews editor is undoubtedly the key entry point for new acts. They invariably gatekeep their first wave of press coverage as well as that of new writers by filtering test reviews and monitoring fanzine writers. On traditional news titles, new writers are not as reliant on any single individual for their career devel-opment. The key criticism of White's (1950) 'gatekeeping' study was that he considered one 'gate' and, as Gieber (1964) notes, he missed out on the complex dynamics of the chain of 'gates' (conditioned by both structural bureaucracy and strict deadlines) that make up the newsroom. This inter-relationship between these gates is of particular and unique interest within the music press.

The reviews desk is at the sharp end of shaping the reader/title homology for two reasons: it introduces new acts and also new writers. The occupational trajectory of new writers exactly mirrors the progress of new acts through a title. They begin by submitting live or album reviews, and their abilities and progress are monitored by the other section editors. When they have proven their professional and (crucially) socio-cultural worth, they will be approached to write small introductory band features, then one-page features and eventually lead/cover features, possibly at this point making the transition from a freelance 'gathering' role to a full-time 'gathering' or 'processing' role. In terms of the socio-cultural dynamics of the freelancer environment, the reviews editor plays an essential role here. They must be proactive in creating an inclusive atmosphere as the other section editors contribute little to this dynamic in the early stages of a freelancer's career (monitoring their progress and approaching them only when they are seen as 'ready' to take the next step within the structural hierarchy).

Reviews editors tend to be the immediate point of contact for freelancers and it is an intense relationship of co-dependence, informed as much by personalities as professionalism. The reviews editor occupies a key gatekeeping role here in relation to new writers and new acts, thereby shaping the title/readership homology from the bottom up. They contribute to, re-evaluate and police the overall title aesthetic/agenda in a number of important overt (through formal and semi-formal consultation with the other editorial staff) and subtle (where autonomous personal judgement informs professional decisions) ways. While their criteria of inclusion and exclusion (of writers and artists) will be shaped within the general editorial vision for the title, they can cause alterations at the periphery that will eventually leak into and later shape the title's overall direction.

The News Editor

The post of news editor (more typical of the weeklies than of any other type of music publication) is the only post within the music press that has formal journalistic training as a prerequisite. As such, it is the post that has the most parallels with traditional journalism, but there are also important differences in terms of their position within the overall structure. On the weeklies the production cycle is highly intensive and routinised around at least three sets of deadlines stretched across the cycle. The news pages are the final section sent to the printers. Their importance for weeklies lies in their delivery of an up-to-date news service that monthlies, due to their more protracted production cycle, simply cannot provide.

A high – but particular – sense of professional rivalry exists between the news editors on titles. They, as Tunstall (1971) argued of all journalists, want to cover every story that their rivals cover if they fit the title aesthetic, but also to have a story their rivals missed out on to ensure aesthetic differentiation between titles. Such 'exclusives' are really only possible when working outside of the normal (generally official) information channels. Many news stories tend to be broken by long-standing contacts within the industry, and the longer news editors work in the industry, the more regular contacts and news sources they accumulate. The world the critic and journalist operate within as cultural intermediaries is a small, self-referential and incestuous one.

As noted above, in the music press the same small groups of people (press officers, journalists and label managers) meet and speak on a regular formal and informal basis. Such subtle blurring of the professional divisions between writers, sources and subjects is typical of the music press and is considered as essential to their jobs rather than, as traditional journalists would argue, a compromise of professional distance and objectivity. This means that the same stories tend to circulate very quickly in what (former *NME* news editor) Jody Thompson calls 'a ridiculously small world'. Press officers will only contact the press about their own acts when they have some positive news or must work towards 'damage limitation'. They will also, as news editors admit, contact the press and leak stories about another press officer's acts. The news desk is an enclosed world, reflecting and reinforcing the title's homology with its readers rather than contributing to it. As a result, they are rarely considered a 'talent pool' and therefore do not experience the same upward occupational dynamic as reviewers do.

The Staff Writer and the Freelancer

The post of full-time contracted 'staff writer' barely exists within the music press. As Rivers (1973) notes, most writers are bureaucratically and spatially removed from their publishers; indeed, freelance contracts are increasingly the norm throughout the print media industry (Trelford 2000). Ultimately, this means that the rules of the professional and organisational structures are imposed from above with freelancers working under, rather that contributing to, them. The issue of age as a key factor in ensuring cultural empathy with readers as well as increased professional and economic insecurity has led to a greater, more regular and institutionalised turnover of freelancers in the music press than in the traditional press. With the increased proliferation of titles, editors have suggested that entry standards have slipped and music journalism no longer attracts the quality of writers it did twenty years ago. The number of (national) traditional news titles has not mushroomed to the same extent, meaning an exponential decline in 'quality control' factor that is more pronounced in the music press (Forde 2001).

Review editors argued strongly for the need for freelancers to come into the office to be introduced to the other processors and use this socio-professional interaction to build their careers. This, however, seldom happens. Freelancers were treated differently across titles with certain magazines taking their opinions and editorial suggestions very seriously while others do not. Several freelancers and former freelancers I spoke to suggested they were hierarchically distanced from the power centres within titles. Because of this, it often happened that ideas they proffered formally during editorial meetings or informally to section editors would be declined only to appear in the title in a slightly amended form a few weeks later. This invalidation of the freelancer (Forde 2001) has had a very obvious impact on the nature of the newsroom as a living organism. Staffers increasingly (and almost exclusively) patrol the newsrooms of all music titles on both a regular and semi-regular level. The admission of gatherers is wholly at the discretion of processors, although a high degree of important social and professional interaction takes place outside the office at concerts, after-show parties and bars.

Conclusion

Music magazines are complex socio-professional organisations where the delegation of editorial responsibilities across a number of distinct roles is conditioned by cultural, commercial and socio-professional demands. Within the major publishing organisations, editors are increasingly under pressure to view their titles as merely one part of a carefully structured corporate portfolio rather than as stand-alone magazines. Titles must contribute to the overall survival and development of the portfolio within which they exist. As a result, strategic long-term planning is conducted between the publishers and all the editors within the portfolio to avoid inter-title cannibalism and to ensure that each title 'inherits' readers from the title before it in the chain and encourages readers to 'graduate' to the next title in the chain. This filters down into each individual newsroom, affecting in particular ways how each of the section editors operates and how both their individual and collective goals are defined and realised. Such unique pressures, expectations and dynamics mark out music journalism as a unique and distinct type of journalism that has previously remained invisible. This chapter has taken this previously invisible and under-theorised world and placed it as central to bringing about a revision of the dominant organisation and professional-production paradigms within both journalism studies and popular music studies.

Within each newsroom there are particular socio-professional discourses that are affected by staffing policy as well as both formal and informal editorial negotiation. Titles must continually evaluate and revise the homology that exists between them and their readers. This key issue has not previously been considered in news production studies but is central to an understanding of this particular type of journalism production. At the heart of this recruitment and professional-organisational dynamic within the music press is a constant and carefully monitored turnover of new writers and section editors who, through their perceived position as 'ideal readers', represent points of cultural empathy and proximity for new generations of readers at the bottom end. There is a symbiotic process in operation here between new writers and new artists as a title's aesthetic can never be static and must shift in order to accommodate new acts within its cultural mix and agenda. This high and institutionalised turnover of writers automatically marks the music press out as different.

The subtle, often mercurial, division of labour and editorial responsibility among the key 'processor' roles within the newsroom is characterised by degrees of both conditional dependency and conditional autonomy. Music title newsrooms, while governed by occupational goals and norms set by editors and publishers, cannot purely be seen as rigid and unresponsive to change. There is a degree of both professional and aesthetic fluidity in operation in the news-room, as each section editor will simultaneously operate independently and co-dependently, contributing to the evolution of the title's homology with its readers in overt/formal and subtle/informal ways. Indeed, appointments will be made on the understanding of this need to revisit and revise the title/readership homology.

The changing terms and conditions of employment within the UK music press since the mid-1990s have had important repercussions on how newsroom power is both negotiated and accessed. While the dominant trend has been towards the de-democratising 'casualisation' of labour at the level of writers (and, in certain cases, section editors), at certain points within particular titles there is a blurring of the division between the personal and the professional. Within this, a process of inclusion and exclusion will mean that section editors professionally prioritise particular writers over other writers. Writers and section editors can and will find themselves caught between the pursuit of individual goals of career advancement and the pursuit of collective goals. They must, therefore, be con-sidered simultaneously as individuals with a personal cultural agenda to write about music, and as part of a collective professional unit contributing to the profit-maximisation strategies of major publishing organisations. These tensions between individual goals and collective goals can be a cause of professional and cultural frustration and while there is some room for resistance to editorial and bureaucratic imposition of policy, it is both limited and conditional.

Finally, then, this chapter has isolated the 'music journalism profession' from the 'traditional journalism profession'. In doing so, it has argued that while there are points of similarity, it is by pointing out and analysing their fundamental dissimilarities that a full and rich theoretical understanding of this unique strand of journalism can be arrived at.

CHAPTER SUMMARY

- Music journalists working for the consumer music press in the UK are a particular and unique type of journalist and must therefore be considered outside of the dominant paradigms within journalism studies. The entry requirements, career trajectories and dynamics of routinisation are all very different from traditional 'hard news' journalism.

- In order to understand popular music journalism, we must attend to the professional and organisational contexts and conditions that inform the work of music journalists, particularly in relation to increased bureaucratisation and corporate movements towards branding and brand extensions.

- Adopting a political economy approach, we can begin to understand why magazine publishers structure their titles in the ways that they do and how they evaluate their market performance.

- The concept of 'cultural intermediaries' is also useful and more accurately designates the role and performance of music journalists and helps us to understand how they work, how they approach their profession, define their goals and write about their subject matter.

- 'Music journalism' not only is a distinct form of journalism but is also characterised by internal complexities. Examining the key posts within music magazines, analysing how they operate both individually and collectively within the newsroom structure and within the music journalism community, helps us to understand the wider socio-cultural dynamics of the field and how this is constituted in practice.

Note

This study is based on the author's PhD research, 'Music Journalists, Music Press Officers and the Consumer Music Press in the UK' (May, 2001), undertaken at the University of Westminster (UK). It involved interviews with music magazine professionals (magazine editors, magazine section editors, magazine publishers, freelance and staff journalists and music press officers) as well as participant observation at a number of music titles and music press offices in London.

CHAPTER 8
Cultures of Production: Making Children's News

Julian Matthews

Jon Snow, a respected UK journalist and news presenter, has argued that children 'have a watershed to protect them but no mechanism to inform them' (Snow 1994). Observing that there is a disproportionate amount of news and current affairs programmes for adults in comparison to those for children, he concludes that broadcasters are failing to inform this important constituency of society. This general argument usefully focuses attention on the quantity of news information available for children. However, it fails to discuss the child audience's regular diet of news through specialised children's news programmes on both terrestrial and non-terrestrial television channels – whether BBC1, Channel 4 or Nickelodeon. Likewise, the media communication research literature has little to say about the nature and content of these special children's news programmes. Hence, this chapter will report on an in-depth study into one of the most popular, and certainly the longest running, of children's news programmes – BBC1's *Newsround*. It deliberately focuses on the programme's construction of the children's environmental agenda as a way of both exploring and explaining how the 'professional visualisation' (Cottle 1993a) of this children's news form shapes the nature of its output. These insights are important not just because they address the under-researched form of children's news but also because they provide a deeper understanding of how differentiated news forms condition and constrain television news in different ways. This has theoretical relevance for our understanding of how news production shapes and conditions democratic representation and processes of citizenship.

The chapter begins by making a case for seeing children as emergent 'cultural citizens', who ideally should have information rights and forms of cultural representation. It then reports findings from recent research into the production of children's news, illustrating how the professional visualisation of this programme is produced with a particular understanding of the relationship between children, news and nature – a conception that impacts in identifiable and often deleterious ways on the construction and representation of environmental concerns and agendas.

The Need to Know: Children, Citizenship and the Environment

Before we discuss the production of children's news, it is important to step back and explore the relationship between news, children and citizenship – a relationship that has tended to receive little serious scrutiny, notwithstanding the recent turn to Habermasian ideas about media approached as 'public sphere' (Habermas 1974, 1989). The present enquiry is in sympathy with David Buckingham's study, *The Making of Citizens* (Buckingham 2000), which recognises the inadequacy of seeing children simply as an immature audience or as non-citizens, especially if this is based on ideas of poor political knowledge. It must be said that adult citizens too are often found to have poor knowledge of political processes and actors. Buckingham also questions the idea that the media are effective agents of political socialisation, and argues that a more appropriate approach is to examine how news programmes position their audience in relation to issues. This relationship between programme and child, I think, is best understood through the term 'cultural citizenship' (Murdock 1991, 1995, 1999), where cultural citizenship is defined in terms of media audiences and their interrelated cultural 'rights' to mediated information, experience, knowledge and participation.

If we accept therefore that children are 'cultural citizens' who need to be informed about the world by news programmes, then we must also accept that they should be exposed to the pressing social problems of our age. This proposition is supported by a number of commentaries that point out that children are in fact already exposed to 'adult' issues and concerns (Postman 1983; Winn 1985). To paraphrase the ideas of Joshua Meyrowitz (1985), the media today, and TV particularly, take children around the world before they have permission to cross the street. Our concern here though is not to examine this wider background information supplied to children by 'adult' media, but to focus on the particular way that specialised children's programmes represent these wider issues. In this chapter, specifically, we shall focus on concerns of environmental degradation.

Therefore, this research is interested in the professional mediation of environmental issues. The environment without doubt has become the most visible problem of the age (Beck 1992; Goldblatt 1996; Lash et al. 1996) and television has played its part here, beaming 'global' pictures of environmentally related death, destruction and devastation into 'local' sitting rooms. In academic terms, theorists see the media as having played a key role in increasing the visibility of risks and the potentially catastrophic effects of 'risk society' (Beck 1992). More specifically, it is conceptualised as a cultural site for the continual contestation and social construction of risks and the natural world (Macnaghten and Urry 1998; Allan et al. 2000). This study contributes to the wider, and often theoretically abstract, literature on the social construction of risks by attending in more focused and empirical terms to the production practices of journalists and how these actively shape 'the environment' for a particular news audience.

A few foundations have thus been laid down for the study that follows. It is assumed that children's news programmes can provide an important service by introducing children to wider social problems, and that children's news pro-grammes can thereby also help to position children as cultural citizens. Environmental concerns are also assumed to be of crucial importance to children (as much as to the rest of us) in that these often demand behavioural changes in present and future lifestyles as well as political involvement. These normative assumptions guide the analysis that follows.

News, Form and the Imagined Child Audience

In considering the potential of children's news to inform and address children as citizens, we need to examine the construction of news as a 'communica-tive space'. This approach departs from previous research and a generalising assumption that news can be theorised as a homogeneous entity. On the contrary, it will be argued here that we must approach news as highly differentiated by form and that these differences profoundly influence the 'communicative spaces' of news.

First it should be said that although it is true that TV news programmes are made up of principal elements, and that these are instantly recognisable as 'the news' (cf. Corner 1995), it is also important to recognise that professionals produce different forms of news and that these shape news output in iden-tifiable ways. It is this basic insight that has often been overlooked in the substantial ethnographic studies of news that were carried out in the 1970s and 1980s. These tended to focus on how production routines of high-profile news organisations shaped news as a relatively standardised form (Schlesinger 1978; Tuchman 1978; Fishman 1980). Such studies failed to recognise or explain, however, the vast array of different news forms in the larger ecology of news (Cottle 2000a) that are now becoming the subject of research. This new approach to the study of news has started to explain the changing production of news, the news form (Corner 1995) and its differentiation (Cottle 1993a, 1993b; MacGregor 1997; Harrison 2000).

In this, the term 'genre' – a French word meaning type or kind – is used as a starting point to understand the 'repertoire of elements' (Lacey 2000) that group news texts together. News is seen as a communicative repertoire of 'narrative, visualisation and talk' (Corner 1995), and it is these elements in combination that help us to understand the various types or sub-genres of news on offer (Harrison 2000). The problem with approaching news entirely as genre, however, is that it tends to conceal the forces that go into shaping news behind the scenes, and it offers few clues to explain how the different forms of news are produced and change through time. It is important, therefore, to operationalise a term that recognises the elements of news genre but which can also be applied to the production environment. Hence this chapter prefers the term 'news form' to that of 'genre', and through the account of the production of children's news that follows, it will demonstrate how a 'professional visualisation' of form decisively shapes news representations.

Producing the Children's News Form

In interview, children's news producers maintain that it is important for any new recruit to the children's news programme to understand fully both the rules of news in general as well as the particular requirements of their distinctive form of children's news. This essential combination of professional knowledge is illustrated in a recent advertisement for a new *Newsround* producer.

Figure 8.1   Job advertisement in the *Guardian* (3 July 2000)

BBC

Producer, Newsround

Children's Programmes

London

Newsround needs a dynamic new producer. It is a rare opportunity for a creative and skilled journalist to play a key role in one of the best known programmes on TV.

We are looking for someone who can find new and exciting ways to bring challenging and fun stories to our audience. You will output the live programme, help lead the team, have plenty of ideas, an understanding of what children are interested in, and be able to keep a cool head.

You should have first class news judgement and editorial skills, and know what makes a good film. An ability to target relevant stories to a young and discerning audience is essential.

Include with your application a short critique of the programme, along with what you think would be a 'perfect' running order for **Newsround**.

For further details and an application form, contact BBC Recruitment Services by July 25th (quote ref. 46311/G and give your name and address) Tel: 020 8740 0005. Textphone: 020 8225 9878. Postcard: PO Box 7000, London W12 8GJ. E-mail: recserv@bbc.co.uk Online: www.bbc.co.uk/jobs/e46296.shtml Closes: July 28th.

The advertisement asks potential applicants to demonstrate their knowledge or 'judgement' of what constitutes the (adult) news genre as well as their understanding of a particular children's news form. Moreover, it also serves to underscore the claim above that journalists invariably work to a developed sense of the particular news form that they are producing. In the context of the research literature, this finding qualifies two contradictory claims made in earlier studies of news production: the view that journalists are either relatively autonomous and battle against organisational imperatives and editorial impositions, or that they are relatively passive and unconsciously conform to bureaucratic structures and routines. My study, as documented elsewhere, suggests that news workers are in fact knowledgeable about, and actively reproduce, a professional visual-isation of their particular form (Cottle 1993a, 2000). In the case of children's news production, a shared 'programme visualisation' was reinforced by processes of multiskilling, in which boundaries between roles of researcher, journalist and producer became blurred and required each member of the team to understand fully the nature and core elements of the children's news programme. Obser-vations of news practice also revealed how their 'programme visualisation' was reinforced through such 'production rituals' as morning meetings, news-gathering discussions and other daily practices of making news, thus reaffirming the norms and values of this particular news form. In such ways, then, the professional visualisation of children's news informs the shaping of news representations.

In examining the professional visualisation more closely, we find that journalists appropriate the elements of the general adult 'news genre' to produce their distinctive form of TV children's news and are aware of a need for prag-matism in so doing. A BBC *Newsround* journalist describes the ethos of the programme at its inception:

> There wasn't a great debate about whether *Newsround* should primarily try and be funky and excite and be like every other children's programme, or whether it should be grown up and serious like any other [adult] news programme. We knew we were somewhere between the two and if we tried to be too serious and too newsy, we would lose our audience. But if we tried to be entertaining and too children [department] oriented, we would lose our credibility. So we knew we had to strike a balance.

The professional visualisation of the children's news form is thus informed by the tension between the perceived credibility of the adult news programme and the entertainment value of the children's programme. This mix is con-sidered as the essential difference between children's news, with its aim to produce a highly entertaining and visual news programme, in contrast to the standard BBC public service news provision. Also incorporated into this mix are the professional views of the news audience. Observing this, we find that the professional understanding of the 'imagined' news audience is based on an amalgam of two competing views: the 'ideal' and 'real' audience. Practically these serve as useful reference points in the production, selection and inflection of programme content. The professional conception of the 'ideal' child audience is described below:

> I kind of think of having a funky 12 year old who is not too funky but has aspirations to be funky. They are quite interested in the news agenda, quite good at school, you know all those sorts of things; someone that comes from quite a stable background, whose family probably read newspapers and has general newsy things around in the house. They've got a little bit of willingness, and appreciate an explanation. (BBC *Newsround* journalist)

The journalist's construction of the 'ideal' child news audience as mature, academically able and middle class practically serves, therefore, to define the 'ideal' programme content and style of presentation. However, in practice this view of the audience competes with a further professional view of the 'real' audience. This will be elaborated further below, but essentially we can say that this professional view imagines the 'real' audience to have limited intellectual capabilities as well as attention span and that these inform the audience's preference for entertainment rather than information-based programmes. The imagined 'real' audience therefore shapes the production of the news programme in ways designed to attract and maintain a child audience. In practice this process sugars the pill of information-led news with the production values of the entertainment programme; while the producers' wilful imagination of the more appreciative 'ideal' audience serves to bolster the journalist's professional esteem as a serious news provider. With these general observations on children's news production in place we can now examine in more detail how the production of a characteristic news form impacts on the construction and representation of the environment.

Form and the Construction of the Environmental Agenda

To construct the children's news agenda, news workers draw on the perceived needs and wants of the imagined child news audience(s). These inform the news selection process whereby judgements are made about the relevance and interest of possible news stories for their news audience, as well as whether they visibly include children and have potential entertainment value. These professional considerations are also at play in the following illustration of the production of environmental news stories.

In the last thirty years *Newsround* has consistently covered environmental issues. Together with the factual magazine programme *Blue Peter*, it has helped to reveal the risks and problems associated with the natural world. Professionally this is acknowledged and has been undertaken with the aim of equipping children with the information needed to make informed decisions.

> There are various issues in the world – the most obvious is the environment – which I think are of critical importance to our audience in that they are going to inherit the planet from adults and therefore what's happening on a global scale in those sorts of areas whether it be pollution, or more recent genetic engineering . . . are very important. In a sense, when one is addressing these issues, one is stepping into the future and therefore it is important that we educate the young people of the pros and the cons and so on and so forth of all those sorts of issues. (BBC *Newsround* editor)

This editor describes the professional commitment to present a range of environmental issues, including the seemingly important issues of pollution and genetic engineering, to an audience of future citizens. If the comments are taken at face value, then they describe a commendable news practice. Yet, as the following analysis of news practice reveals, the editor's comments tend to conceal the principal programme goal of attracting and maintaining the news audience.

A historical analysis of the frequency of the environmental issues in children's news, for example, shows that the news programme overwhelmingly features a particular issue – the animal story. In fact, in its first seven years the programme featured many long-running stories that examined the threat to wildlife including: the campaign to save the tiger and the extinction of the bald eagle in 1973; the plight of giant pandas, swallows and sea lions in 1974; the threat to grizzly bears, the destruction of the habitat of the giant panda and the threat of an oil slick to birds in 1975; the killing of seals and the dangers of pesticides on wildlife in 1976; endangered brown pelicans and the dangers posed by a Scottish oil slick to wildlife in 1977; the danger of a Brittany oil spill to wildlife, whaling and the culling of seals in 1978; the campaign to save the tiger and pandas in 1979; and the slaughter of dolphins in 1980. This is an interesting finding because it begins to undermine the claim that the programme aims simply to reflect the range of environmental information for the audience – a point that is confirmed by the first *Newsround* presenter's recollection that the animal story was selected because it was deemed to be popular and could attract a large news audience:

> I think basically because . . . children are keen on wild animals and anything to do with saving the planet, and saving the creatures. We knew from the very start when we did stories about saving the seals, and saving the whales, we would get vast numbers of letters and petitions in from the audience. (ex BBC *Newsround* presenter)

Other journalists who worked on the early programmes also confirm that animal stories were used deliberately to attract a child audience and help differentiate their particular news programme from the adult news genre which was professionally understood to be 'boring' to children. These stories soon became an established way to make bulletins attractive to the audience and, from that point, were essential parts of the *Newsround* news agenda for the child audience. In the 1980s, global environmental issues were also seen as resonating with children's interests; issues such as acid rain, global warming, and the ozone layer all featured prominently across this period. These were often presented in ways designed to emphasise their emotional or affective appeal. For example, the opening words accompanying a story about the depletion of rainforests – 'The world's rainforest – the lungs of the plant earth – are being destroyed faster than anyone thought' (BBC *Newsround*, 16 August 1982) – uses the anthropomorphic metaphor of human lungs and breathing to represent the relationship between the rainforest and the planet earth. Its presentation, like other environmental stories of the time, positions the child viewer to see the environmental problem in emotional terms.

A historical analysis of the environmental news agenda shows therefore how the professional desire to maintain and attract the news audience informs the selection and inflection of certain environmental issues. In the case of the selection of the animal and later global environmental issues, news producers have been attracted to the possible sentimental appeal of such stories for their particular audience. More recently, however, we also find that the current news team have become more reflexive towards the selection practices of the past. They recognise that the last thirty years have seen the continued presentation of the environment problem and an increase in environmental consciousness among the young audience, a trend that they have both contributed to and to which they have responded.

> You could say that is it us who is making it important to children, and I suppose . . . *Newsround* and *Blue Peter* have an acute environmental awareness. Clearly, it is a bit of a two-way street. We could bang on about all sorts of things. But all children will do is switch off instantly – it's clearly touching a nerve. (BBC *Newsround* series producer)

Today, however, journalists admit that they now question the long-held assumption that children are naturally attracted to environmental issues, and as a consequence they are reassessing, for example, the routine selection of animal stories. A producer explains:

> There is a cliché associated with *Newsround*: we always have a laugh if there is a panda story in the programme just because that's something that *Newsround* has been associated with – animals – because they are all targets for children. Perhaps what we have done is moved off in other directions, looking at what really interests children rather than making an assumption . . . [about what] will dramatically interest them. (BBC *Newsround* producer)

Producers' comments such as these illustrate how there has been a gradual change in the professional thinking over the selection of environmental stories. Today, a new policy seemingly moves beyond the established and routine focus on selecting animal stories for a new selection approach. The discussion pursues this new selection policy further below.

Selecting the Environment

Based on observations of the production of *Newsround* conducted over the two-year period (1998–2000), it was evident that the journalists and producers involved worked with core selection criteria that enabled them professionally to assess the newsworthiness of particular stories. These criteria concerned the extent to which potential news stories could be presented in terms of 'personalisation', 'simplification' and 'popularisation' or suffered from perceived news 'fatigue'.

Personalisation

In selecting news, *Newsround* journalists recognise that the most important element of a news story is its perceived 'connection' with their child audience. Questions asked about possible news stories therefore typically include the following:

● Is it relevant, or does it have elements that are relevant for children?

● Is it interesting, or does it have elements that are interesting for children?

● Are, or could, children be involved in the story? These particular questions isolate what is professionally assumed to be 'newsworthy' for the child audience, and are part of a process that I call 'personalisation'.

This professional pursuit of personalisation can see enhanced newsworthiness in, for example, a celebrity presenting an environmental issue or, as was the case in the 1980s, the activities of a popular environmental group such as Greenpeace. The first presenter of *Newsround* is clear, for example, that Greenpeace became 'the audience's heroes', and in terms of coverage its visibility on the programme increased in frequency across the 1980s. In this way stories were included that concerned Greenpeace's various campaigns, including dramatic scenes of confrontation with whaling ships and polluters, various court actions, and struggles with different international corporations and governments. In short, it provides a good example of how the professional desire to personalise news for its audience has actually increased the coverage of certain issues supported by groups and individuals.

In addition to the selection of environmental events that featured environmental personalities or groups, the study also found that journalists deliberately prioritise and select news stories that either made reference to, or featured children. A typical story is the following:

> Now to the 8-year-old boy who's becoming something of an environmental crusader. Ben Middleton has been involved in environmental campaigning since he was very young, camping at protest sites around the country. [reporter] went to meet him. ('Eco-boy', BBC *Newsround*, 9 Sept. 1998)

The story dubbed 'Eco-boy' was clearly selected because it was thought to help personalise a story, that is 'connect' in individualised terms and appeal to the watching audience. Children are often accessed onto the programme and within news stories as a way of 'personalising' environmental news and increasing its newsworthiness for a child audience. Stories here include, for example, children interviewing environmentalists, politicians and other children on their environmental views; as well as items involving children protesting and engaging in green activities.

As well as the selection of stories based on their association with popular environmental groups, celebrities or children, the practice of personalisation leads to the selection of news stories assumed to have a direct impact on children's lives. The producer's comments below, on the long-running story that features the French government's ban on the export of potentially infected British beef and concerns surrounding the human form of Bovine Spongiform Encephalopathy (BSE), is a case in point:

> The . . . thing we use more than ever before [is] the yardstick: how does it impact on kids? Well BSE impacted on kids when they took beef off the menu in schools; that was the way that kids really got it, and when McDonald's banned it. But, beef now is a political wrangle, so we don't do it as a story – and I don't think that is a problem either. (BBC *Newsround* producer)

The producer above clearly outlines the informing professional visualisation of its audience and how this informs the selection and inflection as well as de-selection of different story themes concerning BSE. Whether a story can be personalised or not figures in the construction of a specifically child-focused news agenda. This selection practice leads to the exclusion of a wide range of environmental stories from the *Newsround* bulletin. The practice of personalisation can also, however, on occasion enhance the likelihood of a story being selected that otherwise would not feature in the programme. In an item based on a BBC adult news story about the government's commitment to decrease pollution in Britain, *Newsround* journalists connect the rise of pollution with the growth of asthma among children in a revised version. The story now moves to focus on the experiential effects on young people of air pollution, as illustrated in its opening words:

> An ordinary day in London, as usual it's raining and there's loads of traffic. Most of us never think about the air that we're breathing in areas like this. But for people with asthma it's a different story. They say that air pollution is one of the things that makes their asthma worse. Asthma is causing breathing problems for more and more young people. A shocking one in four children suffers from asthma – a figure which has almost doubled since 1990. No-one knows why – but we do know pollution makes symptoms worse. (BBC *Newsround*, 8 June 1999)

The story serves as an example of how personalisation can help to broaden the range of stories selected for *Newsround* inclusion, but it also demonstrates how the same process can delimit and de-emphasise information that the child audience receives. In the example above, the adult thrust of the story was relegated to a line at the end of the *Newsround* version.

> The Government's announcement today that they want to cut down on dangerous chemicals from car exhausts . . . but though that news has been welcomed by environmental groups, they say the real answer is to reduce the number of cars on our roads. (BBC *Newsround*, 8 June 1999)

The story illustrates how most of the space granted to the discussion of the impact of the rise of pollution on children also sidelines the presentation of the government and environmental groups' discussion of the political policy to cut car pollution. In such ways, environmental stories are often rendered apolitical and lose their connection to informing social contexts and political processes. With this in mind, the following section explores how another selection practice – simplification – also serves to shape the environmental news agenda in decisive ways.

Simplification

In addition to the professional desire to select stories that connect with the lives of children, journalists also work with the idea that children have a simplistic understanding of news issues. This view of children's cognitive capabilities leads the news producers to produce news in 'a way that makes it interesting and intelligible for children' (*Newsround* 2000). This is a process I call simplification. It involves the use of particular journalistic skills that are unique to the production of children's news and these contribute to the professional esteem of *Newsround* journalists.

It's the hardest programme in the world to write for, because you can't take anything for granted. You have to explain everything without explaining it. (BBC *Newsround* reporter)

The skill of the *Newsround* journalist, according to this account, lies in the ability to translate news into a form that is readily understood by children. This practice informs their professional evaluation of potential news stories and serves to identify geographic references, international treaties and other facts and features important to stories that will need to be explained.

It's jargon that I can't include because why would a 10-year-old understand that statement? Or if something is quite technical, you would never say the 'breakaway republics of Chechnya' – they wouldn't understand that. So, it's just always reminding yourself that a 10-year-old is just not going to take it in. (BBC *Newsround* journalist)

This professional aim to simplify news has serious implications for the selection of news stories. Although, in describing the news selection process, journalists often deny that the practice of simplifying news stories can lead to the sidelining or ignoring of complex story elements, their own views of the news audience contradict this. In interview journalists reveal how they think the child audience conceptualises the environment, that is, in simplistic, morally judgmental, politically naïve and emotional ways.

A child would see the environmental as blue skies and green fields and cows in fields. They would also see the environmental as pollution – as little birds full of oil – that's how they see the environment. In fact, the environment to children is only their back garden. They have a very limited view of the world. They don't see it split up into different socio-economic regions. So they won't understand why Uzbekistan is pumping out all this [pollution] – because they are an old power source, because they don't have the infrastructure or any money to put in. They just see them as baddies. (BBC *Newsround* journalist)

When applied to the selection and presentation of environmental news stories, such a conceptualisation of the child audience's capacity to understand social and political contexts and determinants of environmental problems leads to an impoverishment of the range of information presented to the audience:

The fact is, how do they understand that we as nations have caused the infrastructure to be fucked anyway? . . . So we just have to do it in a way that is palatable. (BBC *Newsround* journalist)

In practice, this professional perception of the child audience's inability to grasp complex environmental issues informs processes of news selection and the presentation of simplified, 'palatable', environmental stories. Conflicts of interest, arguably endemic to most if not all environmental issues, are in such ways either simplified or, as in most cases, completely ignored. Journalists often concede as much when apologetically declaring 'we must do it some time' (BBC *Newsround* journalist).

Fatigue and Popularisation

Alongside the criteria of personalisation and simplification, the professional assumption of the 'fatigue' status of environmental issues across time also informs processes of environmental story selection. For example, a journalist describes how the selection policy in the 1970s often worked as 'a knee-jerk reaction to any environmental story' whether it was local, national or global. But today this has changed. The new news practice seeks to question the continuing 'relevance' of the environment for their news audience:

> Look at how nuclear power was portrayed immediately after the war in the context of everyone exploiting the environment, and not feeling embarrassed about that. Then there was the backlash against that . . . green politics or whatever that's become . . . So it was something that was different that was newsworthy, because it was new. The environment is not new any more. It's more of a general approach to life that we all more or less follow – because we know the rules more or less, even if we don't necessarily follow them. (BBC *Newsround* producer)

Producers, evidently, perceive that environmental concerns today have become generally shared and widely endorsed background assumptions of news producers and audiences alike and, as such, no longer require the prominent exposure of earlier years. The point is further reinforced by another producer referring to an earlier story about the Eco label marketing scheme and its subsequent failure:

> There is no doubt that environmental stories are seen as less important. I did a story about three years ago about the launch of something called the Eco-label, which is a government/ European wide scheme to have one standard way of labelling environmentally friendly products. We went all the way up north and I did a piece on giving toilet rolls and washing machines Eco-labels, and Novel toilet paper was the only toilet paper to have this Eco label – and we thought it might take off and everything. Well, the whole Eco-label has completely died a death, and even Novel has taken it off their packaging. (BBC *Newsround* producer)

Here the producer sees the decline of the environment-marketing scheme in supermarkets as symbolic of the general demise in the importance of environmental issues. Such remarks support the general assumption held by news workers that the environmental issue has become old-hat, an assumption that informs today's news story (non-)selections. During the period of newsroom observation it also became apparent that the news team had sought to change the age of the target audience and this too impacted on the selection of environmental news stories. A producer describes the strategy under way:

> The funny thing with *Newsround* is that we tried to go more streetwise and go 'older' about two years ago; make ourselves a bit more kind of 'in there', a bit more aiming at 13 and 14-year-olds. I think that was seen as a bit of a mistake because there are not so many of those older kids watching. (BBC *Newsround* producer)

Acknowledging their mistake in increasing the age range of the programme, the team decided that it should revert to the younger imagined target audience of

10-year-olds. In doing so, it reintroduced the environmental animal story into the news bulletin with the aim to attract the younger viewing audience, and also reduced the selection of other environmental stories that were presumed to be uninteresting for the slightly older child audience:

> There is a feeling that . . . environmental stories are for quiet young kids – the whole thing about recycling and picking up litter and stuff like that. By the time kids get to 10, 12-year-olds they are a bit more kind of savvy, and they think 'well it's maybe a thing that my mum worries about and my little brother'. It's a thing that . . . 12-year-olds are not quite so bothered about. (BBC *Newsround* producer)

According to the news team, industry audience research shows that those children who are over 12 years old are generally apathetic to the plight of the environment, and in practice this has led to a policy of reducing the number of general environmental issues in the programme. This policy, more specifically, has led to the non-selection of stories about major environmental issues, especially if involving overtly educational messages or a campaigning focus. Such types of stories, it is commonly believed, can provoke today's child audience into changing channels for easier viewing. A producer articulates this view:

> Yeah, it does come to a stage – as an experienced producer – when you have seen these stories again, again and again – and you think: what is there to say about them? Also, if you present only a very dry story it's gonna have them switching off – it's not going to entertain. (BBC *Newsround* producer)

News producers, then, are today selecting or not selecting environmental news stories on the basis of shared professional programme criteria: personalisation, simplification and environmental fatigue. However, they also see that major environmental stories are often at odds with their professional aim to present news items in an upbeat, visually attractive and entertaining manner. Consider, for example, the newsroom's view of the issue and concerns around genetically modified (GM) food.

> It's a bit dull to look at . . . It's people in laboratories; it's . . . talking minuscule – it's microscopic obviously; and it's difficult to explain. I think that it's almost the kind of thing that works better as a background . . . on the *Newsround* web site explaining GM foods for people who want to know about it. But it's got a kind of yawn factor. (BBC *Newsround* producer)

The producer argues that GM food stories are inherently difficult to popularise and raises a number of reasons why it wouldn't fit the programme's ambition to entertain – not least of which is the perceived 'yawn factor' of this and similar other major 'invisible' environmental risks. It is evidence of the practice of popularisation that, in addition to the efforts to personalise, simplify and avoid established news stories, selects news for its perceived ability to attract and maintain the child audience.

Conclusion

At the outset of this discussion I argued that children should be viewed as emergent cultural citizens with information rights, and that it is a responsibility of children's news programmes to inform them of major social problems – including environmental issues and risks. To conclude the discussion we can now evaluate how the production of *Newsround* has enhanced the cultural citizenship of children through its shaping and presentation of its environmental news agenda and, in so doing, we can also help to productively reorient theoretical approaches to the study of news production. Findings from the discussion above demonstrate that it is the professional visualisation of the children's news form that principally constructs and delimits the 'communicative space' of *Newsround*. The news producers have combined elements from the adult news genre with ideas of the child audience and its needs, wants and capabilities to create a unique form of news. This, as we have seen, has had a direct impact on the selection of environmental news agendas and how environmental stories have been constructed and presented across time. When we examine close up, and from the point of view of the production context, the selection of environmental issues, we see how the professional imperative to attract and maintain a target child audience has become the overriding factor shaping and delimiting the programme's environmental news agenda and presentation. More specifically, we also see how the identified professional criteria of newsworthiness characteristic of this particular news form facilitate journalist practices of child news story selection and storytelling. When operationalised, these criteria of personalisation, simplification, fatigue and popularisation all impact to delimit and shape the environmental agenda for the watching audience – and they do so often in deleterious ways. If children's news is one of the main ways to introduce children to the social problems of the age, the present programme strategy of *Newsround* and other children's news programmes like it have yet to live up to the ideal of cultural citizenship rights for emergent citizens – children.

CHAPTER SUMMARY

- Traditional research into news programmes has ignored children's news. This failure needs to be redressed with an approach that investigates children's news and its ability to inform an audience of emergent future citizens.

- Attending to the characteristic and differentiated features of news forms provides new insights into the study of news production and professional journalist practices. The concept of the 'news form' draws on the principal elements of news approached as genre, but moves to ground these within the context of professional news selection and construction and as a professionally understood and particularised 'form' of news.

- The empirical examination of the production of a particular children's news programme demonstrates that news workers share a working visualisation of their news form and that this is an amalgam of core elements of BBC public service news and views of the child audience and its needs, wants and capabilities.

- At the heart of the production of this children's news form are competing imagined 'ideal' and 'real' audiences that inform processes of story selection and presentation. The 'ideal' audience is professionally perceived as mature, academically able and middle class. The 'real' audience is seen as its opposite, having both a limited attention span and a disinterest in news. The latter generally wins out in the programme's pursuit of entertainment production values designed to attract and maintain a large child audience.

- Characteristics of the children's news form help to explain how the early environmental agenda was constructed to attract and maintain the child audience. Professionals sentimentally linked the audience with the plight of animals and later the global environment to justify their place in the news agenda.

- Today's environment news agenda is selected and presented according to core *Newsround* criteria: personalisation, simplification, fatigue and popularisation. The process of personalisation informs the selection of issues that are perceived to be relevant to children's lives. Simplification polices the levels of complexity of environmental stories. Popularisation and fatigue regulate the selections of stories in pursuit of the profession goal of constructing a lively and appealing news programme.

Note

1   This study is based on the author's PhD, 'Infantilising the Environment: A Study of Children's News', Brunel University, submitted in 2002. The research included a two-year empirical study of *Newsround* involving field observation and interviews with thirty programme producers, both past and present, and a detailed quantitative and qualitative analysis of news programmes broadcast across the period 1973–2000.

PART V

CHANGING INTERNATIONAL GENRES AND PRODUCTION ECOLOGIES

CHAPTER 9

International TV and Film Co-production: A Canadian Case Study

Doris Baltruschat

In today's global economy, media organisations increasingly respond to global market pressures. In the field of TV programme and film production – which constitutes the focus of this chapter – foreign competition, industry deregulation and convergences in technologies and content have all led media producers to adapt traditional production practices to international modes of programme development. As a result, media producers are increasingly seeking international TV and film co-productions as a way of accessing new funding and markets, and enhancing their competitiveness. This change in production organisation and practices, from a local production model to a model of international collaboration, can be linked to fundamental changes in the political economic context in which media producers now operate. Since the early 1990s, national policies in Canada and Europe have increasingly favoured deregulation and a *laissez-faire* approach to industry management. This has shifted the focus from public service mandates to commercial production practices. Within this changing production context, commercial media organisations have faced funding cuts for programme development, and production and public service broadcasters have also had to seek new ways to manage their operations with smaller funding allocations. Technical convergences, based on the ability to transfer digital information across a variety of platforms, have offered new possibilities for delivering programmes but in practice these have tended to be exploited as a means of maximising market opportunities. What we have witnessed across recent years, then, is a shift of emphasis from fostering *culture as a public good* to marketing *culture as a commodity*.

Both expressing and contributing to this wider shift towards the commodification of culture is the increasingly export-oriented production practices of the television and film industries and the production of 'global' products based on entertainment values rather than critical reflection on 'local' issues.[1] These developments are clearly discerned in the rise of international TV and film co-productions. Co-productions represent a new way of developing film and television programmes for international markets. Media organisations have sought to capitalise on this production mode as a way of raising new funding, accessing additional markets and competing globally for exposure and revenue. This chapter sets out to examine empirically these trends in a case study of television and film production in Canada. It does this by:

- charting the rise of Canadian co-productions and relating this to the changing production environment of film and television;

- consulting with television and film producers about the nature of co-production;

- analysing the shift from 'local' to 'global' content in terms of genre, represented issues and narrative structures; and

- critically reflecting on these developments in terms of their impact on forms of cultural and political representation and their contribution to a public sphere of engaged citizenship.

First though it is important to elaborate further on the context, rise and nature of Canadian co-productions.

Co-productions: A New International Production Mode

Co-productions are based on the collaboration between producers for the creation of film and television programmes. The pooling of financial, creative and technical resources allows them to increase budgets and access new markets. There are two types of co-productions in Canada: official treaty co-productions and non-treaty co-productions. Both modes are used for big-budget films and television programmes, predominantly of the drama, animation and documentary genres (Hoskins et al. 1997: 102). Treaty co-productions are guided by bilateral agreements that are negotiated by governments for the development of cultural goods and content productions.[2] Here, the goal is the creation of productions that are of national relevance to all partners involved, so that producers can access benefits from legislation and government assistance – such as tax incentives, investments and grants (Ferns 1995). Non-treaty co-productions, also referred to as co-ventures, include collaboration with countries currently not covered by a bilateral agreement. Co-ventures allow for greater production flexibility, but may not be eligible for public funding. They may, however, be considered as a Canadian content production if specific guidelines are met, such as equal decision-making responsibilities and budget administration (Telefilm 1999a).

The use of co-productions in a context of dwindling local resources is of course appealing to many commercial producers who seek to access global markets. Recent research suggests, however, that co-productions differ from film and television programmes developed for local audiences. In pursuit of global audiences they tend to emphasise drama, human emotions and the dynamics of close relationships (Strover 1995: 11); they also tend to prefer the production of particular genres such as science fiction, adventure, horror and fairy tales. Co-produced documentaries tend to be about nature, sports, international celebrities and common histories (Binning 1998; on nature, see Cottle this volume). As we shall see, in contrast to local programmes, international co-productions also tend to feature narratives that are neither spatially nor temporally bound – thus minimising their local cultural or political content and relevance. Even though co-productions aimed at global audiences have the potential to address global issues such as environmental degradation and the effects of world trade and represent cultural diversity and hybridisation, their commercial orientation undermines this critical potential (Murdock 1996: 107). In comparison local and independently produced programmes often prove to be more critical in focus, highlighting issues of public concern at local, national and international levels.

Co-productions have increased in the era of media deregulation, privatisation, conglomeration and convergence, a period that has also seen the development of narrow-casting delivered via multi-channel cable and satellite systems.[3] In a climate of reduced licence fees for television programmes, co-productions met the need for new programming, especially in markets seeking to protect economic and cultural interests through trade barriers against US products. In 1992, Europe's *Television Without Frontiers* initiative set a quota of 50 per cent for foreign programmes. The Canada-US North American Free Trade Agreement (NAFTA) exempts cultural industries to 'prevent the cultural standardisation of content and the complete foreign control of distribution' (Government of Canada 1993: 33). Co-productions between Canada and Europe increased dramatically during the 1990s, consolidating regional markets and integration of media organisations. Alliance/Atlantis, Canada's major co-production company, expanded its operations through co-producing feature films, such as *eXistenZ* (a science-fiction/horror feature) with Natural Nylon Entertainment in England. Salter Street Film co-produced the television science fiction series *Lexx* with Time Film and TV Produktion Gmbh in Germany, and Filmline International collaborated with Talisman Crest, England on the adventure series *The Secret Adventures of Jules Verne* and with Gaumont Television in France on *Highlander*.

In a global economy, economic interests and regional competition drive cultural protectionism even though, officially, policy often emphasises culture as a national good within a liberal, democratic paradigm. However, within this paradigm, culture is treated as a *commodity* rather than a *common good*. The concept of culture as a tradable commodity is based on profit motives and international markets where audiences are addressed as consumers rather than citizens (Garnham 1990: 105). This commodity logic also underpins productions that have a broad appeal and avoid critical reflection – such as co-productions – since they act as 'fillers' in a commercial system where audiences are sold to advertisers (Dahlgren 1995: 29). In contrast, ideas of culture approached as a common good provide the basis for creative works, the development of a body of knowledge and collective memory for communities and nations. Here, 'cultural works allow for current realities to be explored, reflected, debated and contested, thereby laying secure foundations for independence and democracy'

(Audley 1994: 317). Local productions are often able to reflect contemporary challenges and changes in society; they are crucial for maintaining a viable public sphere in which current issues are mediated for critical reflection and debate.[4]

The rise of co-productions is practically facilitated by the growth of international networks between media organisations and producers. Producers regularly convene at trade shows, conferences and markets, such as the *Marché International des Programmes de Télévision* (MIP or MIPCOM) in Cannes, France and the National Association of Television Executives (NATPE) in the US, where they meet distributors, government representatives and policy-makers to exchange information, forge financial relations, and create linkages for the development of cultural products for regional and international markets (Perlmutter 1993; interview with St Arnauld, Director, International Relations, Telefilm Canada on July 2000).

Co-productions are often developed for regional markets that are linked by cultural and linguistic traits and, in many cases, extend beyond neighbouring countries and include diasporic and migrant populations worldwide (Straubhaar 1997). In the case of Canada, cultural proximity allows producers to collaborate with English and French counterparts to create films and programmes suitable for both markets. However, marketing strategies and the deliberate production of 'global genres' indicate that producers also target global markets. Co-productions, global genres and conglomeration of media organisations create the basis for further consolidation of professional practices and commercialisation of cultural productions. The rise of co-productions can therefore be seen as an expression of the surrounding forces of globalisation – processes that have not gone uncontested.

The globalisation of cultural productions creates a 'new communication geography' that is increasingly 'detached from the symbolic spaces of national culture, and realigned on the basis of the more "universal" principles of international consumer culture' (Morley and Robins 1995: 11). Local independent productions represent, in many instances, a reaction – in format and content – to globalisation by reclaiming media spaces to sustain the 'integrity of local and regional cultures' (ibid.: 18). They express their own styles, techniques and narratives that reflect local issues and culture, and thereby help to preserve a public sphere in which debates between citizens can be mediated.

Local media are important, especially since trade liberalisation marginalises communicative spaces (Dahlgren 1999: 507) and undermines the aim of democratic societies to provide open media access for the presentation of cultural diversity. Media commercialisation replaces public speech with *corporate speech*, *infotainment* and *tabloid-style television*, which address audiences as consumers rather than citizens. Public service media and local, independent media are therefore necessary to reflect common experiences and collective memories. They are essential for expressions of diversity and plurality, especially in the face of continued pressures to liberalise the trade of cultural goods, such as reductions in foreign investment restrictions and content quotas (The Canadian Film and Television Production Association and *l'Association des producteurs de films et de télévision du Québec* **[CFTPA and APFTQ]**, 2000: 11).

Charting the Rise of Canadian Co-productions

Currently with over forty-seven co-production agreements with fifty-five countries worldwide, Canada is at the forefront of countries involved in international co-production. Since the early 1990s, Canada's co-productions have increased dramatically, making the latter one of the most prominent modes of production deployed by larger Canadian media organisations today. For these reasons Canada makes an ideal case study for examining the nature, rise and impact of international productions. Even though Canada's first co-production dates back to 1963 (a film co-production with France), it only developed an additional thirteen productions between 1974 and 1983 (Pendakur 1990: 198). Then, coinciding with drastic changes in the film and television industry across the 1990s, Canada's co-production activities quadrupled, indicating a clear departure from traditional production practices to international collaboration and a focus on global markets (Table 9.1).

Table 9.1   Canadian co-production activity 1992–2000 in film and television

Year	Co-productions Numbers	Total budgets in millions $	Canadian Share	
			in millions $	as % of budget
1999–2000	111	621.0	345.0	55.5
1998–1999	135*	762.0	423.0	54.0
1997–1998	71	493.0	246.5	50.0
1996–1997	45	290.8	133.4	45.9
1995–1996	38	246.3	135.9	55.2
1994–1995	48	340.8	156.8	48.1
1993–1994	28	212.3	99.9	49.2
1992–1993	24	186.0	80.0	43.0

* Figure includes some projects for the year 1999/2000 due to Canadian Television Fund (CTF) deadline

Sources: CFTPA and APFTQ 2000: 31; CFTPA and APFTQ 2002: 6, 16, 34; Telefilm Canada 2000.

Telefilm, Canada's cultural agency responsible for the development and promotion of film, television and multimedia, is committed to finance co-productions for global markets: 'The international market is a strategic priority for Canada' (Telefilm Canada 1999b: 6) and co-productions are seen as a tool 'to finance high-quality products for distribution in the global marketplace' (ibid.).

Even though financial statements of the decade depict an increase in overall production, the actual public commitment to develop film and television programmes remained the same or declined (Table 9.2). Local media production continues to be challenged by large volumes of foreign production which increased from 30 per cent in 1994–95 to 44 per cent in 2000–01 (CFTPA and APFTQ 2002: 34). In addition, US distributors earn up to 85 per cent of the profits from Canadian theatres, whereas Canadian films in comparison make up only 5 per cent, outside of French-speaking Quebec (Mandate Review Committee 1996: 201). In television, 95 per cent of programming is foreign and consists predominantly of US drama (ibid.: 196; Juneau 1993).

Table 9.2   Canadian production activity 1992–2000 in film and television

Year	Foreign Locations in CDN$*	Total budgets in mill. CDN$**	CAVCO Share***	
			in mill. CDN$	Public % of total financing
1999–2000	1,506	4,564	1,920	16%
1998–1999	1,096	3,673	1,888	14%
1997–1998	818	3,222	1,413	16%
1996–1997	768	3,098	1,340	20%
1995–1996	534	2,698	1,249	14%
1994–1995	539	2,320	984	11%
1993–1994	318	1,937	876	12%
1992–1993	223	1,573	667	15%

* Foreign location (shooting or production) refers to film or television productions shot in Canada by US or foreign producers and independent producers.
** Figures include production budgets of CAVCO and non-CAVCO certified productions, foreign location shooting, and coventional broadcasters' and speciality channels' in-house productions.
*** CAVCO – the Canadian Audio-Visual Certification Office; productions that are certified 'Canadian' for the purpose of utilizing tax credits.

Sources: CFTPA and APFTQ 2000: 31; CFTPA and APFTQ 2002: 6, 16, 34.

The increase of co-productions coincided with funding reductions for local productions and public service broadcasting. In the 1990s, Telefilm's annual parliamentary appropriation was reduced by 50 per cent (Mandate Review Committee 1996: 241; Telefilm Canada 1999a), forcing the agency to embrace a more commercial mandate. The Canadian Broadcasting Corporation (CBC) also faced a 30 per cent funding reduction and the loss of over 3,000 jobs (Gurd 1998: 47; Mandate Review Committee 1996: 130; Posner and Bourette 2000). These reductions posed a serious challenge to Canada's film and television producers, who increasingly sought funding outside of Canada:

> The model makes sense. You can find partners. You can bring financing to your project, soft money, from another source. It means that you'll be able to more quickly get your project made. You can only raise so much money out of Canada. (Scott Kennedy, producer, interview, 22 June 2000)

Access to foreign markets is also key. Canadian producer Michael Parker found that co-producing with Hong Kong allowed his film to be exhibited in more countries:

Lunch with Charles had probably a larger release in Asia than in Canada. Except for Japan and India, it has been sold and released in China, Taiwan, Singapore, and Malaysia. (Michael Parker, interview, 15 March 2002)

Some film and television productions are considered 'natural' co-productions in the sense that their narratives lend themselves to this form of production. Parker's film *Lunch with Charles*, for example, deals with the topic of immigration and resulting separation between a husband and wife. In spite of different approaches to production time-lines – Hong Kong producers tend to move faster from pre-production to project completion than Canadian producers – the film, none the less, benefited from a larger budget and additional exposure throughout Asia. British producer Nick Powell (*The Crying Game, Little Voice*) points out that co-productions are ideally based on 'materials' that naturally fit this mode.

You can't just say 'I've got this story set in Halifax, Nova Scotia, but I think it could be set in Halifax, Yorkshire' . . . The most famous successes, especially in the low-budget films, have been very specific in terms of local character and colour of the places in which the films are set in. . . . I would have hesitations to move a story from Manchester to Liverpool, or from Glasgow to Edinburgh, because they are different places in terms of character and people. (interview, 2000)

However, 'natural' co-productions are the exception rather than the rule, especially in television production. Most producers seek to collaborate solely for financial reasons, and content is created to fit the co-production mode. British producers seem to be interested in working with Canadian organisations to increase budgets, and to use Canadian locations because they can be 'dressed up' as US cities (British Council 2001). In addition, co-productions are suited for a particular genre:

There are particular genres such as horror, sci-fi that are perfect for co-production because they are not set in a particular place. The German-Canadian co-production Lexx works great because you never have to leave the studio set. (ibid.)

Co-productions rely on a global genre and narratives that are not culturally specific but can be adapted to international markets. The television series *Lexx* is based on a sci-fi plot: set in outer space, two men and a woman pursue a quest for a new home in the universe. *Highlander*'s immortal heroes and heroines encounter adventures throughout the world and centuries. A new television co-production between Canada and Australia, *Sir Arthur Conan Doyle's The Lost World*, creates adventures in a pre-historic world. Another Canada-Australia television co-production, *Guinevere Jones*, features a teenage heroine as a reincarnation of a legendary Arthurian character who travels back in time to meet Merlin. Genres such as science fiction, adventure, horror and fairy tales are thus suited for co-production because of their global appeal and marketability.

Producing 'Global Stories'

The increased collaboration between Canadian producers with European, Australian and Asian counterparts has led, in many instances, to content conversion and the creation of global genre. Many co-productions reflect styles and techniques of US films and television programmes that through extensive global distribution have become a global blueprint for commercial productions (Straubhaar 1997). The co-produced television series *Lexx* (Episode: *Little Blue Planet*), and *The Secret Adventures of Jules Verne* (Episode: *Southern Comfort*; see Figure 9.5) tend to produce at least one episode which relates to the US. The 2001/02 season of *Highlander: The Raven* goes as far as depicting an American flag in its opening scene. Co-productions reflect these popularised narratives and styles to make them easily transferable between countries and attractive for the US market. The adaptation of these global formats actually undermines the original intention for co-productions – to create regional competition for US cultural productions – and integrates them into a global market.

Many other co-productions are about 'global stories' that are defined neither by spatial nor temporal dimensions but occur 'anywhere' – out in space, in prehistoric times, or in changing locations and temporal dimensions.[5] These global stories are useful because they can be shown in diverse cultural environments and markets. As Robert Wong, funding agent for British Columbia Film, explained:

> I think producers that do international treaty co-productions are looking for global stories – stories that don't necessarily pertain to our country. They may be set in Canada or outside Canada, but I don't think it really matters too much. If you actually just change the country's name, it wouldn't make a difference. (Robert Wong, interview, 29 June 2000)

Canadian producers state that working on an international basis inevitably shifts the focus from Canadian content to an emphasis on global audience appeal:

> This is a project I found, it was Irish. It is set in Ireland. . . . There's really nothing Canadian to it at all. I saw it and liked it. And we put Dan Akroyd in it. He is Canadian, but overall it was Irish. So we immediately shot there. Plus the co-production treaty gives you an opportunity to maximize two countries . . . and also put together a cast that is going to have a global appeal. (Scott Kennedy, producer, interview, 22 June 2000)

The shift to global stories as a means to appeal to international audiences is problematic in the context of reduced funding for local and independent productions. In Canada, where local media have been traditionally dominated by foreign programmes, this is of real concern as many local issues – from First Nations[6] topics to representation of diversity in Canadian society – are increasingly marginalised, and films and television programmes are saturated with commercial content and global stories aimed at international markets.

Initially, co-productions were seen as a means to improve and enhance film productions in countries with weak production industries. Even though co-productions are made around the world, activities are now especially pronounced in countries with stronger economies and viable production sectors (Taylor 1995: 414). The drive to compete internationally, on the one hand, and to protect regional markets, on the other, has led to increased co-production activity in Canada, Europe and Australia. Canadian co-producers collaborate especially with their English and French counterparts as they share the *auteur* tradition of European cinema.[7] Moreover, from a European perspective, Canada is appealing since it exhibits North American sensibilities due to its proximity to the US.

> European movies tend to be a little more melodramatic. They tend to be shot with a lot of wide lenses, longer shots, slower build-ups in terms of storyline . . . You don't need to have a car crash in the first 30 seconds. You can build characters and it actually works. Whereas in North America, if you don't have some action in the first minute or two, your audience is off to a different channel or walking out of a theater. (Kevin DeWalt, producer, interview, 15 June 2000)

Many producers complain about the loss of creative control when collaborating on a production (Hoskins and McFadyen 1993: 231). This compromise in technical, creative and stylistic means is probably inevitable when producing for international audiences.

> People who make a production want to keep creative control of that production. When you take on a partner, there have to be compromises . . . I think that the natural reaction of anyone driven by their passion for a particular story is to keep complete control; people that want to stay in business will look at marketing and the potential for making money to be able to make another show. (Tom Adair, President, BC Council of Film Unions, interview, 8 June 2000)

In addition to creative compromises, co-productions are also more expensive to produce. Some of the drawbacks include higher co-ordination costs such as long-distance travel and communications, and dealing with additional government bureaucracies. However, the potential for higher production dollars and access to additional markets outweigh these disadvantages, hence the rise of co-productions witnessed across recent years.

Global Stories: What's at Stake?

To understand better the relationship between Canadian co-productions and changing forms of media content, we can turn to a systematic and qualitative examination of co-production film and television programmes and their forms of output in comparison to locally produced films and television programmes. In this way we can see how international co-production delimits, shapes and inflects media representations and so can begin to appraise the influence of this in respect to cultural diversity, political representation and citizenship. A note on how we approach local and global culture is perhaps useful here.

Morley and Robins emphasise the necessity of local interaction and debate with global culture (1995: 41) and Robertson (1995) points to the 'local' as an aspect of the 'global' in respect of the inevitable exchange of concepts, social and cultural practices based on prior contact and migrations between and within countries. Too often notions of 'pure' culture have underpinned ideas of 'cultural racism' – the elevation of national myths and values to the exclusion of other cultures. Such ideas are untenable: 'modern nations' as Stuart Hall reminds us, 'are all cultural hybrids' (Hall 1992: 297). Therefore, *inclusive* definitions of culture are essential in a context of worldwide migration and diasporic cultures, and it is this definition that informs the present study. The point here is that rather than challenging international co-productions because they are not (by definition) local, we need to examine carefully their actual performance in respect of representations of cultures, on the one hand, and their missed opportunity critically to address globalisation processes and issues, on the other hand.

For the purposes of this comparative study, 1,151 films and television programmes (compiled from catalogues from federal and provincial funding agencies, distributors and film festivals) were selected from the period 1990–2000 – the period that witnessed the most dramatic changes in the regulatory, economic and technical environment of film and television as well as the rise in international co-productions. This sample was then categorised according to the six following categories (Table 9.3).

Table 9.3   Categories of film and TV programmes

Co-produced	(1) Films (8.25%)	(2) Television Drama (6.42%)	(3) Documentaries (5.12%)
Locally produced	(4) Films (14.24%)	(5) Television Drama (19.28%)	(6) Documentaries (46.56%*)

* The relative high percentage of documentaries needs to be understood within the context of Canadian local markets which consist of theatrical, broadcast and non-theatrical (educational video) sectors. Many local documentaries are never broadcast, but are used solely for educational purposes in schools and universities.

Note: Per cent indicates relative proportion of each category from 1,151 sample.

In order to examine in more detail the possible differences of representation informing locally and co-produced programmes and films, thirty randomly selected titles – equally representative of the six categories above – were examined in terms of their local or 'global' reference and appeal using three key dimensions.

1 Main Character (costume/dress, speech/accent);

2 Place/Location (mise-en-scène, props/objects);

3 Plot/Story (time/historical setting, themes/issues, focus (of dialogue), treatment/development).

1,941 scenes that comprised the films and programmes in this sample were then analysed and scored according to the above categories. A scene was defined as a series of continuous acts, in time and space, not broken or interrupted by the addition or departure of characters, or by a change in setting (Greenberg et al. 1980). These key categories of main character, place/location, plot/story, as well as their sub-categories, were next analysed according to a five-scale measure which defined a degree of local or global focus (Table 9.4).

| Table 9.4 | Five-scale measure establishing *global* or *local* focus |

1 = definitely, clearly local
Identification of character's heritage and place of residence; the mention, visually or verbally, of place/location; plot/story based on historical facts, and/or local themes/issues.

2 = appears to be local, tentatively local
Depiction of place (no direct mention) but apparent through (1) place/location and local characteristics – for example, the red soil of Prince Edward Island and (2) plot/story and themes/issues, as in the case of a programme based on a novel, providing intertextual references.

3 = neutral/inconclusive
Not identifiable in regards to (1) character and heritage, (2) place/location, and (3) plot/story, especially in the time/historical setting category; for example, science fiction plots or adventure stories.

4 = appears to be not local (tentatively not local)
Apparently non-Canadian locations identifiable in architecture, landscapes and props – the mise-en-scène; and indication that characters are residents of another country.

5 = definitely, clearly not local
Identification of character's heritage and place of residence; the mention, visually and verbally, of a different place/location providing the backdrop for the plot/story; themes/issues pertaining clearly to another place and historical events.

The comparative study clearly indicates that co-productions have a greater global orientation than local independent productions. Both film and television co-productions featured more prominently in the *apparently not local* and *definitely not local* categories. Local independent productions, on the other hand, showed an *apparently local* and *definitely local* orientation. This was true for all main categories and their sub-elements (Figure 9.1).

Differences between media were also apparent. Co-produced television programmes scored more frequently on the *appears to be not local* and *clearly not local* scale than co-produced films (Figure 9.2). Co-produced television programmes were mainly of the science fiction (28.5 per cent) and adventure genres (42.8 per cent), whereas drama (14.8 per cent) and horror (14.8 per cent) genres were less frequent. Co-produced films, on the other hand, tended to be set in

Figure 9.1   Mean scores for local and co-produced programmes

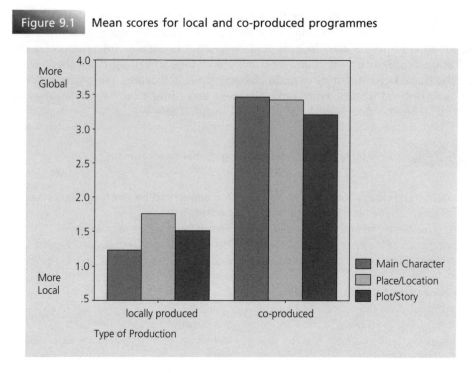

Figure 9.2   Place/location mean scores for television and film

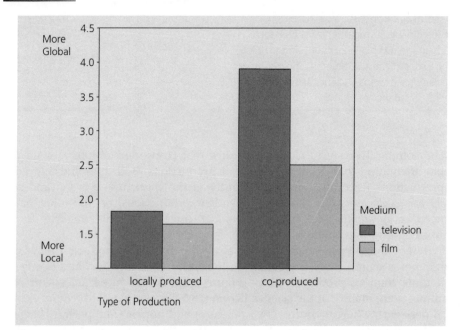

real-life locations – often more than one. In comparison, both local independent film and television productions clearly exhibited a local and culturally specific orientation.

Co-produced drama and documentaries scored predominantly in the *apparently not local* and *definitely not local* categories. However, differences between genre became evident – drama was less specific in local and culturally specific orientation than documentaries. Drama tended to be based on fictitious narratives, whereas documentaries were set in real-life locations. Scores for co-produced documentaries reflected a split between a clearly local orientation and a global focus because at least two locations were featured. In contrast, local drama *and* documentaries showed a clear focus on local and culturally specific issues (Table 9.5).

The scores highlight that co-productions are located predominantly in the 3–5 scale of *appears to be not local* to *definitely not local*, whereas local productions are more in the range of 1–3, *definitely local* to *appears to be local*. Differences between television and film are also apparent. Co-produced television scores dominate in the 3–5 range, whereas co-produced film are in the 3–4 range (also see Table 9.4: Five-scale measure).

Most programmes had received funding from federal and provincial agencies. Where applicable, programmes were predominantly aired during the evening prime-time hours, designated for programmes with Canadian content. Both co-productions and locally produced programmes were featured on public service broadcasting and commercial stations; however, local programmes were predominantly shown on Canada's public service broadcaster, the CBC.

The analyses above have demonstrated how co-productions are more global in focus. Local productions, on the other hand, clearly exhibited a focus on local issues and often critically reflected on social topics and offered more representations of cultural diversity and difference. They portrayed First Nation's issues (*North of 60, The Trickster*), critically reflected on historical and social developments (*Milgaard*) and commented on the importance of community and political action (*The Hanging Garden, The Last Streetfighter: The History of the Georgia Straight*).[8] Local productions also featured predominantly on public service broadcast stations, highlighting the importance of these outlets for local and independent producers.

To identify how co-production and local production practices differ and influence genre and narrative development, the study next explores how programme narratives create a global versus local focus, and how they represent cultural-specific and critical issues. In particular, the analyses identify how narratives transcend spatial and temporal dimensions (and therefore, minimise their local references, cultural specificity and political relevance), first in comparing two film productions (*The Red Violin* and *The Hanging Garden*), followed by two television dramas (*The Secret Adventures of Jules Verne* and *Milgaard*).

International co-produced programmes can often entail complex narrative constructions consisting of sub-plots which tie storylines together and which occur in several spatial and temporal dimensions. For example, *The Red Violin* (a tripartite film co-production between England, Canada and Italy), reveals such a multi-layered narrative. Here the story about a musical instrument allows for a

Table 9.5 Summary of scores for both production modes

Mean Scores for co-productions and local independent productions	Drama		Documentary	
	Co-prod.	local prod.	Co-prod.	local prod.
MEDIUM: Television				
Main Character	3.90	1.20	2.68	1.23
Costume/Dress	3.54	1.82	3.13	2.54
Speech/Accent	3.85	1.22	2.76	1.54
Place/Location	4.13	2.07	3.66	1.56
Mise-en-Scene	4.13	1.95	3.65	1.56
Props/Objects	4.12	1.94	3.65	1.54
Plot/Story	3.89	1.54	3.21	1.21
Time/Historical Setting	3.62	1.50	3.05	1.18
Themes/Issues	3.89	1.59	3.15	1.17
Focus (of Dialogue)	3.98	1.59	2.99	1.18
Treatment/Development	3.72	1.37	2.62	1.08
MEDIUM: Film				
Main Character	3.79	1.27	–	–
Costume/Dress	2.89	2.09	–	–
Speech/Accent	2.57	1.37	–	–
Place/Location	2.47	1.64	–	–
Mise-en-Scene	2.47	1.62	–	–
Props/Objects	2.47	1.56	–	–
Plot/Story	2.52	1.80	–	–
Time/Historical Setting	2.50	1.32	–	–
Themes/Issues	2.52	1.83	–	–
Focus (of Dialogue)	2.58	1.97	–	–
Treatment/Development	2.03	1.19	–	–

1 = definitely, clearly local
2 = appears to be local, tentatively local
3 = neutral/inconclusive
4 = appears to be not local (tentatively not local)
5 = definitely, clearly not local (also see Table 4)

multitude of spatial and temporal shifts as the violin travels from seventeenth-century Italy to twentieth-century Canada (Figure 9.3).

The Red Violin's narrative reflects cultural components of each participating co-producer; thus satisfying content requirements of participating countries. This film can be considered a 'natural co-production' – all the more perhaps in respect of its focus on music with its cross-cultural appeal. The narrative also revealed typical characteristics of co-productions as it transcended spatial and temporal dimensions.

| Figure 9.3 | Co-produced feature film *The Red Violin:* narrative breakdown |

1	2	3	4	5
17th century Italy; narrative present	18th century Vienna; narrative future	19th century England; narrative future	20th century China; narrative future	20th century Montreal; narrative future; conclusion in present

| | **Sub-plot I.** The Tarot Reader reveals the future to Anna Buscotti. | |

| | **Sub-plot II. The Red Violin embodies the soul of Anna Buscotti.** |

1. Seventeenth century Italy; Anna Busscotti consults a tarot reader about her future.
1a. The tarot reading underscores the unfolding of subsequent events – **Sub-plot I.** begins.
1b. Anna dies and her husband varnished the violin with her blood, imbuing the instrument with her soul – **Sub-plot II**.
2. The violin travels to 18th century Vienna and is played by a young prodigy of master George Poussin.
3. The violin is played by a 19th century virtuoso, Frederick Pope, in Oxford, England; a romantic triangle ensues.
4. The violin appears in China where it becomes part of the dramatic unfoldings during the cultural revolution.
5. The violin is sold at an auction in Montréal. Art expert Charles Morritz reveals its secret – **Sub-plot I.** ends.

In comparison, locally produced films tend to focus on one particular place. In the film *The Hanging Garden*, for instance, a small town in rural Nova Scotia remains a cultural anchor for the duration of the film. Celtic music, the idiosyncrasies of community and familial relations are all key elements in conveying the story. In spite of sub-plots and multiple narrative developments, the focus on one place and community is essential to the storyline and identity of its characters (see Figure 9.4).[9]

In comparison to television co-productions, co-produced feature films are less tied to specific genre and tend to be situated in clearly defined locations. Co-produced television narratives, on the other hand, tend to be defined by movement through time and space to facilitate greater cross-cultural appeal and potential commercial success. Television narratives are also underscored by genre hybridisation and new programme formats which are developed for speciality channels and target audiences.

In the co-produced television drama series *The Secret Adventures of Jules Verne* (a Canada-England co-production), a group of adventurers travel across continents and through centuries in a helium balloon combating the 'League of Darkness' – a conspiracy of powerful aristocrats dating back to the Middle Ages. Based loosely on the adventure stories by Jules Verne, the series borrows from a variety of genre – horror, adventure and science fiction – and changes locations and eras from episode to episode. From the outset, the co-producers sought to appeal to global audiences by keeping control over production: 'We wanted to keep it international, because as soon as any one jurisdiction gets a hold of it, they turn it into their product and it kills it for the rest of the world' (Rice-Barker 1998).

Figure 9.4	Locally produced feature film *The Hanging Garden*: narrative breakdown

1	2	3	4	5	6	7	8
past narrative; flashback	past narrative; flashback	present narrative	present narrative – magic realism	present narrative	past narrative – magic realism; flashback	past and present narratives fuse into one	present narrative

Sub-plot 1. A garden used as a metaphor for a small town community, and family unit; describing seasonal changes, growth and death.

Sub-plot 2. William's past and his emerging identity crisis, expressed in the form of flashbacks and magic realism (10) in the present narrative.

1. William as a young boy in the garden with his father, studying the name of different flowers and plants.
2. William as a teenager, watering the plants in the garden.
3. Scene titled: 'The Lady in the Locket'; William returns, after a 10 year absence, to attend his sister's wedding.
4. William first visualises himself as a young boy, and then as growing teenager – use of magic realism.
5. Williams mother leaves the family after the wedding is over.
6. Scene: 'Lad's love'; William as a teenager; his first sexual experience with Fletcher.
7. William's suicide attempt. He awakes with an asthma attack – past and present narrative fuse into one, underscored by elements of magic realism.
8. Scene: 'Mums'; William's family become aware of William's flashbacks and psychological trauma. He leaves his family to return to Toronto.

This focus on international markets affects the series' narratives that are filled with hybrid elements and digital effects.

In the episode 'Southern Comfort', the adventurers are thrown into the heart of the Civil War where they prevent 'The League of Darkness' from perpetuating slavery (Figure 9.5). The episode focuses on the struggle between good and evil (also the series' theme), and the personal relationships between the characters, especially the emotional ties between Phileas Fogg and Saratoga Brown.

In contrast to television co-productions, local television programmes tend to focus on issues pertinent to Canadian society, its history and collective memory. For example, *Milgaard*, a docudrama about the wrongful conviction of David Milgaard, who spent twenty-three years in prison for a crime he did not commit, establishes a local focus from the beginning through highlighting locations throughout Western Canada. The story is part of Canada's history, and *Milgaard*'s critical stance adds a new viewpoint to the collective memory of Canadians.

The narrative's opening scene depicts David Milgaard dancing as a free man outside a diner in British Columbia, anticipating the final scene in the same location – a circular construction typical for television. The narrative then looks

Figure 9.5	Co-produced television drama series *The Secret Adventures of Jules Verne*: narrative breakdown

1	2	3	4	5	6	7	8
Telegraph message disrupts equilibrium	League of Darkness poses opposi-tional force	The Aurora crashes, causing further disruption	Verne et al. on a quest to restore equilibrium	Prometheus attacks; further disruption	Prometheus fights Aurora and Union army; disequi-librium	Quest to rescue Brown fails	Prometheus is damaged; new equilibrium

Episode sub-plot 1. Fogg's and Brown's doomed love affair.

Series sub-plot 2. The struggle between good and evil forces; Jules Verne, the Foggs and Passepartout against the League of Darkness.

1. U.S. Civil War; Union Lieutenant telegraphs Washington for additional troops. The message is intercepted by Jules Verne, the Foggs and Passepartout who are on their way to the southern U.S. They travel in a helium balloon called the 'Aurora'.
2. The League of Darkness is also heading towards the battle grounds of the Civil War – in a flying war machine called 'Prometheus'. They intend to aid the southern troops and perpetuate slavery.
3. The Aurora crashes on a southern estate, called 'Arcadia', owned by Saratoga Brown; Phileas Fogg falls in love with her.
4. Verne, the Foggs and Passepartout meet with Union General Steel to warn him about the Prometheus.
5. Prometheus first attacks the Union Camp, then The League of Darkness change their plans to fight their adversaries Verne and Fogg instead; the Prometheus attacks the estate 'Arcadia'; Brown is taken hostage.
6. The Prometheus, Aurora and the Union army engage in battle.
7. Fogg seeks to rescue Brown and enters the Prometheus; Brown is killed during their escape.
8. The Prometheus is damaged; all convene around a camp fire; Fogg is holding the deceased Brown.

back at different stages of Milgaard's life: his arrest, his time in prison and, finally, the reopening of his legal case leading to his release (Figure 9.6).

Television drama for local markets tend to identify place, visually and verbally, from the beginning and develop a narrative anchored in that location. They feature narratives based on local topics that reflect critically on historical or contemporary issues of concern. They also tend to be based on more 'realistic' themes, and are spatially and temporally bound, rather than featuring genre from the science fiction or adventure category.

In many cases local productions also have a global dimension by connecting issues, values and ideas between cultural diaspora – especially when they address sub-cultural themes (such as First Nations topics, women's issues etc.). The narrative analyses, therefore, revealed that local and independently produced programmes were more critical and reflective of contemporary conditions than co-productions with their global market orientation and resulting non-critical commercial narratives. Co-produced narratives were structured around

Locally produced television docudrama *Milgaard*: narrative breakdown

Figure 9.6

1	2	3	4	5	6	7	8
narrative present	narrative past; flashback	narrative past perfect; flashback	narrative past; flashback	narrative past; flashback	narrative past; flashback	narrative past; flashback	narrative present

1. Milgaard in British Columbia in 1992 outside a diner, dancing in the rain. He is a free man again.
2. Milgaard back in 1969 in Saskatchewan. He has been arrested for the murder of Gail Miller.
3. Milgaard at the police station; he tells his story through flashbacks.
4. Milgaard in prison, the years go by.
5. Joyce Milgaard, his mother, tries to prove his innocence, initial attempts fail.
6. Joyce Milgaard approaches lawyers Hersh Wolch and David Asper. Through their work together and growing media attention surrounding the issues, the case is re-opened.
7. Milgaard is back in court, and his name is cleared.
8. Milgaard in British Columbia in 1992, dancing in the rain.

genres that are spatially and temporally non-specific. Science fiction, adventure stories and fairy tales, therefore, predominated in this production mode. In contrast, local narratives highlighted the importance of place, cultural identity and collective memory. They focused on specific topics that are of social or historical interest and offered new perspectives and insights.

Conclusion

In conclusion, this case study of Canadian TV and film international co-production points to a number of key findings. Co-productions have increased over recent years in direct response to changing market conditions and regulatory environments. Squeezed for funds and encountering increased international competition, producers – both commercial and public service – have deliberately sought new sources of funding and markets. Canadian international co-productions have increased dramatically across the period 1990–2000 in response to increasingly deregulated markets and heightened international competition. With a view to winning new sources of funding as well as finding international markets for their productions, the films and programmes produced in these new forms of international production arrangements have tended to assume 'global' characteristics. That is, they tend to assume forms that are relatively culturally indistinct and which eschew political content. Some genres are preferred over others – drama, adventure, science fiction, documentary – and these tend to focus on human relationships and emotional storylines to increase their universal appeal. Narrative structures are also affected in terms of their temporal organisation and spatial reference. These features combine to marginalise 'local' production and the representation of local issues and concerns, whether played out in local, national, regional, international or global arenas. They also tend to displace cultural representations of diversity and difference. Films and TV programmes produced by local producers, though increasingly in short supply, demonstrate a capacity to provide a space for public engagement with local issues and concerns and the representation of cultural diversity. In short, the market-driven orientation and appeals of international co-productions contribute to the undermining of that public space deemed central for critical reflection, cultural representation and public deliberation. This erosion of the public sphere is injurious for democracy and public well-being.

We need to shift the current emphasis away from film and broadcast communication as *culture as commodity* to *culture as public good*. This can only be achieved if we manage to sustain and support a broad range of cultural institutions and production arrangements. Stable funding structures for independent productions and public service broadcasting are, therefore, essential in maintaining an accessible cultural infrastructure. Public policy should 'promote cultural development because it is essential to democratic public life' (Raboy et al. 1994: 310), and because it can prevent media monopolisation limiting diversity and plurality.

The increase of co-productions, as we have seen, is linked to changing production practices and the globalisation of media organisations. While co-productions have increased, the commitment to local independent productions has decreased. Co-productions with their current financial structure and commercial market orientation cannot be permitted to replace local productions.

However, co-productions could be developed into a vehicle for local independent producers – as was originally envisioned for this production mode – to collaborate on international programmes that critically reflect on contemporary issues of local, national and international concern. Collaborative programmes about global issues, such as cultural diversity and the hybridisation of cultures, could yet provide insight into the changing natures of globalised societies. New narratives could be found to open up discussions about the environment, media commercialisation, the World Trade Organization, and other issues of international concern. The development of new technologies, such as digital video and web-casting, also provides accessible venues for production and dissemination. Official commitment to support and provide open access to a multitude of diverse media channels is, therefore, an essential aspect of the successful integration of old and new production methods within democratically inspired cultural frameworks. The future does not have to be confined to an extension of the present.

CHAPTER SUMMARY

- International co-productions in Canada, as in many other countries, have increased dramatically in recent years, reflecting changing market conditions and processes of deregulation, privatisation, conglomeration and convergence.

- International TV and film co-productions are principally designed to secure sources of new production funding, new markets, enhanced revenue and international product exposure.

- International TV and film co-productions tend to prefer certain genres over others – drama, adventure stories, science fiction, documentaries – as well as human interest content and inflections. Narrative structures are also affected in terms of spatial and temporal dimensions and their local reference.

- Local productions have become increasingly marginalised in comparison to international co-productions and the importation of foreign products. In consequence, there is less representation of local concerns and issues and opportunities for engaged debate and deliberation conducted in relation to these at local, regional and global levels.

- International co-productions informed by the logic of *culture as commodity* rather than the pursuit of *culture as public good* have tended to erode the public sphere of engaged citizenship, critical reflection and the representation of global issues and concerns.

Notes

This chapter is based on the author's Master's thesis: 'Co-productions in Film and Television: A Canadian Case Study'. Leicester University, England, 2000.

1 The terms 'local' and 'global' used in this discussion are defined as follows. **Local** refers to cultural specificity of locations, persons and social arrangements, underpinning identity and engaged citizenship. **Global** refers to the increasing interconnection of the economy, polity and culture defined predominantly within a commercial paradigm and consumer culture.

2 Canadian content productions and content rules stipulate a Canadian presence in film and television programmes. To qualify as a Canadian content production, key positions have to be filled by the director, writer, producer or actor(s). Co-productions are exempted from general content rules. However, as long as they follow overall treaty guidelines, they none the less qualify as Canadian content productions.

3 **Deregulation** of media industries refers to new regulations based on economic and entrepreneurial imperatives rather than the public interest.
Privatisation refers to the dismantling, sale or restructuring of public organisations along commercial and entrepreneurial lines.
Conglomeration or the merging of media companies results in the control over production, distribution and exhibition of media (vertical integration), as well as ownership and control across a variety of media and related industries (horizontal integration), by a few media giants.
Convergence – *Convergence of technologies* refers to the ability to transfer digital information across a variety of platforms. *Convergence of content* refers to content that tends to be based on global stories, styles and techniques popularised predominantly by US film and television productions.

4 **Public sphere**, a concept developed by Jürgen Habermas, constitutes a space of social life that is determined neither by market forces nor the state. It is a free forum, accessible to all citizens for the exchange of ideas, information and debate and underscores the formation of public opinion and citizenship.

5 **Transcending spatial and temporal dimensions**: A narrative that is set in more than one place or era, and/or in which characters move from one spatial and/or temporal dimension to another, either within one film or television episode or, with regard to television series, from one weekly episode to another. Interestingly, these types of narratives reflect concepts such as time-space distanciation which relates to the disembedding of social relations from local contexts and their restructuring across time and space (cf. A. Giddens' globalisation theory).

6 **First Nations**: Aboriginal or Native Canadian.

7 **Auteur**: The focus on the creator and director of a production rather than the actors/stars.

8 *The Last Streetfighter: The History of the Georgia Straight*: A local documentary chronicling the turbulent history of Canada's oldest alternative newspaper. *North of 60*: A local television series which revolves around the lives of members of a First Nation community, addressing controversial issues from conflicts with non-natives to a history of oppression. *The Trickster*: A local documentary by Gordon McLennan features an aboriginal artist, Edward Poitras, and his works amidst discussion about cultural hybridisation, identity and native spirituality.

9 **Magic realism**: the combination of realism and surrealist, dreamlike or fantastic elements in a narrative.

CHAPTER 10

Producing Nature(s): The Changing Production Ecology of Natural History TV

Simon Cottle

In keeping with the other chapters in this book, this final chapter further explores the complexities of media organisation and production.[1] It deliberately adopts a case-study approach to the production of a particular genre of television: that of natural history programmes. This long-established but 'neglected tradition' (Bousé 2000) has undergone dramatic evolution and change in recent years, reflecting wider processes of industrial reorganisation and cultural shifts within national and international television marketplaces. New technologies of production and delivery, heightened competitiveness, industrial centralisation, fragmenting audiences and internationalising markets have all, as we shall hear, dramatically impacted on the 'production ecology' of wildlife programmes. As such, this case study serves to underline many of the themes and findings already raised in previous chapters.

The case study also affords, however, a rare glimpse into how these wider forces are professionally managed and creatively negotiated by programme-makers working within a particular and differentiated organisational field. Here a 'production ecology', characterised by a set of competitive institutional relationships and co-operative dependencies, informs the organisation, production and output of natural history programming. Key players include national public service and commercial broadcasters and their respective natural history units; international satellite and cable TV distributors, co-producers and co-financiers; and a plethora of medium and small-scale production houses and independent producers. These all operate within a dynamic field characterised by co-existence and co-operation, competition and rivalry and played out in response to strategies of self-interest and the imbalances of scale and market opportunity. This leads to processes of organisational restructuring, including take-overs and mergers as well as, for some, extinction. The concept of 'production ecology', based in part on Bourdieu's notion of a 'cultural field' (Bourdieu 1993), is here thought to be particularly apposite.[2] Theoretically it helps to signal the importance of attending to organizational relationships and dynamics that exist *within* a particular field of media production, as well as attending to those inside individual media organisations. Studies of selected production domains and associated professional practices are invaluable for improved theoretical understanding of media output, as we have already seen in this book. But 'production ecologies' extend beyond the immediate sphere of production of any one organisation and we also need to attend to these if we are to understand better how cultural forms are reproduced, differentiated and adapted through time by organisations working within the same field.

This approach is in sympathy with the recent position of Peter Golding and Graham Murdock, when they argue from a 'critical political economy' approach that if we are to understand the nature of the 'cultural industries', then we need to 'explain how the economic dynamics of production structure public discourse by promoting certain cultural forms over others' (Golding and Murdock 2000: 84). Such an approach is essential for understanding the *general* market dynamics of media organisation and production and it also needs to be deployed in more focused ways in respect of *particular* fields of cultural production. But so too do we need to pursue how the *organisational structuration* of a particular field as well as the *professional enactment and negotiation* of wider forces within it, impact on the production and evolution of cultural forms.

This study of natural history programming, then, aims to demonstrate the usefulness of attending to 'production ecologies' for improved understanding of media organisation and production more generally. It also serves as a case study of the social construction and social evolution of public representations of 'nature'. Nature, as contemporary sociologists have documented, is susceptible to a diversity of social constructions (Eder 1996; Macnaghten and Urry 1998; Allan et al. 2000), and the study of natural history programmes provides important insights into the changing 'nature(s)' of public representation and understanding of the natural world. Derek Bousé (2000) has charted the history and informing cultural narratives of wildlife films and argues, 'wildlife film producers, working in a competitive, commercial setting, have perfected and come to rely upon narrative formulas, if only to systematize production'. He goes on to say that, 'the regular application of these formulas, along with consistencies of theme and character give wildlife films the rule-governed coherence of a full-fledged film genre' (ibid.: 20). Today though, the fast-changing nature of natural history programmes renders problematic both the notion of a relatively settled genre defined by predictable formulas, consistencies of theme and character and rule-governed coherence, as well as its functionality for systematising production. The 'genre' of wildlife programming has, if anything, become decidedly 'ungenre-like' if this is taken to be a relatively settled combination of textual elements and appeals, industry inscriptions and audience expectations.

This chapter does not imply that a 'golden age' of natural history programming, defined perhaps in terms of so-called 'blue-chip' programmes, has recently been eclipsed or has mutated into something less 'pure'. The term 'blue-chip' has come to refer to programmes devoted to observing 'spectacular' animal behaviour within 'timeless' natural habitats and all relatively 'untainted' by human intervention, whether presenters in front of the camera, producers and animal trainers behind them, or humans interacting with, or on, the 'pristine' animal habitats depicted. The problem with this, as Bousé demonstrates, is that natural history programmes have always undergone evolution and change. In any case, the scientistic pretensions of earlier forms of wildlife documentary do not really stand up to much scrutiny; and nor could they, given the inescapable artifices of TV production and the medium's predilection for storytelling over science.

By attending to the changing production ecology of natural history TV production and the responses of programme-makers, we can begin to discern processes of cultural negotiation and adaptation at work. We can see how genres become transformed through time, particularly in times of production instability and organisational change. In this way, we can also begin to build a better sense of how media production, though inevitably conditioned and shaped by wider forces – whether technological, regulatory, commercial or cultural – in practice is actively managed and 'creatively' negotiated by organisations and programme-makers operating within particular fields of cultural production.

The study draws upon diverse sources of data and insight. These include: industry updates and interviews reported within the broadcasting trade press across the five year period 1997–2002; a small sample of in-depth interviews conducted with UK independent, commercial and public service natural history producers; in-house documents and organisation web-pages; and, of course, samples of natural history programmes produced and broadcast across recent years[3]

Changing TV Landscapes: *Survival* and the Fittest

In recent years established production companies and successful natural history units noted for their production of so-called 'blue-chip' wildlife documentary programmes have been subject to powerful, sometimes devastating, forces of change. These pressures often emanate from outside the immediate sphere of natural history production; however, their impact on the fortunes and survivability of established production teams has been no less dramatic for that. Within the ITV commercial sector, *Survival* is a case in point.

Commercial Television: Apex Predators and Prey

Since its inception in 1961, *Survival* had established itself as a respected and influential natural history production team based within the ITV commercial broadcaster Anglia Television. During its forty-year existence the unit produced over 1,000 *Survival* programmes and sold in 112 countries, for which it collected over 160 major awards including prestigious Emmys. Producing this 'respected' output was a team of forty staff based at Norwich. Films could take up to three years to make, often requiring teams in the field for up to 18 months, were conceived and put together here. For much of its history, *Survival* set the standards for natural history programming whilst demonstrating that this genre has the potential to win large, prime-time audiences. Its high standing within the field of natural history production, and with past television audiences, failed however to prevent it from becoming, like the subjects of many of its programmes, an endangered species. Its demise is illustrative of the wider forces of change that have reshaped the TV landscape and the ecology of natural history TV production.

In 2000 one of the largest production teams of wildlife programmes outside of the BBC's Natural History Unit (NHU) was Granada's 'United Wildlife', producing up to 50 hours of production annually (estimated to be worth £10 million in 2000). United Wildlife, in keeping with Granada's business success within the entertainment field, had established relationships with Discovery, Animal Planet, National Geographic and PBS as well as ITV, Channel 4 and Channel 5. The Director of United Wildlife summed up his company's view of the changing nature of wildlife programmes in 2000:

> Viewers are no longer looking for big-budget films which concentrate on animal behaviour in isolation. They want identifiable stories and strong people-based narratives. We are introducing more science, history, animation and fantasy into our films. (Paul Sowerbutts, quoted in *Broadcast*, 6 October 2000: 21)

In 2001 Granada acquired for £1.75 billion United News and Media's (UNM) franchises, Meridian, HTV, and Anglia – the host company of *Survival*. This brought Granada's total franchises to seven and made it the largest company in the UK television commercial sector. Granada subsequently sold the HTV franchise to Carlton PLC, the second largest franchise owner, for £320 million to reduce its share of the total national audience to below 15 per cent, in line with regulatory requirements. As part of this centralisation process, Granada then pooled its wildlife television production at its factual production facilities at HTV studios in Bristol with the loss of thirty-five jobs, announcing that the company expected to rely more on freelance staff recruited project by project in the future. Granada had earlier also acquired Partridge Films in 1997, a respected independent production house making popular wildlife films, founded in 1974 under the directorship of Michael Rosenberg (who subsequently resigned following the dilution of the Partridge brand). The trade press reported on this latest Granada acquisition and consolidation of its business interests as follows:

> Granada has dumped its inherited United Wildlife brand and is overhauling the division as a major supplier of 'blue-chip' films shot on video tape under the new name of Granada Wild. The move . . . also sees the disposal of former United Wildlife brands Partridge Films and Survival. (*Broadcast*, 6 April 2001)

This prompted Head of Granada Wild, Paul Fairclough, to complain publicly about the way this change had been represented, revealing something of the market logic and programming rationale informing United Wildlife's future production stance towards wildlife programming.

> Contrary to the impression given . . . we are not 'disposing' of the *Survival* and *Partridge* brands. We are rebuilding the best bits of both firms into a new, powerful and efficient wildlife production company, which will be equipped to deal with the needs of a rapidly changing marketplace. If we hadn't taken this action now, our business and the wildlife television industry as a whole could have been severely damaged. . . . By renaming ourselves *Granada Wild*, we are signalling the firm's commitment to this genre and that we intend to pursue new ways of making wildlife programmes which better meet the needs of the market, both here and abroad. . . . We are still making high-end programmes for *ITV*, *Discovery* and *Animal Planet* among others, and intend to retain *Survival's* relationship with the best wildlife film-makers in the world.
>
>   However, we believe that attention to storyline, character and innovative approaches are much more important than simply filming the natural behaviour and habitats of animals – the traditional focus of many natural history shows. (*Broadcast*, 20 April 2001: 17)

This public justification of Granada's natural history programming production arrangements and programme emphasis perfectly illustrates how wider commercial and corporate forces have forced a re-evaluation of the genre, and a public defence of the same.

These forces are not confined to the UK or even European marketplaces but also impinge from further afield. The world's two largest cable and satellite distributors of natural history programmes on multi-channel TV, US-based Discovery's Animal Planet channel, and National Geographic Television (NGT), exert a global influence on the marketplace of natural history programming. NGT has partnerships with key broadcasters; its main channel is broadcast in 133 countries, in 21 different languages and reaches 27 million homes in Europe. Its principal rival, Discovery Communications Incorporated (DCI), is even bigger. Since the Discovery Channel first went on air in 1985 it has grown exponentially. Today it has services in 155 countries and, according to its own estimates, reaches over 650 million total subscribers. Discovery Networks, in the US alone, reaches almost 85 million households and produces 2,100 hours of original programming. In 1996 DCI launched Animal Planet; this has proven to be one of the most successful networks ever and is now available in 74 million homes.

In the fight for global pre-eminence, natural history programming has become an important market in which to win audience ratings and revenue. Wildlife programmes are commercially useful because they generally have a long 'shelf-life': their subject matter and universal appeal can seemingly cross different cultures, and they can easily be repackaged and dubbed. Both Discovery and NGT have therefore become major international players in the production ecology of natural history programming, commissioning natural history pro-grammes and co-producing with major broadcasters. This includes a global partnership with BBC Worldwide Ltd, recently extended in 2002 for a further ten years, which includes the co-ownership of Animal Planet. Both NGT and DCI have sought to buy up precious programme libraries and programme rights to satisfy the insatiable multi-channel TV environment. While Discovery's approach has been to buy up entire libraries, including the back catalogue of *Survival*, NGT's approach has been to cherry-pick selected series. In 2001 UNM sold 180 hours of programming from the Survival catalogue worth £34 million.

New appointments reported in the trade press frequently serve to underline important shifts in the production ecology of natural history programmes and reveal how developments in one organisational sector are often replicated and capitalised upon in another. For example, when Oxford Scientific Films (OSF) appointed former United Wildlife producer Mark Strickson as head of programming for its natural history unit, this was announced in terms of increasing the range of productions at OSF to include lower-budget, high-volume programming in its science and adventure strands. Strickson had previously been the producer in charge of such presenter-led programmes as Steve Irwin's *The Ten Deadliest Snakes in the World*. OSF, in contrast, had previously built a reputation for blue-chip natural history programmes.

> The appointment means that we can proceed with building the business, with OSF and Southern Star [parent company] working much more closely together. This allows us to access international funding and co-produce programmes in a commercial environment. (Head of factual programmes at Southern Star, *Broadcast*, 9 November 2001, p. 6)

Independents in the TV Food Chain

During the late 1990s and early 2000s the trade press also reported on how independent producers and production houses were struggling to survive in the face of the changing demands of the marketplace and increased competition. *Broadcast*, for example, regularly reported on companies forced into mergers, redundancies and cost-cutting measures. In 2000, for instance, Café Productions (maker of natural history programmes for, amongst others, National Geographic and Discovery) was reported to be in deep crisis. The so-called 'Green Hollywood' of Bristol (because of the numerous natural history production companies based in and around the city including the BBC's Natural History Unit and United Wildlife's Partridge Films), witnessed a number of casualties. Green Umbrella, a blue-chip production house which had employed forty staff, halved this, and the company Ammonite merged its film-making wing with factual producer Scorer, while Zebra Films also cut back its staff by half. Before it was subsumed under Granada Wild, Partridge had also been forced to make redundancies. These difficulties are widely attributed within the industry to the downturn in international demand for 'blue-chip' programmes, based in part on a previous oversupply of these 'heavy investment' programmes by a proliferation of small-scale independents, and the shift in commissioning to low-cost programmes.

> Independent companies cannot rely on the occasional supply of blue-chip factual programming. To create a viable business you need a high volume of good, low-cost popular programming because that's what the market wants. (General Manager, Southern Star Wild and Real, *Broadcast*, 5 Oct. 2001)

A reduction in commissioning by broadcasters in such countries as the US, Germany, France and Japan – traditionally key markets for natural history programmes – as well as a decline in commissioning in the UK by the BBC and the NHU and Channel 4, and with ITV rarely commissioning such programmes at all, and Channel 5 only interested in low-budget programmes, the market-place for wildlife programmes had become highly competitive. Even the big players, such as Granada Wild and the BBC Natural History Unit, were increasingly seeking out co-productions with international partners such as Discovery and National Geographic as a means of reducing costs – a trend that continues to this day. But this only exacerbated the problems confronting small independents lower down the food chain that could ill-afford to devote resources to compete for large-scale projects and international co-finances and co-productions.

Traditional blue-chip programmes, which can take up to 2–3 years to produce and which require considerable time in the field, are relatively expensive to produce. At the top end of the market in 2001–02, a spectacular BBC/Discovery series like *Blue Planet* cost £850,000 per programme (£7 million for the 8 × 50 series) and was produced over five years, while the maximum commission a respected independent company could probably command was around £550,000 per programme. A sum of £40,000 to £50,000 per programme is more likely at the lower end of commissions, while library and archive-based programmes and very cheap commissions can be as little as £15,000 pounds per half-hour programme. In 2001, Animal Planet's European director of programmes had 50 hours to commission on budgets averaging only £30,000 an hour. The director commissioned a series about vets in Abu Dhabi called *Vets in the Sun*, *Wildlife Police Undercover*, a video-clip series on *The Planet's Funniest Animals* and *Adopt a Wild Animal* (reported in *Broadcast*, 24 August 2001, p. 2). In such commercial circumstances, independent producers struggled to stay afloat whilst trying to meet changing market conditions and programme commissioners' requirements.

BBC Natural History Unit: a Protected Species?

The BBC's Natural History Unit (NHU) in Bristol is the world's leading production unit of its kind in the world. Employing up to 300 people on the development and production of natural history programmes, it produces around 1,000 hours of footage a year and has the largest natural history archive in the world. Since its inception in 1957 it has established a reputation for the production of blue-chip programmes and series that are sold around the world, including spectacular series presented by David Attenborough, such as *The Living Planet*, *Life on Earth*, *The Life of Birds*, *State of the Planet* and *Life of Mammals*. The collaboration between BBC Worldwide/Discovery has resulted in BBC natural history programmes being shown on Animal Planet around the globe. Currently headed by Keith Scholey, the NHU seeks to position itself as the world's leading producer of natural history programmes aimed at different channels and markets. Scholey endorses the view that an oversupply of wildlife programmes stimulated by the growth of TV channels and markets led to the collapse in the market, but he also suggests that the poor production values of many of these programmes served to further erode audience appreciation, prompting a re-evaluation of ways of making 'traditional' wildlife documentaries as well as innovations of form across the spectrum of programmes.

> There was a kind of a shock about four years ago [1998/9] when people suddenly realised that the traditional wildlife film bubble had burst. That has put a lot of creative pressure on producers. We're trying to create new formats and using new technology to move us on. . . . I would [also] say the modern way of doing the traditional format has proved to be as successful as ever. So that is our strategy now. It's not to put all your eggs in one basket, it's to spread it around, to have lots of diversity. (Keith Scholey, head of NHU)

Following the success of *Blue Planet*, which at the time of production was widely thought to be the last of the BBC's spectacular, mega-budget, 'blue-chip' programmes, Scholey maintains that programmes such as these can in fact buck the trend, and even help reverse the trend originated in the US of commissioning one-off natural history programmes to 'punch through schedules' and hook audiences.

> We were coming to a point of doing short sharp things, but now you will see the BBC review that, and we will continue to do big landmark pieces. . . . We may end up being kind of unique suppliers of them though, because I don't know if there is a profitable business for other people to make them in the future. (Scholey, head of NHU)

With *Blue Planet* costing £7 million, such spectacular programmes are invariably dependent on co-production. According to the head of the NHU, typically 40–50 per cent of the finance required for such a project would come from the BBC, world sales/marketing could generate a further 25 per cent and 25–30 per cent could come from the co-producer. Within the public broadcasting system, spectaculars such as *Blue Planet* can perform a function over and above the generation of large ratings. The BBC NHU, though intimately bound up in the changing international production ecology of natural history programmes, also occupies a unique programming space. Symbolically, programmes such as *Blue Planet* can therefore help to promote the 'public service value' of the BBC, and was literally used to do so when, for example, shark scenes from the series were used in the corporation's on-air promotions.

> We need to be distinctive, we need to be public service, and we need to claw in larger audiences. And the BBC gets rewarded in all sorts of ways for productions like *Blue Planet* which is important in audience terms but is very, very important in terms of overall BBC public perception terms; that we are there to provide and to inform, educate and entertain. And so there is a lot of support to carry that on. (Scholey, head of BBC's NHU)

The NHU, however, notwithstanding its privileged status and 'relatively' protected position within public service broadcasting, cannot escape entirely the changing TV marketplace of programmes and wider trends. Programme diversity, channel scheduling and niche demographics are no less pertinent to the NHU's commissioning and programme developments than to others within the pressurised TV marketplace.

> You want to get a lot of BBC2 audience, but it is nothing like the BBC1 audience and we ought to hit different kinds of buttons. Also the demographics; I look really carefully at the range of shows that we are doing. That is why I was so pleased with *Ultimate Killers*; it was

'hitting' a lot of teenagers, we don't normally draw them in. . . . So I think it is a complicated thing. There are the channel needs and we do want to serve those, we do want to stay on 'platforms'. . . . And I think *Blue Planet* must have demonstrated to everyone that you do not have to compromise what you are doing to get a big audience. (Scholey, head of BBC's NHU)

Producing Nature(s): Killer Content and Kissing Snakes

As we have heard, the production ecology of natural history programmes is characterised by a differentiated organisational field. This encompasses some of the world's leading global media conglomerates, national public service and commercial broadcasters, and a plethora of medium and small-scale production companies. These all co-exist and compete (or go to the wall) within this 'production ecology', as they seek to position themselves advantageously both in relation to one another and in response to the changing international and national marketplaces of natural history programming. Exactly how they do this is crucial for an understanding of the changing nature(s) of natural history TV and how this field has become reconstituted in particular ways. The next part of the discussion therefore attends to the changing forms and output of natural history TV, and how these express this changing production ecology.

Migrations: Presenters to Celebrities

Within the evolution of natural history programmes, on-screen presenters have come and gone, and come again. In some quarters programme presenters have migrated from 'presenting' the subject of their programmes to arguably becoming the subject itself.

The Americans aren't buying anymore, they're not buying into blue-chip natural history films anymore; not at the sort of money you would need. So then there is this huge change in so-called presenters of wildlife. You have got to do things like Steve Irwin, sort of kissing snakes and nearly getting eaten by crocodiles. (Independent producer)

The use of personalities to enhance the appeal of natural history programmes has become almost a stock response of programme-makers in their bid to win commissions and enhance programme attractiveness. This trend is most evident within the commercialised sectors of cable and satellite history programme delivery, though it now extends across all sectors. Discovery, for example, is in no doubt about the popularity of its most successful programme, nor of the role of the 'presenter' within this. Under a close-up picture of Steve Irwin holding a deadly snake inches away from his face, Discovery promotes the programme series, and markets the video of the same, as follows.

Watch the Croc hunter tackle these slithering killers with unmatched bravado and fearlessness while displaying his unique wit. As the most watched program on Discovery, the Croc Hunter Series has taken Steve Irwin across the globe to find the world's most deadly creatures. Now he's reached new heights with these African snakes with some of the most deadly venom on earth. Let's hope he has his anti-venom handy!

Many producers in the field are highly critical of such programmes:

I've not seen one of those programmes where there has been a good reason for that Australian presenter to go there with a film crew and grab a snake or kiss it or swim in a river with it or whatever. I do not understand that. (Independent producer)

This 'personalised' approach to wildlife programming has none the less helped to make *The Crocodile Hunter* Animal Planet's highest-rated series and served to propel Steve Irwin to celebrity status with appearances on such US shows as *Saturday Night Live, The Tonight Show, Rosie O'Donnell* and *Late Night with Conan O'Brian* as well as featuring in *South Park*. This commercial value of celebrity was then partially cashed-in by Discovery with a global partnership with Toys R Us, with its chain of 1,500 outlets around the world selling toys and products modelled on the series.

Independent producers have also seized on the increased ratings that apparently follow the incorporation of celebrities. Tigress Productions, for example, has produced a string of such programmes seeking to replicate its initial successes in this vein. Programmes include *Born to be Wild – Operation Lemur with John Cleese*, and, under its *In the Wild* series: *Orang Utans with Julia Roberts, The Galapogas Mystery with Richard Dreyfuss, Cheetahs with Holly Hunter, Dolphins with Robin Williams, Asian Elephants with Goldie Hawn*, and *Wolves with Timothy Dalton*. Even producers of 'high-end' natural history programmes, such as Scorer Associates, have felt obliged to incorporate 'attractive' presenters into their programme presentations.

It's been quite difficult for Scorer Associates the company because we've always had a reputation for making high-quality, high-budget documentaries and we've never been seen as a company that churns out Animal Planet type, ten thousand pound, half-hour programmes. . . . We made a film about chimps a few months ago with a primatologist called Charlotte Uhlenbroek who'd previously done a successful series called *Cousins* at the BBC. She's very good, she's very presentable, and she's young and attractive and she's somebody that the BBC has been trying to mould into a presenter who will attract more viewers to wildlife films. (Production manager, Scorer)

The BBC's involvement of the respected naturalist David Attenborough as a presenter of its landmark series has extended over many years. However, the NHU is now deliberately seeking out new presenters, some of whom have already become minor celebrities on the basis of their presentation of other popular TV genres. All of them are young, all of them attractive: Phillipa Forrester (*Robot Wars*), Trude Mostue (*Vets in Practice*), Steve Leonard (*Vets in Practice*), Charlie Dimmock (*Ground Force*) (reported in *Broadcast*, 6 October 2000, p. 2). This generalised attempt to enhance programme appeal across the industry of wildlife programmes is plain enough, though it is interesting to note that the migrations of presenter to personality and celebrity have reached different destinations across the different sectors of the programme environment. David

Attenborough continues to present occasional BBC series along with a growing cast of 'professional' BBC presenters; naturalists – albeit attractive ones – are sought out to present independent, 'high-end' programmes; celebrities have been used to front more populist programmes; and flamboyant 'entertainers' have assumed the focal point of interest in mass appeal shows.

Jaws, Claws and Mauls: Killer Content

The wildlife genre has always had to deal with 'adult' themes of sex, violence and death; it goes with the territory. In pursuit of audiences, ratings, subscriptions and advertising revenues, broadcasters have recently begun to overcome earlier conceptions of audience squeamishness and/or moral discomfort and most now actively seek out, albeit in different ways, the drama and pathos as well as the action and excitement that attend the life and death struggles of animals.

> Natural history films are like a football match, with a beginning, middle and end, and predation is like the goal being scored. In this series we are producing a *Match of the Day*, putting all the goals, or predation sequences, together, because in these moments you get to see what the animals are built for. (Producer, *Predators*, BBC1, *Broadcast*, 28 April 2000, p. 30)

Such scenes, like the 'money shot' in pornography, are widely thought to be what the audience wants and this helps account for their increased prevalence within recent programmes as well as the increased numbers of programmes devoted to the big predators, often sharks, and even more specifically the Great White. To put it another way, the political economy of natural history programmes disenfranchises invertebrates.

> There is an enormous pressure on getting that shot, that money shot, that kill, that television moment which is going to get you ratings. (Independent producer)
>
> There's been a pressure, that's the kill, kill, kill pressure. It's certainly the case that the natural history programmes have been increasingly sold on their ability to deliver the kind of wham, bang, killer shot. (Documentary/film-maker)

In recent years countless programmes have focused on, or included, sharks – perhaps since the film *Jaws* the most deeply feared of all species. Here are just a few of them: *Maneaters: Sharks* (Tigress Productions), *Blue Water Predators* (Granada Wild/Animal Planet), *Predators* (NHU/Discovery); *Ultimate Killers* (BBC NHU), *Killers of . . .* (Granada Wild), *Shark Encounters* (BBC1/Animal Planet), *Shark Summer* (BBC1), *Sensitive Sharks* (Wildlife on One, BBC). Again, however, a discernible differentiation in the extent and use of killing scenes is found across these programmes dependent on the commissioning organisation and channel outlet. A producer of two programmes about sharks explains:

> Discovery is much bloodier. Animal Planet is gentler. Animal Planet reckons to have a different audience profile from the Discovery Channel in that they have more women and

kids. They don't go for the sort of same blood and guts things. So at the moment one of their most successful is *Animal Frontline*, which is about cruelty inspectors working for the American Society of Prevention of Cruelty to Animals in New York. That's a really popular one for them because it's a natural way I suppose of putting together people and animals in a dramatic kind of way, and that's really what Animal Planet's brief is. Discovery certainly likes more kills per acre. I mean, Animal Planet is quite likely to either tell you to take a shot out because it's too gory, whereas Discovery will put it the other way. And yet they both belong to the same parent outfit. (Independent producer)

The BBC has also increasingly focused on deadly predators and killing across a number of its programmes. However, given its public service reputation to uphold, it is also careful to distance itself from any possible criticism that it is simply following wider market trends or base cultural appetites. The six-part NHU BBC1 series *Ultimate Killers* (2001) covered themes of 'speed', 'strength', 'chemical killers', 'pack hunters' and 'deadly offenders' before climaxing with a programme devoted to 'man-eaters'. Across the series Steve Leonard shortlisted the world's deadliest animals, his six 'ultimate killers'. In the same year BBC1 broadcast another six-part series, *Predators*. According to the BBC's on-line promotion, '*Predators* captures for the first time the moment where life hangs in the balance, the split second that the human eye would never normally see', and went on to say, 'This is not a story of blood and guts – it is the behind-the-scenes drama of a gripping battle of wits that decides which animals get a meal and which escape becoming one.' While these and other BBC programmes are careful to distance themselves from the most gratuitous use of predatory behaviour and scenes, it is also apparent that the BBC has sought not to be left behind in the competition for audiences attracted to programmes about large predators and killer content TV.

Human Habitats: Wither Environment?

A recurring complaint about earlier nature programmes, especially those that appeared to endorse the blue-chip representation of humanly untouched environments, was that these 'timeless' representations failed to provide any means for understanding how animal habitats and behaviour are in fact influenced by human activity and processes of environmental degradation. More recently, as we have heard, the return to presenter-led programmes and dramatic storylines has led commissioners and programme producers to explore various forms of animal–human interaction.

The old-fashioned biology lesson approach has to change. We want to find strong emotional storylines and more interaction with people. (Granada Wild, managing director, *Broadcast*, 24 August 2001, p. 2)

The pursuit of emotional storylines and interaction is apparent in the recent spate of programmes about sharks, as well as elsewhere. The producer of *Shark Encounters* outlines the informing ideas set out by the commissioning organisation, Animal Planet:

> They wanted me to work in Michaela Strachen [TV presenter] in a slightly more grown-up role than she had been in kids' programmes; and they wanted to get close up to the sharks. And we went back to the shark attack victims, we went back to scientists and a photographer who was actually attacked by the shark while he was filming it, so he's a good story. . . . I wasn't constrained only to the Great White, but they wanted the man-eaters basically. They wanted the big three – the Tigers, the Bulls, and the White.

Though constrained by the commissioning programme brief, this particular producer seeks to overcome the evident play on deep-seated cultural myths and fears about sharks embedded in so many programme treatments. Her next programme about sharks, currently in production, aims to move the genre on, though to what extent it too still trades in popular myths of sharks in the very act of trying to dispel them is a moot point.

> Our working title is *Sharks Beyond Jaws*. And the whole idea is that you can get behind this image of the teeth and find out what the whole animal is about. I'm learning about the importance of the apex predator. . . . So the film is going to try and develop the idea of the shark as an individual, and I'm also trying to develop the idea of shark researchers as individuals. This film is going to say, 'Here's a shark. His name's Rip Torn'. . . . I suppose that's why I'm doing it because we haven't seen sharks as individuals. (Producer, *Sharks Beyond Jaws*)

A very different strategy to incorporate emotional storylines and human inter-action draws more on the dramatic devices and narratives of soap opera than the documentary tradition of film-making. And this also has the commercial benefit of being incredibly cheap to produce. A series of 15 × 30 minute programmes, *Safari School*, produced by Cicada Films for Animal Planet, follows eight young trainee safari tour guides as they learn survival skills in an African game reserve. Soap opera angles are used to hook audiences into the unfolding narrative across the episodes. The series was produced on a micro-budget of £15,000 per 30-minute episode, with the director herself shooting much of the DVcam material, before editing each programme in five days. The 'shaky-cam' effect that results from using a hand-held camera was felt by the director to give the programme an '*NYPD Blue on Safari*' feel, music introduced mood, and slowed-down sequences helped to give pace to action scenes. The director also explains how:

> We only had a five-day edit so there was no way that we could produce something that flows in the traditional way – with perfect cut-aways, etc. – so we chose a more dynamic, vital style using visual effects, jump cuts, and music very much like they do in drama productions. This creates real immediacy and excitement. (*Broadcast*, 6 July 2001, p. 16)

Here we see how constraints of budget and commissioning have in fact been creatively negotiated by this director to produce, in this instance, a blend of TV genres whilst pushing the boundaries of the wildlife genre in new directions. Human interactions with animals and nature are also on the horizons of producers working for the BBC. As the producer of BBC1's *Bear Crime: Caught in the Act* explains:

> It's not enough just to show lifecycle stories anymore, because people have seen all that. We're very interested in showing the interface between humans and animals, because landscapes are changing and wildlife and humans are being pushed closer together all the time. (*Broadcast*, 28 August 2000, p. 30)

As the producer also explained, 'I'm very aware of the legacy of *Wildlife on One*. There was no way I was going to do anything to alienate our core audience, but it was very important at this time, when so much has changed in television, that we looked at the format, because we're going out on BBC1 and we have to compete' (ibid.).

The pursuit of mass audiences can also take natural history programmes into the domestic habitats of ordinary viewers. The producer of an LWT production for ITV explains:

> Instead of the Serengeti plains as our landscape, we have our ordinary semi-detached house in Hitchin, Herefordshire. It's a real house, where a real family live. What we wanted to do was a kind of science/natural history/wildlife programme for a popular mainstream audience. That was central to the brief. It's a way that ITV can get a handle on popular science. (Producer/director *Infested*, *Broadcast*, 22 June 2001, p. 20)

These programmes and many, many more produced in recent years have deliberately sought to increase their appeal for audiences by including presenters and peopled landscapes that both interact with animals in interesting, or preferably, dramatic ways. While this may be thought to be an important development on the 'timeless' portrayals of habitats depicted earlier in 'blue-chip' productions, the absence of a politicised environmental agenda across most of these programmes is all too apparent, and strangely out of step with the known growth in environmental politics and wider public environmental concerns.

> Any proposal that had the word 'environment' or 'conservation' in it was immediately in the bin. What wasn't permitted was to look at a story within a wider context, environmental or ecological. (Independent producer/director)

> I'm wary about these 'e' words, the 'environment' and 'ecology'. I've been told explicitly that I can't have a strong conservation message. (Producer/director)

In part, the failure to produce programmes informed by environmental and political issues relates to the shelf-life, and hence longevity, of these programmes as a commodity as well as their potential international appeal; those that engage with current political concerns and developments, like news, will soon date and become unsaleable, and they may also have an 'unhelpful' national inflection. But of course there is more to it than that. Entertainment-based channels and distributors seeking to maximise audiences are generically disposed to avoid contentious, audience-splitting issues, while a general avoidance of 'gloom and doom' series (such as those thought to have turned away audiences in the 1970s) acts as a further barrier to the production of environmentally engaged programmes. These are barriers that commercial companies and independent producers find difficult to overcome. Even so, the differentiated production ecology of natural history programme-making permits some variation of output. Indeed, occasional BBC series such as *State of the Planet*, as well as occasional independent productions, have managed to introduce themes of global environmental threat and engage with the politics of conservationism. These, though, are a rare sighting on the populist plains of natural history TV rolling across channels and schedules. What is chronically lacking, and surprising given the rise of environmental new social movements and a growing environmental consciousness over recent years (Lash et al. 1996), are programmes actively engaging with the evident rise in ecological politics.

Blue-chip to Micro-chip: Future(s)

The production of natural history programmes has always been intimately dependent on the development of new technologies that have allowed film crews to record animal behaviour in their natural settings or examine certain aspects of behaviour in microscopic detail under laboratory conditions or slowed down to the nth degree within the editing suite and so on. Blue-chip films were as dependent on the arrival of new portable recording technologies as today's programme-makers are on miniaturised cameras and new post-production technologies facilitating the construction of virtual habitats, simulated animals and interactive applications. The BBC's *Walking with Dinosaurs* and *Walking with Beasts* are the best-publicised of what is anticipated to be a long line of simulated animal portrayals (3D animations) artificially recreated and narrativised entirely in the studio. The two high-profile series mentioned visually trace the evolution of mammals and the appearance of early man. As a way of promoting the series, the BBC also trailed the programmes showing prehistoric beasts in modern environments to exaggerate their 'weirdness', including a sabre-tooth tiger walking across a zebra crossing, and a prehistoric whale emerging from a park pond.

In pursuit of broad audiences, these and other animated programmes have pushed the natural history genre in new directions. These technological applications, however, are deployed within the changing production ecology of natural history programmes and, as such, do not escape the shifting priorities and approaches informing the producers' pursuit of commissions, audiences and market success, as well as the disadvantages of scale and resources to capitalise upon new technologies.

Computer graphics are increasingly being used, for example, to enhance the viewers' perspectives on animal killing, continuing current 'killer content' enthusiasms as well as, it seems, the fascination with shark attacks. An independent producer ironically comments on this continuing fascination:

> The next thing that I'm going to do is about sharks and what we're doing between very, very expensive graphics is we are looking in intimate detail at a shark killing a particular thing. What we're trying to do is look at that from the point of view of all the other animals on the reef. 'Give me a break'! But it will go down well; the public will be wowed by the graphics.

Anyway, it's 16 weeks' work over the next 6 months. Yeah, that's the next 6 months sorted, thank you very much!

Miniaturised electronic cameras and high-speed photography running at 500 frames a second in contrast to the normal 100–150 can be deployed to capture all manner of forms of animal behaviour.

It has been a dream in natural history for many years that one day, when the technology is small enough, it will be possible to film from the animal's point of view. . . . It's revolutionary. In the past it has been rather cumbersome so the animals have not behaved normally. (Cameraman quoted in *Broadcast*, 28 April 2000, p. 30)

This technical capability however is more often than not put to work in the service of the current production ecology and its general pursuit of dramatic scenes and split-second killing moments, especially if these can subsequently be slowed down and explored in detail (for example, BBC1 *Predators*).

Digitalisation, electronic archiving of previous films and out-takes combined with new post-production techniques such as computer graphics represent a major opportunity for new programmes to be constructed either without, or with minimal, new filming. Depending on the extent to which these make use of expensive graphics and so on, they can also be produced relatively cheaply if the producer has access to library and archive materials ('electronic museums') – and these, as indicated above, have recently become a prized resource acquired by major players in the competitive natural history TV environment.

The head of the NHU is in no doubt, however, that interactive TV will be the next main advance. 'Technological improvements will continue to surprise in series like *Predators*', but 'to attract the younger multimedia audience, interactive wildlife shows are the way forward.' How interactivity develops in natural history provision will depend on the capability of different organisations to take advantage of new technological capabilities. The boundaries of the wildlife genre, as we have seen, are highly fluid and these most recent developments only look set to further erode notions of wildlife programming as a settled form. Differentiation within the field of natural history programme output continues, and this is both constituted by and is constitutive of, the informing field of natural history programmes and its changing production ecology.

Conclusions

Wildlife programmes have clearly undergone a dramatic evolution across recent years and these changes and adaptations can be related to the changing production ecology of natural history programmes and the wider forces that are expressed and negotiated within and through this production environment. Attending to how these forces are actively addressed and negotiated by organisations and programme-makers is crucial for understanding exactly how changing representations of nature have come about, and how the boundaries and content of television wildlife programmes have become redefined in recent years.

It is at the level of production ecology, comprising the relationships and responses of differently positioned media organisations, that we can begin to understand how and why the genre has been reconfigured and also differentiated in the ways that it has. It is within and through the production ecology of natural history programmes that production choices have been enacted that have changed and inflected the nature(s) of wildlife programmes in sometimes innovative, sometimes unimaginative ways. The genre, like the nature(s) that it represents, continues to evolve.

CHAPTER SUMMARY

- Natural history programmes have undergone dramatic change and evolution in both representations of nature(s) and form across recent years.

- In order to understand better how cultural forms change and evolve through time we need to attend not only to the determinations of the marketplace, but also to the organisational field and professional responses that both express and actively negotiate these and other wider forces of change.

- The concept of 'production ecology' helps to orient research precisely to the organisational dynamics and relations characterising a particular field of cultural production and how these can permit differentiated responses and creative adaptations towards specific forms of cultural production.

- Attending to the changing production ecology of natural history programmes illustrates how this is composed of a dynamic interplay between different players in an unequal field. This includes: national public service and commercial broadcasters and their respective natural history units; international distributors and co-producers of wildlife programming; and medium- and small-scale production houses and independent producers.

- This organisational field has responded to the changing commercial and cultural environment in discernible and differentiated ways and these have impacted on the changing nature(s) of natural history programmes. Attending to the production ecology of natural history programming reveals how and why these transformations of genre have been enacted.

Notes

1 This chapter is based on research reported more fully in a forthcoming article under the same name in 'Media, Culture and Society'.
2 For the purposes of this research, eight semi-structured interviews were conducted between

November and December 2001 with managers, programme-makers and independent producers working in natural history programming. These included: the head of the BBC Natural History Unit, Keith Scholey; wildlife and documentary film-maker Brian Leith; wildlife production manager Mandy Leith; independent wildlife film-maker Jenny Jones; and independent producer Chris Godden. Sincere thanks to all the above and to the others who preferred to remain anonymous.

3   This argument builds on the author's previous work that has sought to examine the production of news as a distinctive cultural form and how this indirectly impacts on the mediation of diverse social problems (Cottle 1993a, 1993b, 2001b), as well as a schema for renewed ethnographies of news, exploring how the differentiation of news forms is actively produced inside news domains (Cottle 2000a).

References

'Ad spend growth' (2000) *Advertising Age International*, January, p. 1.

Addicott, R. (1999) 'Harris quits as select editor for a writing career', *Press Gazette*, 12 November, p. 4.

Adorno, T. and Horkheimer, M. (1972 [1944]) 'The culture industry: enlightenment as mass deception', in T. Adorno and M. Horkheimer (eds) *Dialectic of Enlightenment*. London: Verso, pp. 120–67.

Allan, S. (1999) *News Culture*. Buckingham: Open University Press.

Allan, S., Carter, C. and Adams, B. (2000) *Environmental Risks and the Media*. London: Routledge.

Altheide, D. L. (1976) *Creating Reality*. Beverly Hills/London: Sage.

Altheide, D. L. and Snow, R. P. (1991) *Media Worlds in the Postjournalism Era*. Hawthorne NY: Aldine De Gruyter.

Altschull, J. H. (1997) 'Boundaries of journalistic autonomy', in D. Berkowitz (ed.), *Social Meanings of News*. Thousand Oaks/London: Sage, pp. 259–68.

Atton, C. (1999) 'A reassessment of the alternative press', *Media, Culture & Society*, 2 (1): 51–76.

Atton, C. (2002) *Alternative Media*. London: Sage.

Audley, P. (1994) 'Cultural industries policy: objectives, formulation, and evaluation', *Canadian Journal of Communication*, 19 (3): 317–52.

Auletta, K. (1997) *The Highwaymen: Warriors on the Information Superhighway*. New York: Random House.

Austin, A. L. (1962) *How to Do Things with Words*. Oxford: Oxford University Press.

Bantz, C. R., McCorkle, S. and Baade, R. C. (1980) 'The news factory', *Communication Research*, 7 (1): 45–68.

Bardoel, J. (1996) 'Beyond journalism: a profession between information society and civil society', *European Journal of Communication*, 11 (3): 283–302.

Beamish, R. (1998) 'The local newspaper in the age of multimedia', in B. Franklin and D. Murphy (eds), *Making the Local News: Local Journalism in Context*. London: Routledge, pp. 140–53.

Beck, U. (1992) *Risk Society: Towards a New Modernity*. London: Sage.

Bell, A. (1991) *The Language of News Media*. Oxford: Basil Blackwell.

Benjamin, W. (1982 [1934]) 'The author as producer', in Francis Frascina and Charles Harrison (eds), *Modern Art and Modernism: a Critical Anthology*. London: Paul Chapman in association with the Open University, pp. 213–16.

Benson, A. C. (n.d.: *c*. 1910) *From a College Window*. London: Thomas Nelson & Sons.

Berkowitz, D. (ed.) (1997) *Social Meanings of News: A Text-Reader*. London: Sage.

Bianco, A. (2000) 'Deal time at Seagram', *Business Week*, 26 June, p. 60.

Binning, C. (1998, March 9) *Special Report on Documentary Production and Distribution: Who's shopping for docs*, Playback Magazine [Online] Available: http://www.playbackmag.com/articles/pb/20973.asp, 31 January 2000, p. 39.

Bird, E. (1990) 'Storytelling on the far side: journalism and the weekly tabloid', *Critical Studies in Mass Communication*, 7: 377–89.

Born, G. (2000) 'Inside television: television studies and the sociology of culture', *Screen*, 41 (4): 404–24.

Bourdieu, P. (1993) *The Field of Cultural Production*, edited and introduced by Randal Johnson. Cambridge: Polity Press.

Bourdon, J. (2000) 'Live television culture is still alive: on television as an unfulfilled promise', *Media Culture & Society*, 22 (5): 531–56.

Bousé, D. (2000) *Wildlife Films*. Philadelphia: University of Pennsylvania Press.

Boyd-Barrett, O. (1998) '"Global" news agencies', in O. Boyd-Barrett and T. Rantanen (eds), *The Globalization of News*. London: Sage.

Boyd-Barrett, O. and Newbold, C. (eds) (1995) *Approaches to the Media: Reader*. London: Edward Arnold.

Breed, W. (1955) 'Social control in the newsroom: a functional analysis', *Social Forces*, 33: 326–55.

British Council (2001, September) *British Co-production Showcase*, chaired by Andrew Senior, Head, Creative Industries, The British Council, Vancouver, BC.

Brodesser, C. (2000) 'Sony's global gaze pays', *Variety*, 3–9 April, pp. 13, 62.

Bromley, M. (1997) 'The end of journalism? Changes in workplace practices in the press and broadcasting in the 1990s', in M. Bromley and T. O'Malley (eds), *A Journalism Reader*. London: Routledge, pp. 330–5.

Brooke, J. (2000) 'Canadian TV makes a move into papers', *New York Times*, 1 August, pp. C1, C25.

Browne, D. R. (1999) 'The snail's shell: electronic media and emigrant populations', *Communications*, 24 (1): 61–84.

Brown-Humes, C. (2000) 'Bonnier Scotland', *Financial Times*, 20 September, p. 9.

Buckingham, D. (2000) *The Making of Citizens: Young People, News, and Politics*. London: Routledge.

Burns, T. (1977) *The BBC: Public Institution and Private World*. London: Macmillan.

Byerly, C. M. and Warren, C. A. (1996) 'At the margins of center: organized protest in the newsroom', *Critical Studies in Mass Communication*, 13 (1): 1–23.

Campbell, J. and Pedersen, O. (eds) (2001) *The Rise of Neoliberalism and Institutional Analysis*. Princeton: Princeton University Press.

Canadian Film and Television Production Association (CFTPA) and l'Association des producteurs de films et de télévision du Québec (APFTQ) (2000) *The Canadian Film and Television Industry: Profile 2000*. Toronto: CFTPA.

Canadian Film and Television Production Association (CFTPA) and l'Association des producteurs de films et de télévision du Québec (CAPFTQ) in Association with PriceWaterhouse Coopers (2002) *The Canadian Film and Television Industry: Profile 2002*. Ottawa: CFTPA.

Carey, J. (1995) 'Abolishing the old spirit world', *Critical Studies in Mass Communication*, 12: 82–9.

Carter, C., Branston, G. and Allan, S. (eds) (1998) *News, Gender and Power*. London: Routledge.

Case, T. (2001) 'Gains and Aussies', *Editor and Publisher*.

Castells, M. (1996) *The Rise of the Network Society*. Cambridge, MA and Oxford: Polity Press.

Castells, M. (2000) 'Materials for an exploratory theory of the network society', *British Journal of Sociology*, 51: 5–24.

Chapple, S. and Garofalo, R. (1980) *Rock 'n Roll is Here to Pay: the History and Politics of the Music Industry*. Chicago: Nelson-Hall.

Chenoweth, N. (2001) *Virtual Murdoch: Reality Wars on the Information Highway*. London: Secker & Warburg.

Cherney, E. (2000) 'CanWest tightens its media grip', *Wall Street Journal*, 2 August, p. A17.

Chibnall, S. (1977) *Law-and-Order News: an Analysis of Crime Reporting in the British Press*. London: Tavistock Publications.

Clausen, L. (2001) *The 'Domestication' of International News: A Study of Japanese Television Production*. Copenhagen: Copenhagen Business School.

Coleridge, N. (1993) *Paper Tycoons: the Latest, Greatest Newspaper Tycoons and How They Won the World*. London: Heinemann.

Comedia (1984) 'The alternative press: the development of underdevelopment', *Media, Culture & Society*, 6: 95–102.

Corner, J. (1995) *Television Form and Public Address*. London: Arnold.

Cottle, S. (1993a) *TV News, Urban Conflict and the Inner City*. Leicester: Leicester University Press.

Cottle, S. (1993b) 'Mediating the environment: modalities of TV news', in H. Hansen (ed.), *The Mass Media and Environmental Issues*. Leicester: Leicester University Press, pp. 107–33.

Cottle, S. (1995) 'The production of news formats: determinants of mediated public contestation', *Media, Culture & Society*, 17 (2): 275–91.

Cottle, S. (1998) 'Participant observation', in A. Hansen, S. Cottle, R. Negrine and C. Newbold (eds) *Mass Communication Research Methods*. Basingstoke: Macmillan, pp. 35–65.

Cottle, S. (1999) 'From BBC newsroom to BBC news centre: on changing technology and journalist practices', *Convergence: Journal of New Information and Communication Technologies*, 5 (3): 22–43.

Cottle, S. (2000a) 'New(s) times: towards a "second wave" of news ethnography', *Communications: The European Journal of Communication Research*, 25 (1): 19–41.

Cottle, S. (ed.) (2000b) *Ethnic Minorities and the Media: Changing Cultural Boundaries*. Milton Keynes: Open University Press.

Cottle, S. (2001a) 'Contingency, blunders and serendipity in news research: tales from the field', *Communications: The European Journal of Communication Research*, 26 (2): 149–67.

Cottle, S. (2001b) 'Television news and citizenship: packaging the public sphere', in M. Bromley (ed.) *No News Is Bad News*. Harlow: Pearson Education, pp. 61–79.

Cottle, S. (ed.) (2003) *Journalism, Sources and Promotion*. London: Sage.

Curran, J. (ed.) (2000) *Media Organisations in Society*. London: Edward Arnold.

Curran, J. and Seaton, J. (1997) *Power without Responsibility: the Press and Broadcasting in Britain*. London: Routledge.

D'Alessandro, A. (2000) 'The top 125 worldwide', *Variety*, 24–30 January, p. 22.

Dahlgren, P. (1995) *Television and the Public Sphere: Citizenship, Democracy and the Media*. London: Sage.

Dahlgren, P. (1999) 'Public service media, old and new: vitalizing a civic culture?', *Canadian Journal of Communications*, 24: 495–514.

Dahlgren, P. and Sparks, C. (eds) (1992) *Journalism and Popular Culture*. London: Sage.

Davis, A. (1988) *Magazine Journalism Today*. Oxford: Heinemann Professional Publishing.

Dow, G. and Parker, R. (eds) (2001) *Business, Work, and Community: Into the New Millennium*. South Melbourne: Oxford University Press.

Downing, J. (1984) *Radical Media: The Political Experience of Alternative Communication*. Boston, MA: South End Press.

Downing, J. H. D. (2001) *Radical Media: Rebellious Communication and Social Movements*. London: Sage.

Dreyfus, H. (1991) *Being-in-the-World*. Cambridge, MA: MIT Press.

Du Gay, P. (2000) *In Praise of Bureaucracy*. London: Sage.

Duke, P. F. (2000b) 'Robinson explores Asian films for Sony', *Variety*, 28 August–3 September, pp. 7, 128.

Durham, M. G. and Kellner, D. M. (eds) (2001) *Media and Cultural Studies*. Oxford: Blackwell.

During, S. (1999) *The Cultural Studies Reader*. London: Routledge.

Eder, K. (1996) *The Social Construction of Nature*. London: Sage.

Ehrlich, M. C. (1995) 'The competitive ethos of television news', *Critical Studies in Mass Communication*, 12: 196–212.

Eliasoph, N. (1988) 'Routines and the making of oppositional news', *Critical Studies in Mass Communication*, 5: 313–34.

Elliott, S. (2000) 'Publicist plans to buy Saatchi for at least $1.5 billion', *New York Times*, 20 June, pp. C1, C8.

English, J. W. (1979) *Criticizing the Critics*. New York: Hastings House.

Epstein, E. J. (1973) *News from Nowhere: Television and the News*. New York: Random House.

Ericson, R. V., Baranek, P. M. and Chan, J. B. L. (1987) *Visualizing Deviance: A Study of News Organization*. Milton Keynes: Open University Press.

Ericson, R. V., Baranek, P. M. and Chan, J. B. L. (1989) *Negotiating Control: A Study of News Sources*. Milton Keynes: Open University Press.

Fagan, R. H. and Webber, M. (1994) *Global Restructuring: the Australian Experience*. Melbourne: Oxford University Press.

Fairclough, N. (1995) *Media Discourse*. London: Edward Arnold.

Farber, S. (1976) 'The power of movie critics', *The American Scholar*, 45: 419–23.

Ferguson, M. and Golding, P. (eds) (1997) *Cultural Studies in Question*. London: Sage.

Ferns, W. P. (1995) 'Co-production', in B. Hehner and A. Sheffer (eds) *Making It: The Business of Film and Television Production in Canada*. Toronto: Doubleday Canada, pp. 253–71.

Fishman, M. (1980) *Manufacturing the News*. Austin: University of Texas Press.

Forde, E. (2001) 'From polyglottism to branding: on the decline of personality journalism in the British music press', *Journalism*, 2 (1): 23–43.

Foreman, L. (2000) 'Teuton tongues untied', *Variety*, 14–20 August, pp. 39–40.

Foster, J. (1999) *Trade Union/Employment Rights*, Trades Union Congress, 1999 www.tuc.org.uk/congress/.

Fountain, N. (1988) *Underground: the London Alternative Press, 1966–74*. London: Comedia/Routledge.

Franklin, B. (1994) *Packaging Politics*. London: Edward Arnold.

Franklin, B. (1997) *Newszak and the News Media*. London: Edward Arnold.

Franklin, B. and Murphy, D. (eds) (1998) *Making the Local News: Local Journalism in Context*. London: Routledge.

Freeman, C., Soete, L. and Efendioglu, U. (1995) 'Diffusion and employment effects of information and communications technology', *International Labor Review*, 134: 587–603.

Freeman, J. (1972) 'The tyranny of structurelessness', *Berkeley Journal of Sociology*, 17: 151–64.

Frenkel, S. J., Korczynski, M., Shire, K. A. and Tam, M. (1999) *On the Front Line: Organization of Work in the Information Economy*. Ithaca, NY: Cornell University Press.

Frith, S. (1978) *Sociology of Rock*. London: Constable.

Frith, S. (1983) *Sound Effects: Youth, Culture and the Politics of Rock 'n' Roll*. London: Constable.

Frith, S. (1985) 'Behind the times', in I. Cranna (ed.) *The Rock Yearbook (Vol. 6)*. London: Virgin Books, pp. 335–6.

Frith, S. (1996) *Performing Rites: On the Value of Popular Music*. Oxford: Oxford University Press.

Gans, H. (1979) *Deciding What's News*. New York: Pantheon.

Garfinkel, H. (1984) *Studies in Ethnomethodology*. Cambridge: Polity Press.

Garnham, N. (1986) 'Contribution to a political economy of mass communication', in J. Curran, N. Garnham, P. Scannell, P. Schlesinger and C. Sparks (eds) *Media, Culture and Society: A Critical Reader*. London: Sage, pp. 9–32.

Garnham, N. (1990) *Capitalism and Communication: Global Culture and the Economics of Information*. London: Sage.

Garnham, N. (1995a) 'Political economy and cultural studies: reconciliation or divorce', *Critical Studies in Mass Communication*, 12: 62–71.

Garnham, N. (1995b) 'Reply to Grossberg and Carey', *Critical Studies in Mass Communication*, 12: 62–71.

Gieber, W. (1964) 'News is what newspapermen make it', in L. A. Dexter and D. W. White (eds) *People, Society & Mass Communications*. New York: Free Press, pp. 173–82.

Giffard, A. (1998) 'Alternative news agencies', in O. Boyd-Barrett and T. Rantanen (eds) *The Globalization of News*. London: Sage, pp. 191–201.

Gitlin, T. (1980) *The Whole World is Watching: Mass Media in the Making and Unmaking of the New Left*. Berkeley: University of California Press.

Glasgow University Media Group (1976) *Bad News*. London: Routledge & Kegan Paul.

Glasser, T. L. and Craft, S. (1998) 'Public journalism and the search for democratic ideals', in T. Liebes and J. Curran (eds) *Media, Ritual and Identity*. London: Routledge, pp. 203–18.

Goldblatt, D. (1996) *Social Theory and the Environment*. London: Polity Press.

Golding, P. (1999) *The Political and the Popular: Getting the Measure of Tabloidisation*. AMCCS Conference (ed. Tessa Perkins) Association of Media, Communication and Cultural Studies, Sheffield, UK, pp. 2–18.

Golding, P. and Elliott, P. (1979) *Making the News*. London: Longman.

Golding, P. and Murdock, G. (1979) 'Ideology and the mass media: the question of determination', in M. Barrett, P. Corrigan, A. Kuhn and J. Wolff (eds) *Ideology and Cultural Production*. London: Croom Helm, pp. 198–224.

Golding, P. and Murdock, G. (2000) 'Culture, communications and political economy', in J. Curran and M. Gurevitch (eds) *Mass Media and Society*. London: Edward Arnold, pp. 70–92.

Goldsmith, C. (2000) 'BBC forms commercial Internet unit; U.S. firms to take stake in subsidiary', *Wall Street Journal*, 23 August, p. B10.

Goldsmith, J. and Dawtrey, A. (2000) 'Murdoch: Sky's the limit', *Variety*, 28 August–3 September, pp. 1, 130.

Government of Canada (1993) *International Trade Business Plan, 1993–94*. Ottawa: Ministry of Supply and Services.

Greenberg, B. C., Richards, M. and Henderson, L. (1980) 'Trends in sex-role portrayals on television', in B. C. Greenberg (ed.) *Life on Television: Content Analysis of U.S. TV Drama*. Norwood, NJ: Ablex Publishing Corporation, pp. 65–88.

Grey, T. (2000) 'Promo effort key in France', *Variety*, 21–27 February, pp. 30, 106.

Grossberg, L. (1995) 'Cultural studies vs political economy: is anybody else bored with this debate?', *Critical Studies in Mass Communication*, 12: 72–81.

Grossberg, L., Nelson, C. and Treichler, P. (eds) (1992) *Cultural Studies*. London: Routledge.

Grover, R. and Siklos, R. (1999) 'Where old foes need each other', *Business Week*, 25 October, pp. 114, 18.

Groves, D. (2000) 'Star connects dot-coms', *Variety*, 29 May–4 June, p. 63.

'Growing up' (2000) *The Economist*, 12 August, pp. 57–8.

Guider, E. (2000) 'AFMA exports up 22% as global TV booms', *Variety*, 19–25 June, pp. 14, 75.

Gurd, G. (1998) 'Canada', in A. B. Albarran and S. M. Chan-Olmsted (eds) *Global Media Economics: Commercialization, Concentration and Integration of World Media Markets*. Ames, IA: Iowa State University Press, pp. 33–50.

Habermas, J. (1974 [1964]) 'The public sphere', *New German Critique*, 3 (Autumn): 49–59.

Habermas, J. (1989) *The Structural Transformation of the Public Sphere*. Cambridge: Polity Press.

Hall, J. (2001) *Online Journalism*. London: Pluto Press.

Hall, S. (1982) 'The rediscovery of ideology: return of the repressed in media studies', in M. Gurevitch, T. Bennett, J. Curran and J. Woollacott (eds) *Culture, Society, Media*. London: Methuen, pp. 56–90.

Hall, S. (1992) 'The question of cultural identity', in S. Hall, D. Held and T. McGrew (eds) *Modernity and its Futures*. Cambridge: Polity Press in association with Blackwell Publishers and The Open University, pp. 273–316.

Hall, S. and Jacques, M. (eds) (1989) *New Times: The Changing Face of Politics in the 1990s*. London: Lawrence & Wishart.

Hall, S., Critcher, C., Jefferson, T., Clarke, J. and Roberts, B. (1978) *Policing the Crisis: Mugging, the State and Law and Order*. London: Macmillan.

Halloran, J. D., Elliott, P. and Murdock, G. (1970) *Demonstrations and Communication: A Case Study*. Harmondsworth: Penguin.

Hamelink, C. (1996) *World Communication*. New York: Zed Books.

Hansell, S. (2000) 'Murdoch sees satellites as way to keep news corp. current', *New York Times*, 16 June, p. C7.

Hansen, A., Cottle, S., Negrine, R. and Newbold, C. (1998) *Mass Communication Research Methods*. London: Macmillan.

Harding, T. (1997) *The Video Activist Handbook*. London: Pluto Press.

Harrison, J. (2000) *Terrestrial TV News in Britain: The Culture of Production*. Manchester: Manchester University Press.

Hatfield, S. (2000) 'EU turning into battleground over more curbs on marketing', *Advertising Age*, 18 September, p. 60.

Haugeland, J. (1992) 'Dasein's disclosedness', in H. Dreyfus and H. Hall (eds) *Heidegger: A Critical Reader*. Oxford: Blackwell.

Heidegger, M. (1962) *Being and Time*. Oxford: Blackwell.

Heidegger, M. (1999) *Ontology: The Hermeneutics of Facticity*. Bloomington: Indiana University Press.

Hellend, K. (1995) *Public Service and Commercial News: Contexts of Production, Genre Conventions and Textual Claims in Television, Report No. 18*. Bergen: University of Bergen.

Herman, E. and Chomsky, N. (1988) *Manufacturing Consent*. New York: Pantheon.

Herman, E. and McChesney, C. (1997) *The Global Media: The New Missionaries of Corporate Capitalism*. London: Cassell.

Hoag, C. (2000) 'Empire building: the slow track', *Business Week*, 11 September, pp. 126E3–26E4.

Hodgson, J. (2001) *NME and Virgin set for net radio launch*, MediaGuardian.co.uk, 15 August http://mediaguardian.co.uk/newmedia/story/0,7496,536941,00.html.

Hodson, R. (2001) *Dignity at Work*. Cambridge: Cambridge University Press.

Hollingsworth, J. R. and Boyer, R. (eds) (1997) *Contemporary Capitalism: The Embeddedness of Institutions*. Cambridge: Cambridge University Press.

Hoskins, C. and McFadyen, S. (1993) 'Canadian participation in international co-productions and co-ventures in television programming', *Canadian Journal of Communication*, 18 (2): 219–36.

Hoskins, C., McFadyen, S. and Finn, A. (1997) *Global Television and Film: An Introduction to the Economics of the Business*. Oxford: Oxford University Press.

Immergot, E. M. (1998) 'The theoretical core of the new institutionalism', *Politics and Society*, 26 (1): 5–34.

Jacob, R. (2000) 'Star is shooting towards interactive TV', *Financial Times*, 10–11 June, p. 11.

Jacobs, R. N. (1996) 'Producing the news, producing the crisis: narrativity, television and news work', *Media, Culture & Society*, 18 (3): 373–97.

James, P., Veit, W. F. and Wright, S. (eds) (1997) *Work of the Future: Global Perspectives*. St. Leonards, NSW: Allen & Unwin.

Jankowsjki, N. W. and van Selm, M. (2000) 'Traditional news media online: an examination of added value', *Communications: The European Journal of Communication Research*, 25 (1): 85–101.

Juhasz, A. (1995) *AIDS TV: Identity, Community and Alternative Video*. London: Duke University Press.

Juneau, P. (1993) 'Overview of issues in culture and national identity', in R. de la Garde, W. Gilsdorf, I. Wechselmann and J. Lerche-Nielson (eds) *Small Nations, Big Neighbour: Denmark and Quebec/Canada Compare Notes on American Popular Culture*. London: John Libbey & Company, pp. 15–21.

Kirkpatrick, D. D. (2000a) 'HarperCollins plans to buy a small British publisher', *New York Times*, 11 July, p. C6.

Koltsova, O. (2001) 'News production in contemporary Russia: practices of power', *European Journal of Communication*, 16 (3): 315–33.

Koschnick, W. J. (1989) 'As I see it: an interview with Rupert Murdoch', *Forbes*, 27: 98–104.

Küng-Shankleman, L. (2000) *Inside the BBC and CNN: Managing Media Organisations*. London: Routledge.

Kurtz, H. (1994) *Media Circus: The Trouble with America's Newspapers*. New York: Random House.

Landry, C., Morley, D., Southwood, R. and Wright, P. (1985) *What a Way to Run a Railroad: An Analysis of Radical Failure*. London: Comedia.

Lang, K. and Lang, G. E. (1953) 'The unique perspective of television and its effects: a pilot study', *American Sociological Review*, 18: 168–83.

Langer, J. (1997) *Tabloid Television: Popular Journalism and 'Other News'*. London: Routledge.

Larsen, P. T. (2000) 'Little time for a commercial break', *Financial Times*, 25 August, p. 15.

Lash, S. and Urry, J. (1987) *The End of Organised Capitalism*. Cambridge: Polity Press.

Lash, S. and Urry, J. (1994) *The Economy of Signs and Spaces*. London: Sage.

Lash, S., Szerszynski, B. and Wynne, B. (eds) (1996) *Risk, Environment and Modernity*. London: Sage.

Levinson, S. (1982) *Pragmatics*. Cambridge: Cambridge University Press.

Locke, R. and Thelen, K. (1995) 'Apples and oranges revisited: contextualized comparisons and the study of comparative labor politics', *Politics and Society*, 23: 337–67.

Louw, P. E. (2001) *The Media and Cultural Production*. London: Sage.

Lukacs, G. (1968 [1922]) *History and Class Consciousness*. London: Merlin Press.

Lyman, R. (2000) 'No trace of anti-Hollywood bias in French purchase of Universal', *New York Times*, 20 June, p. C12.

McChesney, R. (1999) *Rich Media, Poor Democracy*. New York: The New Press.

McEachern, D. (1991) *Business Mates: The Power and Politics of the Hawke Era*. Sydney: Prentice Hall.

MacGregor, B. (1997) *Live, Direct and Biased? Making Television News in the Satellite Age*. London: Arnold.

McGuigan, J. (1992) *Cultural Populism*. London: Routledge.

MacIntosh, M. (1984) 'Technological change at Advertiser Newspapers Limited', *Work and People*, 10: 29–37.

McManus, J. H. (1994) *Market-Driven Journalism*. London: Sage.

Macnaghten, D. and Urry, J. (1998) *Contested Natures*. London: Sage.

McNair, B. (1998) *The Sociology of Journalism*. London: Edward Arnold.

McNair, B. (1999) *News and Journalism in the UK*. London: Routledge.

Malyon, T. (1995) 'Might not main', *New Statesman and Society*, 24 March 1995: 24–6.

Mandate Review Committee (CBC NFB Telefilm) (1996) *Making Our Voices Heard: Canadian Broadcasting and Film for the 21st Century*. Hull, Québec: Minister of Supply and Services Canada.

Manning, P. (2001) *News and News Sources: A Critical Introduction*. London: Sage.

Manzella, J. C. (2000) 'Negotiating the news: Indonesian press culture and power during the political crisis of 1997–8', *Journalism*, 1 (3): 305–28.

Marcus, G. E. (1995) 'Ethnography in/of the world system: the emergence of multi-sited ethnography', *Annual Review of Anthropology*, 24: 95.

Marcuse, H. (1968) *One Dimensional Man*. London: Abacus.

Marglin, S. A. and Schor, J. B. (eds) (1990) *The Golden Age of Capitalism: Reinterpreting the Postwar Experience*. Oxford: Clarendon.

Marjoribanks, T. (2000a) *News Corporation, Technology and the Workplace: Global Strategies, Local Change*. Cambridge: Cambridge University Press.

Marjoribanks, T. (2000b) 'The "anti-Wapping"? Technological innovation and workplace reorganization at the Financial Times', *Media, Culture & Society*, 22: 575–93.

Marks, N. (1999) 'Summer of love and magazine wars', *The Independent*, Tuesday Review Section, 10 August, p. 11.

Marx, K. (1970 [1852]) 'The eighteenth brumaire of Louis Bonaparte', in Karl Marx and Frederick Engels (eds) *Selected Work in One Volume*. London: Lawrence & Wishart, pp. 94–179.

Marx, K. (1975 [1844]) 'The economic and philosophic manuscripts', in K. Marx (ed.) *Early Writings*. Harmondsworth: Penguin, pp. 279–400.

Marx, K. (1976 [1867]) *Capital (Volume 1)*. Harmondsworth: Penguin.

Marx, K. and Engels, F. (1976 [1846]) *The German Ideology*. Edited and introduced by C. J. Arthur. London: Lawrence & Wishart.

Matheson, H. (1933) *Broadcasting*. London: Thornton Butterworth Ltd.

Matthews, J. (2002) 'Infantilising the environment: a study of children's news'. PhD Submission. London: Brunel University.

Mermigas, D. (2000a) 'International plays take media firms to next level', *Electronic Media*, 31 July, p. 22.

Mermigas, D. (2000b) 'Morgan Stanley banks on media', *Electronic Media*, 15 May, pp. 17, 20.

Meyrowitz, J. (1985) *No Sense of Place: The Impact of Electronic Media on Social Behaviour*. New York: Oxford University Press.

Miliband, R. (1969) *The State in Capitalist Society: The Analysis of the Western System of Power*. London: Quartet.

Minority Press Group (1980) *Here is the Other News: Challenges to the Local Commercial Press* (Minority

Press Group Series No.1). London: Minority Press Group.

Mishra, P. (2000) 'Yearning to be great, India loses its way', *New York Times*, 16 September, p. A27.

Mohammadi, A. (1999) *International Communication and Globalization*. London: Sage.

Molony, D. (1999) 'Utsumi's CEO think-tank to shake up ITU', *Communications Week International*, 4 October, pp. 1, 74.

Morley, D. and Robins, K. (1995) *Spaces of Identity: Global Media, Electronic Landscapes and Cultural Boundaries*. London: Routledge.

Morrison, D. (1994) 'Journalists and the social construction of war', *Contemporary Record*, 8 (2): 305–20.

Morrison, D. and Tumber, H. (1988) *Journalists at War: The Dynamics of News Reporting During the Falklands War*. London: Sage.

Mortensen, F. and Svendsen, E. N. (1980) 'Creativity and control: the journalist betwixt his readers and editors', *Media, Culture & Society*, 2 (1): 169–77.

Mosco, V. (1996) *The Political Economy of Communication*. London: Sage.

Murdoch, R. (1997) 'Chairman's message', *News Corporation Annual Review*, www.newscorp.com.

Murdock, G. (1978) 'Blindspots about Western Marxism: a reply to Dallas Smythe', *Canadian Journal of Political and Social Theory*, 2 (2): 109–19.

Murdock, G. (1990) 'Redrawing the map of the communication industries: concentration and ownership in the era of privatisation', in M. Ferguson (ed.) *Public Communication: The New Imperatives, Future Directions for Media Research*. London: Sage, pp. 1–15.

Murdock, G. (1991) 'Corporate dynamics and broadcasting futures', in M. Aldridge and N. Hewitt (eds) *Controlling Broadcasting: Access, Policy and Practice in North America and Europe*. Manchester: Manchester University Press.

Murdock, G. (1992) 'Citizens, consumers and public culture', in M. Skovmand and K. C. Schroder (eds) *Media Cultures: Reappraising Transnational Media*. London: Routledge, pp. 17–41.

Murdock, G. (1995) 'Across the great divide: cultural analysis and the condition of democracy', *Critical Studies in Mass Communication*, 12: 89–95.

Murdock, G. (1996) 'Trading places: the cultural economy of co-production', in S. Blind and G. Hallenberger (eds) *European Co-productions in Television and Film*. Heidelberg: Universitätsverlag C. Winter, pp. 103–14.

Murdock, G. (1999) 'Rights and representations:

public discourse and cultural citizenship', in J. Gripsrud (ed.) *Television and Common Knowledge*. London: Sage, pp. 7–17.

Murdock, G. and Golding, P. (1974) 'For a political economy of mass communications', in R. Miliband and J. Saville (eds) *The Socialist Register 1973*. London: Merlin Press, pp. 205–34.

Murphy, D. (1976) *The Silent Watchdog: The Press in Local Politics*. London: Constable.

Murphy, D. (1998) 'Earthquake undermines structure of local press ownership: many hurt', in B. Franklin and D. Murphy (eds) *Making the Local News: Local Journalism in Context*. London: Routledge, pp. 80–90.

Murray, R. (1989) 'Fordism and post-Fordism', in S. Hall and M. Jacques (eds) *New Times: The Changing Face of Politics in the 1990s*. London: Lawrence & Wishart, pp. 38–53.

Negus, K. (1992) *Producing Pop: Culture and Conflict in the Popular Music Industry*. London: Edward Arnold.

Negus, K. (1999) *Music Genres and Corporate Cultures*. London: Routledge.

Neil, A. (1997) *Full Disclosure*. London: Macmillan.

News Corporation (1996, 1997, 1998, 2001) *Annual Report*; online at www.newscorp.com.

Newsround (2000) transmission, 15 June.

Niblock, S. (1996) *Inside Journalism*. London: Blueprint.

Nieman Reports (1999) 'Special issue: the business of news, the news about business', *Nieman Reports*, 53: 8–31.

Nieman Reports (2000) 'Special issue: the Internet, technology and journalism', *Nieman Reports*, 54: 4–77.

Nilson, T. H. (1998) *Competitive Branding: Winning in the Marketplace with Value-Added Brands*. Chichester and New York: John Wiley & Sons.

Oram, S. (1987) 'Fleet Street moves on: a managerial perspective', *Industrial Relations Journal*, 8: 84–9.

Pan, Z. (2000) 'Spatial configuration in institutional change: a case of China's journalism reforms', *Journalism*, 1 (3): 253–81.

Patrickson, M. (1986) 'Adaptation by employees to new technology', *Journal of Occupational Psychology*, 59: 1–11.

Pavlik, J. V. (1996) *New Media Technology: Cultural and Commercial Perspectives*. Boston: Allyn & Bacon.

Pedelty, M. (1995) *War Stories*. London: Routledge.

Pendakur, M. (1990) *Canadian Dreams and American*

Control. Detroit, MI: Wayne State University Press.

Perlmutter, T. (1993) 'Distress signals: a Canadian story – an international lesson', in T. Dowmunt (ed.) *Channels of Resistance*. London: British Film Institute in association with Channel Four Television, pp. 16–26.

Perry, J. (2000) 'Shades of 1960 are superficial amid changes in electorate', *Wall Street Journal*, 14 September, p. A12.

Peters, J. D. (1999) *Speaking into the Air: A History of the Idea of Communication*. Chicago: Chicago University Press.

Picard, R. G. and Brody, J. H. (1997) *The Newspaper Publishing Industry*. Boston: Allyn & Bacon.

Pilling, R. (1998) 'The changing role of the local journalist: from faithful chronicler of the parish pump to multiskilled compiler of the electronic database', in B. Franklin and D. Murphy (eds) *Making the Local News: Local Journalism in Context*. London: Routledge, pp. 183–95.

Posner, M. and Bourette, S. (2000) 'CBC announces more layoffs to meet budget restraints', *Globe and Mail*, 26 July, p. A2.

Postman, N. (1983) *The Disappearance of Childhood*. London: W.H. Allen.

Powell, N., Johnson, T. and Parker, M. (2000) 'Co-productions: the second installment', Panel discussion moderated by B. Presner, M. Friesen (Chair/Producer) The 15th Annual Film and Television Trade Forum conducted during the Vancouver International Film Festival, Vancouver, BC, 29 Sept.

Purcell, J. (1993) 'The impact of corporate strategy on human resource management', in J. Story (ed.) *New Perspectives on Human Resource Management*. London: Routledge, pp. 67–91.

Raboy, M., Bernier, I., Sauvagenau, F. and Atkinson, D. (1994) 'Cultural development and the open economy: a democratic issue and a challenge to public policy', *Canadian Journal of Communication*, 19 (3/4): 291–315.

Randall, G. (1997) *Branding*. London: Kogan Page.

Reed, S. (2000) 'A media star is born', *Business Week*, 24 April, pp. 136–7.

Rice-Barker, L. (1998, October 19) 'On set: 21st Century Jules Verne', *Playback Magazine* (Online). Available: http://www.playbackmag.com/articles/pb23428.asp 21 June 2000, p. 16.

Rimmer, D. (1985) *Like Punk Never Happened: Culture Club and the New Pop*. London: Faber & Faber.

Rivers, W. L. (1973) 'The press as a communication system', in I. de Sola Pool, F. W. Frey and W. Schramm (eds) *Handbook of Communication*. Chicago: Rand McNally College Publishing Company, pp. 521–50.

Robertson, R. (1995) 'Glocalization: time-space and homogeneity-heterogeneity', in M. Featherstone, S. Lash and R. Robertson (eds) *Global Modernities*. London: Sage, pp. 25–44.

Rock, P. (1981) 'News as eternal recurrence', in S. Cohen and J. Young (eds) *The Manufacture of News: Deviance, Social Problems and the Mass Media*. London: Constable, pp. 64–70.

Rohwedder, C. (2000) 'Kirch tightens control over German broadcast assets', *Wall Street Journal*, 29 June, pp. A18, A21.

Rooney, D. (2000) 'Ciao time for Italy', *Variety*, 19–25 June, p. 72.

Ross, K. (2001) 'Women at work: journalism as en-gendered practice', *Journalism Studies*, 2 (4): 531–44.

Sabel, C. F. (1982) *Work and Politics: The Division of Labour in Industry*. Cambridge: Cambridge University Press.

Sabel, C. F. and Zeitlin, J. (eds) (1997) *Worlds of Possibilities: Flexibility and Mass Production in Western Industrialization*. New York: Cambridge University Press.

Sacks, H. (1992) *Lectures in Conversation* (2 volumes). Oxford: Blackwell.

Said, E. (1994) *Representations of the Intellectual: the 1993 Reith Lectures*. London: Vintage.

Scannell, P. (1992) 'Public service broadcasting and modern public life', in P. Scannell, P. Schlesinger and C. Sparks (eds) *Culture and Power*. London: Sage, pp. 317–48.

Scannell, P. (1994) *Radio, Television and Modern Life: A Phenomenological Approach*. Oxford: Blackwell.

Scannell, P. (2002) 'History, media and communication', in Klaus Brun Jensen (ed.) *A Handbook of Media and Communication Research*. London: Routledge, pp. 191–208.

Scannell, P. and Cardiff, D. (1991) *A Social History of British Broadcasting, 1922–1939*. Oxford: Blackwell.

'Scardino's way' (2000) *The Economist*, 5 August, p. 62.

Schechter, D. (2000) 'Long Live Chairman Levin!', Mediachannel.org. posted 5 July.

Schein, E. H. (1992) *Organizational Culture and Leadership*. San Francisco: Jossey Bass.

Schiller, H. (1991) 'Not yet the post-imperialist era', *Critical Studies in Mass Communication*, 8: 13–28.

Schiller, H. (2000) 'Digitised capitalism: what has changed?', in H. Tumber (ed.) *Media Power, Professionals and Policies*. London: Routledge, pp. 116–26.

Schlesinger, P. (1978) *Putting 'Reality' Together: BBC News*. London: Constable.

Schlesinger, P. (1980) 'Between sociology and journalism', in H. Christian (ed.) *The Sociology of Journalism and the Press*. Keele: University of Keele, pp. 341–69.

Schor, J. and You, J.-I. (eds) (1995) *Capital, the State and Labor: A Global Perspective*. Brookfield, VT: Edward Elgar.

Schudson, M. (2000) 'The sociology of news production revisited (again)', in J. Curran and M. Gurevitch (eds) *Mass Media and Society*. London: Edward Arnold, pp. 175–200.

Searle, J. (1969) *Speech Acts: An Essay in the Philosophy of Language*. Cambridge: Cambridge University Press.

Sigelman, L. (1973) 'Reporting the news: an organizational analysis', *American Journal of Sociology*, 79: 132–51.

Silverstone, R. (1999) *Why Study the Media?* London: Sage.

Smith, M. A. (1977) 'Organisations', in W. M. Williams (ed.) *The Sociology of Industry*. London: George Allen & Unwin, pp. 75–84.

Smythe, D. (1980) *Dependency Road: Communications, Capitalism, Consciousness and Canada*. Norwood, NJ: Ablex.

Snow, J. (1994) 'Home and away', *Guardian*, 20 September.

Soloski, J. (1989) 'News reporting and professionalism: some constraints on the reporting of news', *Media, Culture & Society*, 11: 207–28.

Sreberny, A. (2000) 'The global and the local in international communications', in J. Curran and M. Gurevitch (eds) *Mass Media and Society*. London: Edward Arnold, pp. 93–119.

Sreberny-Mohammadi, A., Winseck, D., McKenna, J. and Boyd-Barrett, O. (eds) (1997) *Media In Global Context*. London: Edward Arnold.

'Star turn' (2000) *The Economist*, 11 March, pp. 67–8.

Stern, A. (2000a) 'EU questions pubcaster aid', *Variety*, 22–28 May, p. 67.

Stern, A. (2000b) 'EU to change pubcaster financial rules', *Variety*, 10–16 January, p. 105.

Stern, A. (2000c) 'Microsoft/Telewest deal faces high EC hurdles', *Variety*, 3–9 April, p. 79.

Stratton, J. (1982) 'Between two worlds: art and commercialism in the record industry', *Sociological Review*, 30: 267–85.

Straubhaar, J. D. (1997) 'Distinguishing the global, regional and national levels of world television', in A. Sreberny-Mohammadi, D. Winseck, J. McKenna and O. Boyd-Barrett (eds) *Media in Global Context: A Reader*. London: Arnold, pp. ix–xxviii.

Strover, S. (1995) 'Recent trends in co-productions: the demise of the national', in F. Corcoran and P. Preston (eds) *Democracy and Communication in the New Europe*. Cresskill, NJ: Hampton Press, pp. 97–123.

Sullivan, C. (1998) 'Rock bottom', *The Guardian*, 'Media Guardian' Section, 16 March, p. 4.

Sutter, M. (2000) 'Hicks, muse invests $1 bil in Latin American drive', *Variety*, 17–23 January, p. 70.

'Talk Show' (2000) *Business Week*, 2 October, p. 12.

Taylor, P. W. (1995) 'Co-productions – content and change: international television in the Americas', *Canadian Journal of Communication*, 20 (2): 411–16.

Teinowitz, I. and Linnett, R. (2000) 'Eye on mergers: media behemoths up agency ante', *Advertising Age*, 8 May, pp. 3, 105.

Telefilm Canada (1999a) *Co-productions: 20 Years of Co-productions on the International Scene*, International Affairs [Online]. Available: http://www.telefilm.gc.ca/enaffint/coprod/20_ans.htm (October 22).

Telefilm Canada (1999b) *Co-production Guide: Partnering with Canada*. Montreal: International Relations Division of Telefilm Canada with the collaboration of the Communications and Public Affairs Division.

Telefilm Canada (2000) *Annual Report 1998–1999*. Montréal, Québec: Communications and Public Affairs Department of Telefilm Canada with the participation of the Policy, Planning and Research Department.

'The World's 100 Largest Public Companies' (2000) *Wall Street Journal*, 25 September, p. R24.

Thomas, H. (1944) *Britain's Brains Trust*. London: Chapman & Hall.

Thomas, H. (1977) *With an Independent Air*. London: Weidenfeld & Nicolson.

Thomas, R. (1994) *What Machines Can't Do: Politics and Technology in the Industrial Enterprise*. Berkeley: University of California Press.

Thussu, D. K. (ed.) (1998) *Electronic Empires: Global Media and Local Resistance*. London: Edward Arnold.

Thussu, D. K. (2000) *International Communication: Continuity and Change*. London: Edward Arnold.

Tolliday, S. and Zeitlin, J. (eds) (1991) *The Power to Manage? Employers and Industrial Relations in Comparative Historical Perspective*. London: Routledge.

Tomkins, R. (2000) 'Zenith spotlights advertising surge', *Financial Times*, 18 July, p. 21.

Tomlinson, J. (1991) *Cultural Imperialism*. London: Pinter Publishers.

Tomlinson, J. (1999) *Globalization and Culture.* Cambridge: Polity Press.

Traber, M. (1985) *Alternative Journalism, Alternative Media* (Communication Resource, No. 7, October 1985). London: World Association for Christian Communication.

Tracey, M. (1978) *The Production of Political Television.* London: Routledge & Kegan Paul.

Trelford, D. (2000) 'Contacts and contracts', *Press Gazette*, 8 September, p. 16.

Tuchman, G. (1972) 'Objectivity as strategic ritual: an examination of newsmen's notions of objectivity', *American Journal of Sociology*, 77: 660–79.

Tuchman, G. (1973) 'Making news by doing work: routinizing the unexpected', *American Journal of Sociology*, 79 (1): 110–31.

Tuchman, G. (1978) *Making News: A Study in the Social Construction of Reality.* New York: Free Press.

Tuchman, G. (2002) 'The production of news', in K. B. Jensen (ed.) *A Handbook of Media and Communication Research.* London: Routledge, pp. 78–90.

Tumber, H. (ed.) (1999) *News: A Reader.* Oxford: Oxford University Press.

Tunstall, J. (1970) *The Westminster Lobby Correspondents: A Sociological Study of National Political Journalism.* London: Routledge & Kegan Paul.

Tunstall, J. (1971) *Journalists at Work.* London: Constable.

Tunstall, J. (1983) *The Media in Britain.* London: Constable.

Tunstall, J. (1996) *Newspaper Power: The New National Press in Britain.* Oxford: Clarendon Press.

Turner, G. (1996) *British Cultural Studies.* London: Routledge.

'U.S. cable channels tighten their grip on Latin American cable viewers' (2000) *TV International*, 12 June, p. 6.

Volkmer, I. (1999) *News in the Global Sphere: A Study of CNN and Its Impact on Global Communication.* Luton: University of Luton Press.

Warner, M. (1971) 'Organisational context and control of policy in the television newsroom: a participant observation study', *British Journal of Sociology*, 22: 283–94.

Whitaker, B. (1981) *News Limited: Why You Can't Read All About It* (Minority Press Group Series No. 5). London: Minority Press Group.

White, D. M. (1950) 'The gatekeeper: a case study in the selection of news', *Journalism Quarterly*, 27: 383–90.

Williams, R. (1980) 'Means of communication as means of production', in R. Williams (ed.) *Problems in Materialism and Culture: Selected Essays.* London: Verso, pp. 50–63.

Winn, M. (1985) *The Plug-in Drug.* Harmondsworth: Penguin.

Zelizer, B. (1993) 'Has communication explained journalism?', *Journal of Communication*, 43 (4): 80–8.

Index

Aberdeen People's Press 44
Advertiser 63, 67, 68, 70, 71, 72, 73
Advertising Age International 32
Addicott, R. 124
Adorno, T. 9
Akwesasne Notes 45
Alarm 44
Allan, S. 132, 171
alternative media 6, 21, 38, 41–55
Altheide, D. L. 14, 16
Altschull, J. H. 19
amateur journalists 45–47
Anglia Television 172, 173
Animal Planet 173, 174, 176, 179, 180, 181, 182
AOL–Time Warner 3, 29, 30, 34, 36, 66, 119
Atton, C. 20, 21, 41, 46, 51
AT&T 36
Audley, P. 152
Auletta, K. 66
Austin, A. L. 103
auteur tradition 157, 169
author as producer 51

Baltruschat, D. 22, 168n
Bantz, C. R., 14
Bardoel, J. 16
BBC 6, 14, 18, 19, 21, 77–96, 99–112, 131–145
　Any Answers 112n
　Any Questions 101, 112n
　Blue Peter 136
　Brains Trust 99–112
　Question Time 112n
　Natural History Unit (NHU) 173, 175, 176–178,
　　　179, 180, 181, 183, 184, 185, 186–187
　Newsround 131–145
　Wildlife on One 180, 183
　Worldwide 85, 174, 176
Beamish, R. 20
Beck, U. 132
Bell, A. 16
Benjamin, W. 51
Benson, A. C. 108
Berkowitz, D. 18, 24n
Bertelsmann 3, 29, 30, 32, 66
Bianco, A. 29
Big Issue 43, 44, 47, 53
Binning, C. 151
Bird, E. 18

Bollywood 35
Born, G. 11, 13
Bourdieu, P. 19, 116, 117, 120, 122, 123, 170
Bourdon, J. 112n
Bourette, S 154
Bousé, D. 170, 171
Boyd-Barrett, O. 16, 24n
Boyer, R. 60
Breed, W. 14, 15, 113, 123
Brighton Voice 44
British Columbia Film 156
British Council 155
British Socialist Worker 42
Broadcast 173, 174, 175, 176, 179, 181, 183, 185
Brodesser, C. 35
Brody, J. H. 61
Bromley, M. 16, 20
Brooke, J. 32
Browne, D. R. 20
Brown-Humes, C. 33
Buckingham, D. 132
Burns, T. 14, 79
Business Week 29
Byerly, C. M. 20

Café Productions 175
Campbell, J. 60
Canadian Broadcasting Company 6, 154
Canadian Film and Television Production
　　Association 152
CanWest Global Communications 32
Cardiff, D. 104, 105, 108
Carey, J. 11
Carlton PLC 173
Carter, C. 20
Case, T. 66
Castells, M 20, 59, 65.
CD-UK 45
Channel 4 131, 173, 175
Channel 5 173, 176
Chapple, S. 120
Chenoweth, N. 66
Cherney, E. 33
Chibnall, S. 14, 113, 122
Chomsky, N. 8
Cicada Films 182
Cisneros Group 33
Clarin 33

Clausen, L. 16, 17, 19
CNN 6, 21, 77–96
    World Report 92
Coleridge, N. 65
Columbia 33
Comedia 42
commodity fetishism 8–9, 109
communicative intentionality 17, 22, 100, 111
conglomeration/concentration 3, 6, 9, 10, 12, 19, 20,
        21, 29, 34, 152, 167, 168, 170, 173
    horizontal integration 9
    vertical disintegration 19
    vertical integration 9, 29
convergence 3, 6, 16, 22, 29, 74, 77, 84, 92, 149, 167,
        168
conversation analysis 103
co-production 22, 23, 149–168, 170–187
Corner, J. 133
correspondents 14
Cottle, S. 16, 17, 18, 19, 20, 23, 24n, 131, 133, 151,
        187n
Counter Information 47–49
cradle-to-grave publishing 116–120, 125
Craft, S. 18
cultural citizens/citizenship 132, 133
cultural fields/production 12, 19, 23, 117, 122–123,
        170–171
cultural hybrids 158
cultural imperialism 10, 35
cultural industries 4, 9, 10, 171
cultural intermediaries 120–130
cultural milieu 16
cultural studies 4, 6, 7, 10–13, 24, 27, 28
culture as commodity 149, 167–169
culture as public good 149, 151, 167–169
culture industry 4, 9
Curran, J. 13, 42, 124

D'Alessandro, A. 35
Dahlgren, P. 18, 151, 152
Davis, A. 124
Dawtrey, A. 30
de-democratising 120, 129
de-politicisation 36, 48
deregulation 3, 37, 149, 166, 168
deskilling 16
digital/digitalization 3, 6, 10, 16, 20, 21, 30, 77, 84,
        93, 164, 167, 184–185
Discovery 173, 174, 175, 176, 178, 179, 180, 181
Disney 3, 29
disorganized capitalism 19
Dow, G. 59
Dow Jones 32
Downing, J. 20, 41, 42, 45
Dreyfus, H. 112n
du Gay, P. 122

Duke, P. F. 35
Durham, M. G. 11
During, S. 11
Durkheim, E. 13

Eder, K. 171
Ehrlich, M. C. 19
Eliasoph, N. 17
elite access 18
Elliott, P. 14
Elliott, S. 32
Emap 116
Engels, F. 7
English, J. W. 113, 123
Erin Bulletin 45
Enron affair 37
Epstein, E. J. 14
Ericson, R. V. 14, 15, 16
ethnography 4, 5, 16, 18, 19, 20, 22, 24, 134
    formative studies 14
    substantive studies 14
ethnomethodology 103, 104
event orientation 14

Fagan, R. H. 60
Fairclough, N. 46
Farber, S. 123
Fatigue (production) 142–143, 145
Ferguson, M. 11
Ferns, W. P. 150
FHM 119
Financial Times 67
Fishman, M. 14, 15, 133
flexible work regimes/specialization 3, 16, 19
Forde, E. 17, 19, 22, 119, 120, 127, 130n
Foreman, L. 35
Foster, J. 70, 72
Foucault, M. 17
Fourth Estate 32
Fountain, N. 42
Fox TV 30
Franklin, B. 16
freelancers 3, 122, 173
Freeman, C. 60
Freeman, J. 42
Frenkel, S. J. 63
Frith, S. 120, 125

Gannett 32
Gans, H. 14
Garofalo, R. 120
Garfinkel, H. 104
Garnham, N. 11, 151
Gatekeeping 14, 125
Gaumont Television 151
General Electric 29

Gieber, W. 125
Giddens, A. 169n
Giffard, A. 20
Gitlin, T. 14
Glasgow University Media Group 47
Glasser, T. L. 18
global-local 3, 6, 20, 23, 35, 53, 59–75, 149–169
global oligopoly 28
globalization 6, 10, 21, 27–39, 77, 152, 169n
Globo 33
Goldblatt, D. 132
Golding, P. 9, 10, 11, 12, 13, 14, 46, 171
Goldsmith, C. 31
Goldsmith, J. 30
Government of Canada 151
Granada Wild 173, 175, 176, 180, 181
Green Umbrella 175
Greenberg, B. C. 159
Grey, T. 35
Grossberg, L. 159
Grover, R. 34
Groves, D. 30
'Growing Up' 35
Guardian Weekly 8
Guider, E. 35
Gurd, G. 154

Habermas, J. 132
Hall, J. 16
Hall, S. 15, 17, 19, 158
Halloran, J. D. 14, 15
Hamelink, C. 10
Hansell, S. 30
Hansen, A. 63
Harding, T. 51
HarperCollins 32
Harrison, J. 133
Hatfield, S. 31
Haugeland, J. 112n
Hearst and Advance Publications 32
Heat 119
Heidegger, M. 110, 112n
Hellend, K. 16
Herman, E. 8, 16
Hoag, C. 34
Hodgson, J. 119
Hodson, R. 63
Hollingsworth, J. R. 60
Hollywood 35
Horkheimer, M. 9
Hoskins, C. 150, 157
HTV 173
hypercommercialisation 36

ideal readers/audience 116, 128, 135, 136, 145
Islington Gutter 44

imagined audience 11, 19, 22, 135
Immergut, E.M. 62
Indymedia (Independent Media Centers, IMCs) 47, 52–55
instrumentalism 5, 7, 9, 16
IPC (International Publishing Corporation) 113, 114, 115, 117, 118
ITV 172, 175, 183

Jacques, M. 19
Jacob, R. 30
Jacobs, R. N. 18
James, P. 59
Jankowsjki, N. W. 16
Juhasz, A. 51
Juneau, P. 154

Kellner, D. M. 11
Kerrang! 115, 121
Kirkpatrick, D. D. 32
Kirch Group 32
Koltsova, O. 20
Koschnick, W. J. 66
Kung-Shankleman, L. 20, 21, 96n
Kurtz, H. 68

L'Association des producteurs de films et de télévision du Québec 152
Lacey, N. 133
Landry, C. 43, 44
Lang, G. E. 14
Lang, K. 14
Langer, J. 16, 18
Larsen, P. T. 31
Lash, S. 19, 132, 184
Levinson, S. 103
Liberty Media 29
Linnett, R. 32
Liverpool Free Press 44
Loaded 119
Locke, R. 62
Louw, P. E. 65
Lukacs, G. 9
Lyman, R. 35

MacGregor, B. 16, 20, 133
MacIntosh, M. 70
Macnaghten, D. 132, 171
Malyon, T. 50
Mandate Review Committee (CBC NFB Telefilm) 154
Manning, P. 16
Manzella, J. C. 20

Marche International des Programmes de television (MIPCOM) 152
Marcus, G. E. 64
Marcuse, H. 9
Marglin, S. A. 60
Marjoribanks, T. 20, 21, 59, 67, 68
Marks, N.
Marx, K. 7, 8, 13, 109
Mattheson, H. 105
Matthews, J. 16, 17, 19, 22, 145n
McChesney, R. 10, 16, 19, 21
McEachern, D. 72
McFadyen, S. 157
McGuigan, J. 11
McManus, J. H. 19
McNair, B. 16, 20, 120, 121
Mediaset 8, 32, 33
mediation 4, 6, 13, 132
Melody Maker 115
Meridian 173
Mermigas, D. 29, 30, 34
Metal Hammer 115
Meyrowtiz, J. 132
Microsoft 36
Miliband, R. 7
Ministry 115
Minority Press Group 42, 43, 44
Mishra, P. 36
Mixmag 115, 121
Mohammadi, A. 10
Mojo 115, 118
Molony, D. 31
Morley, D. 152, 158
Morning Star 42
Morrison, D. 18
Mortensen, F. 122
Mosco, V. 13
multimedia production 3, 10, 16, 20, 184–185
multiskilling 3, 20, 69, 135
Murdoch, R. 21, 30, 32, 34, 59, 65, 93
Murdock, G. 9, 10, 11, 12, 13, 16, 19, 132, 151, 171
Murphy, D. 14, 16, 19
Murray, R. 19
Muzik 115

National Geographic Television (NGT) 173, 174, 176
National Guardian 45
Negus, K. 115, 116, 119, 120, 125
Neil, A. 66
network society 20
Newbold, C. 24n
New Music Express (NME) 114, 115, 118, 119, 121, 122, 127

new technologies of production 3, 6, 16, 20, 21, 30, 52, 59, 89, 99–100, 167, 170, 177, 184–185
strategizing technologies 21, 59–75
New York Daily News 68
New York Post 63, 64, 65, 66, 68, 73
News Corporation 3, 21, 29, 30, 33, 34, 59–75
News International 6
Star TV 30
news ecology 6, 16, 18, 19, 20, 24
news facticity 16
News of the World 63, 64
news policy 14
news net 15
news sense 15
news values 14
Niblock, S. 120, 123
Nickelodean 131
Nieman Reports 61
Nilson, T. H. 119
North American Free Trade Agreement (NAFTA) 30, 37, 151

Objectivity, 14, 15, 18, 114
strategic use of 14
O'Reilly, T. 32
Oram, S. 70
Organizational functionalism 17
Oxford Scientific Films (OSF) 175
Oz 42

Pan, Z. 20
Parker, R. 59
Partridge Films 173, 175
Patrickson, M. 70
Pavlik, J. V. 59
PBS 173
Pearson 32
Pedelty, M. 17
Pedersen, O. 60
Pendakur, M. 153
Perlmutter, T. 152
Perry, J. 36
personalization 138–140, 145
Peters, J. D. 112n
phenomenology 17, 22, 111
Phoenix TV 30
Picard, R. G. 61
Pilling, R. 20
political economy 4, 6, 7–10, 11, 12, 13, 18, 19, 21, 23–4, 27, 28, 38, 39, 115–120, 129, 171, 180
Posner, M. 154
Postfordism 19, 60
Postman, N. 132
Powell, N. 155
practices 17, 18, 22, 23, 99–112
care structure of 110–112

pragmatics 103, 111
prefigurative politics 42, 53
Prica 32
primary definers/definition 15
problem of inference 5, 23
production ecology 6, 12, 23, 170–187
production rituals 121, 135
professional socialization 13
professional visualization 131, 133, 135, 144
propaganda model 8
public sphere 45, 132, 150, 152, 167, 168
Purcell, J. 116, 123

Q 115, 116, 121

Raboy, M. 167
Radio Times 104
Randall, G. 119
Reed, S. 32
Reed Elsevier 32
Reith, Lord, 81, 82, 93, 94, 95
Republica 45
Reuters 32
Rice-Barker, L. 162, 163
Rimmer, D. 115
Rivers, W. L. 127
Robertson, R. 158
Robins, K. 152, 158
Rock, P. 15
Rohwedder, C. 32
Rolling Stone 120
Rooney, D. 35
Ross, K. 20

Sabel, C. F. 62
Sacks, H. 103
Said, E. 46
Scannell, P. 17, 22, 99, 104, 105, 108
'Scardino's way' 29
SchNEWS 44
Schechter, D. 29
Schein, E. H. 77
Schiller, H. 10
Schlesinger, P. 14, 113, 121, 122, 133
Schor, J. B. 60
Schudson, M. 18, 24n
Scorer Associates 175, 179
Searle, J. 103
Seaton, J. 42, 124
Select 115
Selm, V.M. 16
Sigelman, L. 14
Siklos, R. 34
Silverstone, R. 41
simplification 140–141, 145
Sky Global Networks 30

Small World Media 50
Smash Hits 115, 118, 121
Smith, M. A. 121, 123
Smythe, D. 12
Snow, J. 131
Snow, R. P. 16
Socialist Worker 42
sociology of news production 13–20, 24, 113–114, 120–130, 131–145
Soloski, J. 14, 15
Sony 3, 29, 35
Sparks, C. 18
speech act theory 103
Squall 44
Sreberny, A. 10
'Star turn' 32
strategic ritual 15
Stern, A. 31
stop-watch culture 121
Stratton, J. 119
Straubhaar, J. D. 152, 156
Strover, S. 150
structural determinism 5, 62, 123, 134
Sullivan, C. 118
Sun 63, 64
Sunday Times 63, 65
Sutter, M. 33
Svendsen, E. N. 122

'Talk Show', 29
taste publics 116
Taylor, P. W. 157
Teinowitz, I. 32
Telfornica 36
Telefilm Canada 150, 152, 153, 154
Televisa 33
Television Without Frontiers 151
The Guardian 134
The Times 63
The Wire 117, 121
Thelen, K. 62
Thomas, H. 102, 108, 112n
Thomas, R. 62
Thussu, D. K. 10, 16, 19
Tigress Productions 179
Time Film 151
Tolliday, S. 62
Tomkins, R. 32
Tomlinson, J. 10
Top of the Pops 115
Traber, M. 46
Tracey, M. 14
transnational corporations (TNCs) 3, 6, 21, 27–39
Trelford, D. 127
Tuchman, G. 14, 15, 18, 24n
Tumber, H. 18, 24n

Tunstall, J. 14, 61, 63, 67, 113, 115, 121, 124, 126, 133
Turner, G. 11
Turner, T. 34, 89, 92, 93, 94, 95
TV International
Twentieth Century Fox 30
tyranny of structurelessness 42

Uncut 115, 121
Undercurrents 47, 50–51, 53–55
UNESCO 31
United News and Media (UNM) 173
United Wildlife 175
Universal 34
Urry, J. 19, 132, 171

Variety 34, 35
venture capitalism 19
Viacom 3, 28
Virgin Radio 119
Vivendi Universal Studios 28, 30
Volkmer, I. 16

Wall Street Journal
Warren, C. A. 20
Warner Brothers 33

Warner, M. 14
Webber, M. 60
Weber, M. 13
Whitaker, B. 42, 44
White, D. M. 14, 15, 113, 125
Williams, R. 41
Winn, M. 132
World Economic Forum 37
WTO (World Trade Organization) 30, 31, 36, 37, 47, 52, 167

You, J.-I. 60

Zebra Films 175
Zeitlin, J. 62
Zelizer, B. 121